HACK YOUR BUREAUCRACY

GET THINGS DONE
NO MATTER WHAT YOUR ROLE
ON ANY TEAM

MARINA NITZE
AND NICK SINAI

hachette
BOOKS

NEW YORK

Hachette Go, an imprint of Hachette Books
Hachette Book Group
1290 Avenue of the Americas
New York, NY 10104
HachetteGo.com
Facebook.com/HachetteGo
Instagram.com/HachetteGo

First Edition: September 2022

Hachette Books is a division of Hachette Book Group, Inc.

The Hachette Go and Hachette Books name and logos are trademarks of Hachette Book Group, Inc.

The publisher is not responsible for websites (or their content) that are not owned by the publisher.

Print book interior design by Jeff Williams.

Library of Congress Control Number: 2022940044

ISBNs: 9780306827754 (hardcover); 9780306827778 (ebook)

Printed in the United States of America

LSC-C

Printing 1, 2022

Marina:
To Richard Culatta

Nick:
To Christine, Ellis, and Georgia

CONTENTS

PITCH THE SOLUTION

START SMALL AND BUILD MOMENTUM

BUILD YOUR TEAM

MAKE IT STICK

INTRODUCTION

It was clear President Obama was getting frustrated. Staffers looked down, shuffling paper and refusing to make eye contact. The clock showed only five minutes left until the cabinet meeting was over. You know that feeling when the teacher is going to call on you, and you don't know the answer? The minute hand couldn't move fast enough. Marina's anxiety was sky high.

The president hadn't yet called on Marina to explain why her team at the Department of Veterans Affairs had failed to get traction, and she hoped the meeting would end before the topic came up. Normally, attendance at this quarterly cabinet meeting with the president on veterans issues was restricted to the VA's three most senior officials: the secretary, deputy secretary, and chief of staff. But Marina had been asked to join because President Obama's dissatisfaction with her progress was rumored to be on the agenda.

The chairs in the Cabinet Room are huge and heavy, and because there were so many people packed into the room, the chairs were jammed together. At barely five feet tall, Marina was too short for her feet to reach the floor, and she kept slowly sliding off the slick leather seat. Her attention now turned to how she was *literally* going to escape the room, hoping Vice President Biden might scooch his chair back just far enough for her to slip out unnoticed.

"And just one more thing..." the president started, looking right at Marina. "It's been quite a while now, and I hear your team still hasn't been able to deliver any working software."

Marina knew this was why she was there, but it was still surreal to have the president of the United States call her out.

"It's all about risk frameworks!" Marina blurted out, a bit more enthusiastically than she had rehearsed. "We can't get the signatures we need to proceed, because the normal paperwork doesn't apply to our newer technology. We have to get a whole new approval process cleared first. No one wants to be held responsible if we fail, so they're coming up with every last way to make sure they're not on the hook. It's possible to get through this, but it's just going to take more time."

President Obama listened intently to Marina's explanation. After a short pause, he volunteered a suggestion: "What if I record a video telling them that they *have* to approve your project?"

"I appreciate that offer, Mr. President," Marina said, unsure how to tell him that no civilian employee in their right mind was going to sign off on incomplete paperwork, no matter *who* told them it was okay. By the time the inevitable Inspector General investigation began, a new president would be in office, leaving that employee holding the bag. "I'll let you know if we need that."

Even the power of the presidency has limits. The leader of the free world genuinely wanted to help her—but even *he* couldn't make the bureaucracy of the VA move any faster. Marina was on her own to get this software—which would identify thousands of veterans whose appeals had fallen through the cracks—into production.

What she needed was a set of powerful bureaucracy hacks. And eventually, through trial, error, and a bit of luck, she found them.

=====

In 1944, the precursor to the CIA, the Office of Strategic Services (OSS), published a secret field guide for operatives carrying out sabotage. Suggested techniques included:

1. *Insist on doing everything through "channels." Never permit shortcuts to be taken in order to expedite decisions.*

2. *Make "speeches." Talk as frequently as possible and at great length. Illustrate your "points" by long anecdotes and accounts of personal experiences.*

3. *When possible, refer all matters to committees, for "further study and consideration." Attempt to make the committees as large as possible—never less than five.*

4. *Bring up irrelevant issues as frequently as possible.*

5. *Haggle over precise wordings of communications, minutes, resolutions.*

6. *Refer back to matters decided upon at the last meeting and attempt to reopen the question of the advisability of that decision.*

7. *Advocate "caution." Be "reasonable" and urge your fellow conferees to be "reasonable" and avoid haste, which might result in embarrassments or difficulties later on.*

8. *Be worried about the propriety of any decision—raise the question of whether such action as contemplated lies within the jurisdiction of the group or whether it might conflict with the policy of some higher echelon.*

Millions of people today go to work in an environment indistinguishable from a CIA saboteur master class. However, their managers and coworkers aren't spies—they are everyday leaders and employees trying to do their jobs. The larger or older the organization, the more the bureaucracy seems to have a singular mission of its own: to stop change of any kind in its tracks.

When Marina first became the chief technology officer of one of the world's largest bureaucracies—the US Department of Veterans Affairs—it seemed impossible to get even the smallest thing done. While the Department of Defense (DoD) outmatches the VA in sheer numbers of employees, the DoD is at least designed to operate cohesively—you can't wage war in Iraq and have your navy show up in South Africa, for example. But at the VA, it was not only possible, but commonplace, for a veteran to get healthcare but never even hear about any of the other benefits they had earned, or vice versa. To further complicate matters, Marina didn't at first appear to have many tools for success: at twenty-eight, she had dropped out of college, and formally had zero budget and zero employees.

The department was in a constant state of crisis, with office floors literally buckling under the weight of overdue disability claim paperwork and employees panicked over discoveries of secret patient waiting lists and unprocessed healthcare applications. Everyone from Congress to *The Daily Show* was publicly criticizing the VA for failing its mission.

And yet these crises weren't a catalyst for change—they just made people dig in their heels even harder. With a spotlight on their every move, no one dared veer from established procedures, lest they get singled out and scapegoated. It felt like that CIA manual had been handed out at new employee orientation.

But it *was* possible, in spite of all these obstacles, to make lasting changes. Six months after that painful cabinet meeting with President Obama, Marina's team was able to launch their first software application—and they've launched new functionality almost every single day since then. By the time Marina left the VA in 2017, the agency had achieved seemingly impossible goals, such as enrolling over 600,000 veterans in VA healthcare from their mobile phones; completely revamping the Board of Veterans' Appeals; and consolidating the VA's over 1,500 disparate websites, phone numbers, and wrong doors into a single, veteran-friendly website and phone number. Marina—together with other executives and thousands of colleagues across various divisions of the VA—worked relentlessly over years to create a better experience for veterans. Over a five-year period, from 2016 to 2020, veterans' trust in the VA rose by an astounding 25 percentage points.

Marina first learned how to get things done in a bureaucracy from her former White House boss, and coauthor of this book, Nick Sinai. Nick spent four years in the US chief technology officer's office, spanning all three US CTOs in the Obama administration—Aneesh Chopra, Todd Park, and Megan Smith. Nick's career trajectory before the White House included a Harvard undergraduate degree in government, management consulting, an MBA from the University of Chicago, and then venture capital investing at Polaris Partners in Boston. When Lehman Brothers went bankrupt shortly after he had joined its venture capital arm—on the very first day of his honeymoon!—he decided to follow his earlier passion for government into the Obama administration. After leading a team on a blue-ribbon task force at the FCC, Nick joined the White House in the Office of Science and Technology Policy. He eventually held the fancy title of US deputy CTO, where he had zero budget and zero direct authority over the vast executive branch—similar to the predicament Marina initially found herself in at the VA.

After our time in the federal government, we've worked in and advised several different types of organizations: venture capital, academia, think tanks, and start-ups. Nick is a senior advisor at Insight Partners, a multibillion-dollar software venture capital and private equity firm, where he works with the CEOs and management teams of growing software companies. As an adjunct professor at the Harvard Kennedy School, he also teaches technology and innovation to graduate and college students. Marina is a fellow at New America's New Practice Lab, where she is focused on improving foster care. She also cofounded the crisis management firm Layer Aleph, where she has worked on high-profile problems like the State of California's unemployment insurance backlog during the COVID-19 pandemic. We've seen a lot of organizations, across the public and private sectors, and advised (and learned from) both executive leadership and the rank and file.

From our time in the White House and the VA, our experiences since, and those of many of our amazing colleagues, we've amassed expertise and answers to the question: What makes someone effective in a bureaucracy? Why are some people particularly effective in bureaucracies—companies, universities, or government agencies—and why do some fail miserably?

What's in This Book

In this book we explore one of the central misunderstandings of getting things done: change doesn't happen just because the person in charge declares it should—even if that person is the CEO of your company or, as in our case, the president of the United States. In our experience, too many people think that the president—or your CEO, organization head, or university president—is the instigator of change, the champion of reform, and the catalyst of new initiatives. That happens sometimes, sure, but we've seen just as many occasions when the instigator of massive change is an everyday employee who takes matters into her own hands.

We explain the mindset and principles that enabled us (and our colleagues) to accomplish seemingly impossible reforms. We show you how to get started at defining the root causes of your problems, sell your vision, build a team, build momentum, and make lasting change in any company, university, nonprofit, community organization, or government agency. Alongside our own stories, we offer tried and true bureaucracy-hacking strategies to steer companies and organizations of all kinds, gathered from our fellow bureaucracy hackers who drove change in some of the world's toughest, largest, and most complex environments.

We've organized the book by specific tactics—explaining what they are, why they are important, and how you can use them in your organization. We grouped these chapters into the following six themes:

- **DEFINE THE PROBLEM:** Discover what you should really be working on. Whether you are new to an organization or simply need a fresh lens, understand what problems you really ought to be addressing, the root causes, and potential fixes.

- **LEARN YOUR ORG:** Figure out how things really work and get to know the people in your bureaucracy. Recognize how decisions really get made, why things are the way they are, and what motivates your colleagues.

- **PITCH THE SOLUTION:** Sell your ideas in context. Use the written word, visual design, compelling examples, and hard numbers to sell your project—focusing on what will resonate most with your audience.

- **START SMALL AND BUILD MOMENTUM:** Experiment, learn, and show progress. With a bias toward solving small problems and getting rapid feedback, start where you are, pilot with real demos, and generate the kind of excitement that builds upon itself.

- **BUILD YOUR TEAM:** Do more, together. Bureaucracy hacking is a team sport, especially if you want to make an impact at scale. Recruit informal teammates, deputize doers, and build allies—even in unlikely places.

- **MAKE IT STICK:** Scale smartly while rewiring your organization. Ensure your initiative will last beyond any single individual by changing the rules. Persevere across leadership changes, crises, and other challenges by seeing them as opportunities to advance and solidify the change you are driving.

In each chapter, we'll discuss a single tactic, share some examples or stories, and end with a handful of practical tips that we hope you can use, whatever your industry, your role, or your seniority. You can certainly read this book straight through, but we've also worked to make it useful to revisit individual chapters as necessary. Every tactic might not apply to your situation or fit where you are in your career; pick and choose those that resonate most.

Why Us

But why should you listen to us? There's a whole industry of people peddling and practicing big organization innovation and business management books. Why Marina and Nick?

Between the two of us, we've hacked bureaucracies at scale—at the White House, the Department of Veterans Affairs, foster care, state capitals, Harvard University, and growing software companies. And we've been lucky to work alongside and get to know other world-class bureaucracy hackers in the Department of Defense and elsewhere. We've learned things the hard way, collected advice and stories from other expert hackers, and had our share of successes and failures.

We both benefited greatly from the wisdom and experiences of our colleagues and teammates who themselves have successfully shifted a variety of supertankers, one degree at a time. We're also part of a larger group of people who have figured out how to make an outsized impact inside a large organization—and we are excited to tell their stories, too. In particular, Tom Kalil, who spent sixteen years in the Clinton and Obama White Houses, and his de facto deputy in the Obama White House, Kumar Garg, have been mentors to us on this topic. Kumar kept a whiteboard of bureaucracy-hacking tactics in his White House office (which you can see on our website), and we've included a number of them—like recruiting allies, working from both the top-down and bottom-up, and making it as easy as possible for others to help you—in this book.

We've also counseled people on how to flip the script on an individual scale. CEOs, three-star generals, and national politicians, as well as students, friends, and neighbors, have successfully applied these tactics from boardrooms to condo associations.

We aren't magicians—but it turns out that making a change in a bureaucracy doesn't require magic. It requires doing your homework, building authentic allies, doing the small things to make progress every day, and being attuned to how your organization *actually* works. The most impactful changes also call for significant levels of grit, resilience, and confidence in your vision.

Defining Bureaucracy Hacking

What do we mean when we say "bureaucracy hacking"? We're talking about having an outsized impact—at a rate, scale, and force beyond your immediate resources—within large organizations that others often consider immovable. If Harvard Business School professor Howard H. Stevenson defined entrepreneurship as "pursuing opportunity beyond the resources under your control," then we are talking about doing exactly that in corporations, nonprofits, academia, and government.

The word *hack* has many different meanings in today's world. In this book, we don't use the word to mean an uninspired journalist or the unauthorized accessing of a computer system. Rather, we mean: "a clever tip or technique for doing or improving something." We like this definition because it's expansive: bureaucracy hacking can include doing something new *and* improving something that already exists. In fact, in our experience, the best bureaucracy hackers accomplish both.

Bureaucracy hacking is also sales. Just as successful start-up entrepreneurs are constantly selling—to investors to get capital, to prospective employees to join the team, and to potential customers to win their business—bureaucracy hackers excite others with their vision in order to attract resources, recruit more people, and generate impact. The best bureaucracy hackers have a legendary focus on the problem they are trying to solve and embrace experimentation to continually improve. They are effective at experimenting, selling, and executing because they believe in a better way, and they know how to convert that belief into reality.

What's in It for You

In this book, we will help you unleash your inner bureaucracy hacker by answering the following questions: What are the tactics and tips that will let you move mountains? What are the things to avoid when coming in as a newcomer? What does it mean to have empathy for your existing organization, mission, and culture—while also having a bias for action toward changing them? How can you find and empower existing employees to join your cause? We're here to share with you tools that will work inside any organization, no matter your role or where you sit in the hierarchy, compiled from world-class bureaucracy hackers. The skills you develop as a bureaucracy hacker can also help you personally and professionally; as you earn wins and refine your approach, you'll also grow your reputation at work and in the community. Even if you already know some of these plays, having them all at your fingertips will allow you to experiment with sequencing and combining hacks—ultimately getting even more done.

If you're reading this book, there's probably some change you want to see in the world. Maybe it's at work: you want to transform how your organization delivers a new service, product, or feature—or maybe you just want to digitize that frustrating expense form. Maybe it's related to your local community: you want to improve your local elementary school or serve veterans in your town. Or maybe you're watching the news and want to make a difference on big issues like poverty, climate change, or global health. Whatever your goal, however big or small, odds are that you'll need to hack a bureaucracy or two to get it done—and there's no better time to start than now.

In practice, this means recruiting allies and navigating organizational forces to accomplish your goals. To do this you'll need extreme empathy: for your customers, fellow employees, and the organization itself. At the end of the day, most bureaucratic problems have human solutions. Bureaucracy hacking isn't about being a soulless schemer, but rather about understanding real needs and banding together with real people as you maneuver through a labyrinth of rules, risks, and incentives.

A deep respect for an existing organization juxtaposed against a fierce urgency for change may seem paradoxical, but balancing those conflicting forces is key to making a lasting impact. Maybe you see that tension in your workplace too: the person loudly advocating for change versus the old guard advocating for caution. This book can help you bridge that divide.

Bureaucracies are explicitly designed *not* to change on a dime. There are approvals, committees, policies, procedures, and packets of paperwork. Ignore them at your peril. Instead, *use* them to your advantage—especially to codify the changes you want to make permanent.

We write for the millions of leaders, managers, consultants, and employees around the globe who see the hype about fast-paced start-up culture and wonder how it might be relevant to their slow-moving, risk-averse company or organization, as well as for those feeling stuck in frustrating bureaucracies in their personal lives, like PTAs, neighborhood or city council groups, and condo associations. Everyone is in, or at least alongside, a bureaucracy of some kind. You can keep feeling like change is impossible—or you can start making the changes you want to see.

This book is for everyone, whether you are starting your career, mid-career, or a senior executive. The most powerful change in an organization comes from within. Change is possible, even in the most challenging of environments. But no one else is coming to save the day. It's up to you.

A BUREAUCRATIC NOTE

Our friends warned us about writing a book with the word *bureaucracy* in the title. Who wants to read that, they asked? And who even wants to admit they're in a bureaucracy? Despite so many of us working in or alongside a bureaucracy, we see them as something to be endured, not loved. But however imperfect, bureaucracies are important and highly relevant. The prodigious economist Anthony Downs opens his famous 1967 book on the topic, *Inside Bureaucracy*, with the following observation that still holds true today:

> It is ironic that bureaucracy is primarily a term of scorn. In reality, bureaus are among the most important institutions in every nation in the world. Not only do they provide employment for a very significant fraction of the world's population, but they also make critical decisions that shape the economic, educational, political, social, moral, and even religious lives of nearly everyone on earth.

Let's start with the basics. What defines a bureaucracy? In short, a bureaucracy is a sizable organization—government, business, or nonprofit—with hierarchy, rules, processes, and power. Whether public or private, bureaucracies are characterized by their "complexity, division of labour, permanence, professional management, hierarchical coordination and control, strict chain of command, and legal authority." Sound familiar?

Max Weber, the German sociologist and bureaucracy theorist—yes, that is a thing!—observed that bureaucracies are "distinguished by specialized expertise, certainty, continuity, and unity." Weber thought:

> In the pure form of bureaucratic organization universalized rules and procedures would dominate, rendering personal status or

connections irrelevant. In this form, bureaucracy is the epitome of universalized standards under which similar cases are treated similarly as codified by law and rules, and under which the individual tastes and discretion of the administrator are constrained by due process rules.

While most people focus on the problems to overcome in a bureaucracy—as do we in this book, offering tactics on how to both leverage and reform the existing rules—few focus on the benefits that the stability and continuity of a bureaucracy offer. Bureaucratic structures are resistant to change, for better (resisting external corruption or authoritarian leaders) and for worse (failing to adapt fast enough to meet customer and employee needs). That consistency can be comforting for the employees, stakeholders, and even some customers. We also recognize the value that stability brings and yet see bureaucracies around the world that desperately need to adapt and change, whether to win in the marketplace or to accomplish their important missions. As you hack your bureaucracy to make change, recognize that stability and continuity are often seen by many as a feature, not a bug.

Bureaucracies can be more effective than you think. In an article for *Harvard Business Review*, Amy C. Edmondson and Ranjay Gulati argue that bureaucracies have benefits: "Bureaucracy—characterized by specialized functions, fixed rules, and a hierarchy of authority—has gotten a bad rap: When designed well, it excels at ensuring reliability, efficiency, consistency, and fairness." You probably take for granted your mail being delivered, a Big Mac tasting the same no matter where you order it, or Google Search working instantly—but all of those services and products have some degree of bureaucratic systems behind them.

Bureaucracies are all around us. If you work in an organization of any size, whether as an employee, consultant, or volunteer, you're operating within a bureaucracy to at least some extent. Even the most flexible and innovative start-ups eventually grow into bureaucracies of their own. If you are self-employed or work in a small business, you likely have customers or suppliers that are bureaucracies. And you probably operate within or alongside bureaucratic systems closer to home, like parent-teacher associations, school boards, homeowners associations, and local governments that control zoning rules and how tall your grass can grow.

You probably bemoan the hierarchy, rules, and process. But if bureaucracies are so painful, why are they so plentiful? It's worth considering the alternative. Without rules and specialization—in an organization of any size—how would decisions get made fairly? How would people allocate resources? How would things get done?

Rules and processes enable organizations to scale. If you've ever been at a fast-growing company, you'll recognize the need to create standardized processes. What may have worked on an ad hoc basis when you were selling and serving a handful of users needs to be codified into a standard process when you have hundreds or thousands of customers. As an organization grows larger, defining specialist roles and standardizing their work becomes more important.

As our friend Rohan Bhobe, cofounder of Nava, puts it: when you are faced with a bureaucracy, your first instinct may be to try to "reduce bureaucracy" or "eliminate process or hierarchy." But a sufficiently large organization will always have structure. The challenge is to build a structure that most consistently produces the outcomes you want, while accepting or mitigating the trade-offs. Bureaucracies, in all their variations, are here to stay.

Whether your bureaucracy was created recently or has been around for centuries, each rule and process was created for a reason. People thought about the problem and decided that the current rule you are lamenting made sense. It's easy to assume that the person who created today's broken process was stupid or didn't have accurate foresight. But in truth, they probably made the best decision they could at the time. (You might have made the same decision then, too!) If you're not careful, your innovative solution today can become tomorrow's bureaucratic nightmare.

World War II general Omar Bradley is often credited with the maxim: "Amateurs talk strategy. Professionals talk logistics." In other words, the *how* matters. The same is true for making impact inside, alongside, or against a bureaucracy. We hope our tips on *how* to hack your bureaucracy—whether it's your employer, school, community association, house of worship, or local government—empower you to do great things.

DEFINE THE PROBLEM

TALK TO REAL PEOPLE

Experience is the teacher of all things.
—JULIUS CAESAR

Get out of your office to observe and listen to prospective, current, and former users—ideally in their natural environments. Ground your ideas for change in their real-life experiences.

Get Out of the Office

How do you persuade President Obama's senior advisors to change their minds? Lisa Gelobter, the new chief digital services officer at the US Department of Education, knew that pushing back against the West Wing wasn't going to be easy. As a former product and engineering executive at BET Networks, Hulu, and NBC, Lisa had a lot of experience building compelling digital products. And she knew that to be successful at her mission, she would need to understand the behavior of people not usually represented in the West Wing: students.

Lisa and her team were building the College Scorecard, a second-term addition to President Obama's array of initiatives aimed at decreasing the cost of college, like increasing Pell grants and making financial aid forms easier to use. The president was rankled by the fact that the country's most popular college ranking system, published by *U.S. News and World Report*, values what he considered to be the wrong things, like selectivity (the fewer students an institution accepts, the higher the ranking) and facilities (creating incentives to build new climbing walls and gyms, rather than invest in instructor training).

President Obama wanted a scorecard that would compete with it, but one that would give students and their families the same kind of "value for your money" information that you can find when you are buying, say, a new car or a new refrigerator. Colleges with low graduation rates or whose graduates didn't earn enough to repay their loans would have to disclose that information, presumably causing students looking for good value to give other, higher-performing schools a second look.

It turns out that using the federal government to rank seven thousand post-secondary institutions is trickier than it seems. How do you score the value of degrees from seminaries that are training clergy members who will never seek to earn much money? What about liberal arts degrees, which may ripen into lucrative careers over time, but not at first? What about schools that are serving students from marginalized areas with low-performing high schools? Rather than rank schools against each other, President Obama focused his team on presenting data that would allow students and their families to be better informed consumers.

The College Scorecard, as the initiative became known, is both an official US government website for students to learn about college costs *and* an effort to make the raw data available to the companies and nonprofits that help Americans with college choice—including other ranking systems. Arguably, getting the data into the hands of thousands of companies, nonprofits, and college counseling services could reach more people than an official government website alone. But the website was something that the president and senior West Wing officials could tangibly understand—and make suggestions about.

The original website was launched in February 2013 as part of President Obama's State of the Union speech. And it was a big flop. According to the *New York Times* in 2013:

> ...some of the data in the new scorecard is a few years old, and most of it has been available from other sources, notably the federal

government's own College Navigator site. Further, the information is presented as averages and medians that might have little relevance to individual families. The scorecard does connect to each institution's net price calculator, which allows individualized cost estimates, but it does not provide side-by-side comparisons of multiple schools, as other government sites do.

Further, and perhaps more critically, the website lacked the ability to show how much recent graduates of each college were making—an important feature if you are trying to show a prospective student's "bang for the buck." This was an innovation that the administration had been very excited about: using earnings data available from the Department of the Treasury and applying it to show how much students who attended particular universities actually earned a few years after graduating. But it was proving difficult to effectively use this earnings data alongside the other information the Department of Education was already making available. That's why West Wing officials asked Lisa to help.

Lisa and her team at the Department of Education were sensitive to the fact that they weren't starting from scratch. They did their best to get to know their counterparts across the government who had already been working on this project. But they also knew they would have to get out of the office and talk to real people to make the next version of the tool meaningfully better. Instead of focusing solely on untangling the knots tying up the project internally, Lisa's team took a fresh approach to the scorecard, asking what it would take to achieve its original purpose of being useful to students and their families as they made big investments in their futures.

With paper drawing prototypes—some made from cardboard salvaged from the trash—Lisa and her team walked around the Mall in front of the US Capitol to chat with college-bound students and their parents. After seeing the prototypes of a mobile website, students gave rapid, in-person feedback. Armed with the data from actual students—who weren't shy about saying what made sense and what didn't—Lisa was able to show President Obama's senior advisors insights like their idea for a "compare" button (something that some of them really wanted) wasn't a feature students would actually use, especially on the limited real estate of a mobile phone screen. President Obama's team—not to mention the *New York Times*—genuinely thought that the ability to compare schools would be a useful feature, but it turns out it didn't have any value to the students.

This insight didn't require fancy design or coding skills—the prototypes were literally hand-drawn on leftover cardboard. What it did require was getting out of the office and speaking with the actual target customers to find answers.

As a result of their research, Lisa and her team launched an updated College Scorecard as a mobile website with features that met the needs of actual students, rather than what senior White House officials *thought* students wanted. The team also persuaded the West Wing to release the data as an application programming interface (API), to make the data available to ranking systems, college counselors, and anyone else who wanted to use the data.

The updated website and underlying data were finally making an impact. Three years later, the *New York Times* was singing a different tune:

> Despite the hand-wringing of many in academia, who saw the immeasurable richness of a college education crassly reduced to a dollar sign, the data [underlying the College Scorecard] has wrought a sea change in the way students and families evaluate prospective colleges. Earnings data are finding their way into a proliferating number of mainstream college rankings, shifting the competitive landscape of American higher education in often surprising ways.

Look Beyond Your Organization

Great companies are obsessed with their customers. They know they need to deeply understand their customers' needs and desires if they want to have any chance of winning in a hypercompetitive market. Sometimes a company founder has intimately lived the problem she is trying to solve; other times, the founder is good (or gets good quickly) at talking to as many stakeholders as possible to understand their problems. Over time, companies employ people with job titles like "designer," "user experience researcher," and "product manager," all of whom are laser-focused on understanding customer behavior and attitudes.

But large bureaucracies—like government agencies, nonprofits, schools, and even some companies—are not necessarily designed to meaningfully listen to and learn from their end users. When they do, it's often in a very structured way, such as focus groups, surveys, or commissioned market research. In your organization, it might be the role of the marketing department to listen to prospective customers, and the role of the customer service department to listen to existing customers. These silos can prevent your organization from developing an accurate, holistic view of the real end user experience.

At Harvard, after his White House experience, Nick designed and taught a field class that forced students to get out of the ivory tower and listen to real people in their community. The student teams worked with government clients, like the City of Boston, to understand a specific problem and conduct original field research—doing ride-alongs with cops, interviewing voters in laundromats, talking to parents in libraries, and observing city workers struggling to fill out forms. While the students often hesitated, spending too much time planning these visits, Nick would insist, friendly but firmly, that they leave campus and embed themselves within their target population.

As a result, the students formed much richer understandings of the problem area they were tasked with solving. One student, Berkeley Brown, who spent a considerable amount of time with the Boston Police Gang Unit, observed how valuable it was to escape the "Cambridge bubble" and how her previous assumptions about how the police used technology—and what really mattered—were quickly shattered by spending time with two detectives, John and Brian. She noted:

> The remarkable thing was that, after four or five more visits to the gang unit and countless conversations with other stakeholders in the city, I did start to understand their world. I learned the names of the patrolmen's kids, and learned that the way John and Brian give each other a hard time is actually how they express their deeply entrenched commitment to each other's safety and well-being, a bond I will probably never fully understand. Indeed, a common refrain we heard is: "my first priority is my partner's kids." I learned to adjust my manner of speaking so I could get to the heart of the problems they were facing. I learned how to put their individual narratives into the context of the larger system I was observing, and how to ask questions that were more aligned with their lived experiences. Finally, I learned to take their experience—both the problems with and joys of their job—and turn them into real solutions.

Berkeley also admitted, in her post-class reflection paper, that coming back to Cambridge could be a bit culturally jarring; back in Harvard Square after a several-hour ride-along with the gang unit, she overheard her fellow students debating the pros and cons of taking Dutch versus Swedish as a foreign language, and using phrases like "a priori reasoning." Berkeley believed she was much wiser from having spent real time in the field, beyond the classroom.

Marina's first foray into foster care after working at the VA was thanks to an afternoon of talking to real people. She was invited to spend an afternoon in Rhode Island by her former boss Richard Culatta, who had recently become the state's chief innovation officer. The state was interested in tapping her technical expertise to recruit more foster parents, who were needed badly. Knowing how valuable talking to real people had been to her at the VA, the first thing Marina did was ask to have coffee with anyone who had *dropped out* of becoming a foster parent. It seemed easier to retain current applicants than to recruit brand-new ones, so she wanted to find out: Why had they given up?

After a few coffees, the answers were all the same: potential foster parents shared that they would call asking about the next steps in the licensing process, but the employee answering the phone often didn't know and didn't call them back. If the agency was this disorganized when it was *recruiting* them, the families thought, how would they support them if they had a challenge with a child in their home? This broke trust, and they dropped out.

This insight ended up being good news: it revealed a relatively easy fix that the agency had not yet considered, because it was not talking to the families that had dropped out. Marina shared the feedback with the state team, which quickly responded by making a shared spreadsheet that let everyone in the office see each family's progress as they worked through a series of required steps toward becoming licensed. This made it easy for anyone answering the phone to tell people where they stood in the process. Was this spreadsheet the ultimate solution? Of course not. A couple years later, the state implemented an online foster parent licensing portal from Binti, a software vendor focused on foster care, that let families log on to see their own progress. But that initial spreadsheet let the team get started and make immediate progress toward improving the foster parent experience. Today, Rhode Island has one of the highest foster parent licensing rates in the country.

Get Outside the Office—Literally

Once you're inside an organization, you can't have a truly outside perspective. No matter if you've been there for ten minutes or ten years, you can counter this by *going* outside.

One of Marina's most impactful experiences was meeting a woman on a bench at the Menlo Park VA Hospital. Marina, who is rather shy, was forced to sit on this bench all afternoon for an exercise in a design thinking workshop. She was instructed to keep her VA role to herself and simply make small talk with anyone who sat down. This woman seemed eager to talk. Due to her husband's illnesses, she had essentially lived at the hospital for the last year. As she told her story, Marina racked up a growing mental list of all the VA benefits for which this woman qualified: pension, home loan, and college tuition for their oldest son, to name a few. Yet when asked what other benefits they used besides healthcare, the woman's response stunned her: "What other benefits?"

The realization that it was possible to literally live at the VA for a year and not know about its eighty-two non-healthcare benefit lines was alarming; but it fueled Marina's vision of a VA that could organize itself around a veteran and their family, instead of continuing to force veterans to organize themselves around the agency.

Going outside the building proved a repeatable success play at the VA. In the face of a mounting crisis in which veterans could not enroll in VA healthcare because over 800,000 paper applications had piled up in a warehouse, Mary Ann Brody, a new member of Marina's team, sought answers in an unlikely place: the White House correspondence office. There, every letter sent to the president is meticulously saved and cataloged. Mary Ann pulled a letter from a homeless veteran, Dominic, who was asking for help in obtaining VA healthcare. She arranged to meet him and (with his permission) recorded their interaction, asking him to show her how he had tried to get VA healthcare in the past. Busting all stereotypes of homeless veterans, Dominic was young, personable, and tech-savvy—and he expertly narrated the seemingly impossible task of enrolling in VA healthcare, which he had unsuccessfully tried to do *twelve times*. The application experience was so bad, he likened it to trying to get through a door spiked with IEDs. After demonstrating that there was literally no way for him to enroll, Mary Ann had him try the team's prototype for a new and simpler application. Dominic was able to complete it on the first try, declaring he would use it "over anything the VA would provide."

This video took off like wildfire across the VA and the White House. The focus immediately shifted to: "How do we get this new online application into the hands of every veteran?" Within weeks, every VA employee was directed to point veterans at the new online form instead of paper. Most importantly, Dominic was enrolled in healthcare the very next morning. In a testament to its leadership, the VA even put Dominic's videos online. Faced with his undeniable real-world experience, decision makers were newly motivated to pick up the pace of transformation. Over a million veterans have since enrolled in healthcare, all thanks to Mary Ann getting out of the building and finding Dominic. (You can watch Dominic's videos on our website.)

Observing from a Distance

You should also find ways to indirectly observe your customers' behavior. We aren't proposing one-way mirrors or fancy surveillance systems, though these days there are lots of high-tech solutions to measure where people move in a store, where they linger on a web page, and how much time they spend making a decision. It often doesn't take anything but a keen eye to spot customer dissatisfaction. In 2001, delivery driver Joe Perrone saw frustrated customers walk right past parked FedEx trucks while carrying packages to their nearest drop-off location. He suggested adding drop slots to trucks. Thanks to his idea, FedEx trucks effectively became mobile drop-off locations.

If you have an OXO Good Grips peeler in your kitchen, it's because its designer, Sam Farber, went out and observed real people—starting with his wife. A lifelong entrepreneur, he was looking for a way to break into the kitchen goods space when he noticed his wife, who had arthritis, struggling to peel a carrot. With a bit of clay, he built a prototype— which he then refined by watching many volunteers from the American Arthritis Foundation try to use it. The resulting Good Grips peeler works well for people with joint problems, and *also* works really well for people who don't have joint problems.

This technique isn't limited to observing human users: Canadian officials struggled repeatedly to design raccoon-proof garbage bins until they took the time to observe real raccoons breaking into the bins at night. This ultimately led to a new bin design that the raccoons could not overcome.

Grounding your initiative in the context of real stories of real users (not to mention prospective and former customers) will give you more than survey data—it gives you a narrative that is easy to understand, and easy for others to repeat. Your strongest competitive edge will come from immersing yourself among real customers—*especially* if that isn't part of your job description.

HOW CAN I USE THIS?

» **Do your homework.** Your organization probably has a public engagement, market research, or customer service function. Get a coffee with someone in that department to understand what information they already collect, how they listen to customers— and what they don't know. For example, your marketing depart- ment might have user personas (a fictionalized person with attributes that represents a target customer segment) that can help you determine which people to talk to next.

» **Talk to customers through existing channels.** If your organi- zation has a customer support, customer service, or customer success group, see if you can shadow them, or even do a cou- ple hours of direct customer support. You can also talk to cus- tomers at conferences or trade shows.

» **Go where your customers are.** Marina got some of her best feedback from veterans by simply sitting on park benches or in waiting rooms at hospitals and talking to people. Rather than asking others to come to you, go to their office, home, or community.

» **Be brave.** Users are usually eager to talk and share their feed- back; don't be shy!

» **Get started.** Don't worry about trying to perfectly understand all of your customers at once. Get out there with your first user as soon as you can, and make this kind of interaction part of your routine.

» **Find ways to talk to former and prospective customers, too.** They will have different perspectives on why they left (or why they aren't yet working with you), which can spark a whole new set of ideas and solutions.

» **Use incentives.** Small gift cards can encourage more people to talk to you and can often be purchased through petty cash or other small office supply budgets. It's especially important to compensate people in settings like nonprofit or public sector user research.

» **Cast a wide net.** You can't replace talking with and observing real people one-on-one, but this individual approach can't always scale. Give a wider audience of colleagues or users a way to share feedback or review ideas using digital crowd-sourcing tools like Medallia's Crowdicity, or even simply giving out your email address.

» **Block out time.** Schedule some extra time during your next business trip to visit with users. Build talking to real people into your schedule.

» **Take a human-centered design class.** Still nervous about talking with real people? Different industries call this practice different things—user research, field market research, or ethnographic field work—but they are all fundamentally about observing and listening to your audience. Take a short class to learn skills and practice them.

BE YOUR OWN CUSTOMER

You have to know the weeds, to have lived in
them, to delegate. I wouldn't want to be
a leader who had never lived in the weeds.

—BRIAN GRAZER

---

*Experience your organization's product or service
the way customers or constituents do. You'll
uncover customer service gaps, confusing
instructions, and opportunities for new products,
services, or features.*

In the UK government, it's policy that a cabinet minister must successfully use a website or application before it launches to the public. This serves a few purposes. First, while it's not a substitute for usability testing and quality control, if a minister finds something confusing, the website can still be revised before it publicly launches. Second, it gives the minister an up-close view of the digital experience that he or she is responsible for, so they can be a more informed advocate. Third, it forces the team building the service to make sure it truly is easy to use—despite their privilege and status, ministers aren't exactly known for their digital savvy.

You might be surprised by the number of executives that are responsible for a product or service without any firsthand knowledge of what it's like to be a buyer or user. Simply bringing the end user experience to their attention can be a powerful driving force for improvement and change.

Marina's inspiration to fix digital identity problems at the VA came from her personal experience trying to create an online account for her grandfather, a World War II veteran. World War II veterans have seven-digit ID numbers, but the VA's online benefits system required a minimum of eight numbers. If you put in only seven digits, the resulting error message was a four-inch block of red text containing three separate phone numbers to call. When she raised the issue with the team responsible for that website, they proudly showed her their fix: an even longer error message, with a *fourth* phone number. Undeterred, she used her grandfather's case as motivation to eventually fix this experience for every veteran.

Mystery Shop

No matter where you sit in an organization, there is a lot of value in trying your product or service yourself. While you'll certainly have some unfair advantages over a typical customer or constituent, you can still uncover many opportunities for improvement.

Many companies hire mystery shoppers to act as normal customers, document their experience, and report back on how it went. These undercover customers note how long it takes to be greeted by staff, whether certain items are in stock, whether the restroom is clean, and other details. Since employees don't know who the mystery shoppers are, or when (or if) they are stopping by, this practice can be a useful source of objective information on the everyday customer experience.

Our use of the term *shopping* isn't limited to retail products; being an undercover customer is useful for services as well. Mystery shopping his own practice opened the eyes of Dr. Robert Mecklenburg, a physician in Seattle, to his patients' experiences. "I practiced for 30 years without knowing how long patients waited to see me," revealed Dr. Mecklenburg. The realization that his patients endured long waits prompted him to start a collaborative effort between his hospital and local employers, to embed specialists like physical therapists inside local workplaces like Starbucks to get ahead of problems like back pain and workplace injuries.

Similarly, many school districts have opportunities like so-called learning walks, where teachers throughout the district can sit and observe other teachers during particular classes. Some teaching centers have formal opportunities for instructors to sit in one another's classrooms. This way, instructors and administrators can learn how other schools, districts, and peers approach similar problems and topics. When Nick was first asked to teach, for example, he interviewed other Harvard professors—across the Kennedy School, the Business School, and Harvard College—and watched some of them teach.

The information you gain from mystery shopping can help you make the case that a particular process or product needs changing. Mystery shopping can also uncover reasons why your organization is failing to meet certain metrics, like customer service satisfaction scores. Sometimes mystery shopping simply helps you put your bureaucracy in greater context, which you can use to design and implement more relevant solutions to the problems you care about.

New Businesses in New Jersey

When Giuseppe Morgana, originally one of Nick's first students at Harvard, and E. J. Kalafarski began working for the State of New Jersey's newly formed Office of Innovation, one of their first assignments was to make it easier for people to open new businesses. Colleagues helpfully suggested that they could do this by digitizing business permits, or by making more forms digitally fillable.

But Giuseppe and E. J. weren't convinced that digital forms were business owners' most pressing need. To find out for sure, their team started shadowing real businesses as they tried to register with the state, and spent time meeting with the dedicated and incredibly helpful state employees processing the registration forms. They started to realize that although there was a lot of focus on individual forms, no one owned the end-to-end experience of an entrepreneur interacting with the state across all the required registration steps. Giuseppe, E. J., and their team learned just how many phone numbers businesses had to navigate for support. New Jersey has a long list of requirements for businesses, including permits for construction, hiring employees, and more—but it was up to each business owner to figure out which rules applied to their specific business, complete different processes for each rule, and navigate each helpline when they had questions. Entrepreneurs were understandably confused and frustrated.

The team's first step toward improving this experience was to make the registration requirements more easily understandable to business owners. The team launched a clearly branded, simple website that businesses could go to for help—Business.NJ.gov—which laid out this information in plain language. To launch quickly, the team used open-source code (meaning anyone can copy and use it) from the City of Los Angeles, so they didn't have to start from scratch. Government colleagues were impressed that they could "copy and paste" so much work for free to get started.

Their team was able to pull together the necessary resources because they found a gem in New Jersey: the Business Action Center, a small group of experienced state employees who could capably troubleshoot complex business issues. When they were first introduced, Giuseppe and E. J. sat alongside the Business Action Center and listened to phone calls as the team directed business users across the state. In late 2019, the Office of Innovation added live chat to its new website and trained the Business Action Center experts on how to use it. Now the plain language website also had a knowledgeable, interactive help desk, which they could periodically review as mystery shoppers.

A few months later, the pandemic hit. The live chat became a lifeline for businesses across the state as they struggled to stay afloat, particularly in the first few days before the telephone helpline was updated to allow for remote work. Because they had already launched with their first two representatives, it was possible for the website to scale to over fifty representatives over the course of a weekend, ultimately facilitating over 58,000 live chats in the first year.

Giuseppe, E. J., and their growing team gathered data from the live chat to learn about New Jersey business owners' top questions and concerns and began adding frequently asked questions and answers to the website. They added "How do I…" starter kits for residents with specific goals like opening a food truck or an auto body repair shop. This plain language content transformed the experience of New Jersey business owners—in a pandemic, no less!—and cost comparatively little in

time and money. And all these solutions were inspired by Giuseppe and
E. J. spending time with real business users, trying to navigate state services themselves, and starting with small changes to improve the overall experience.

Being Your Own Customer When You Know Too Much

Admittedly, being an undercover customer is easier if your business or organization offers a product or service for consumers. If, for example, you work for a company that sells complicated technical services to other large enterprises, it would be challenging to experience that firsthand. But you can still ask yourself: Are there elements of the sales, implementation, or customer service process that I *could* experience?

There are plenty of situations where it's hard, or even impossible, to be your own customer. If you are faculty or staff at a university, it's hard to play a student. If you are a medical or administrative professional, it's hard to disappear into the role of a patient in your own hospital—your colleagues would recognize you and give you special consideration (and maybe send you to the psych ward). But you can still:

- sit in the lobby and observe the check-in process;

- listen to the reservation or help phone line;

- try to find directions to a particular building or room number, using only the available signage or customer service staff; or

- try to make a new patient, student, or customer appointment— which you can later cancel.

For most people, especially in the digital age, it's easier than you think to be your own customer—at least for part of the customer experience. A hotel manager may not be able to stay in her own hotel as an anonymous guest, but she can create a fake email address to experience what it's like for a new customer to book a room online, or call the front desk to make a reservation.

Being Your Own Customer Is Not a Substitute for Working with Real Users

Being your own customer is one powerful lens to catch issues and improvement areas firsthand. But no one person's experience can highlight everything you need to know. One limitation: you already know how your organization works behind the scenes—and that's hard to forget. At the VA, Marina found many of her colleagues, who were veterans themselves, had trouble believing *other* veterans struggled to navigate the agency because *they*, as veterans, could navigate it just fine. They couldn't see that their knowledge of acronyms, departments, and even some of their personal relationships meant that they experienced the VA in a fundamentally different way than a veteran on the outside experienced it.

This didn't mean that a veteran working at the VA couldn't still provide valuable insights. Scott Blackburn, a veteran and now senior partner at McKinsey who led many transformation efforts at the VA, was the very first user of the prescription refill functionality on Marina's redesigned digital experience. Her team was thrilled to see a photo of Scott opening his mailbox to find his refill inside. Scott later went on to test a lot more functionality, such as preregistering for a gravesite, to give constructive feedback on the process. Would it make sense for Scott to pretend to be a veteran who didn't know anything about gravesite registration? No; they'd need to talk with other veterans for that perspective. Did he still have valuable feedback to give about the registration process itself? You bet.

Beyond your own experience, there are a myriad of other perspectives you'll want to understand better to make your case for change: perhaps it's people with disabilities, people who speak other languages, or people unfamiliar with your industry. Our friend and former White House colleague Erie Meyer likes to say that you aren't being truly innovative unless you are making it possible for the most vulnerable and marginalized communities to use your service. It's this tactic of being your own customer, *coupled* with other tactics like getting out of the office to talk with all kinds of real people, that together give you the inspiration, and the details, you need to make lasting change.

HOW CAN I USE THIS?

» **Mystery shop.** See if you can navigate your organization's buying process (or user experience) yourself. Take notes about your experience. What was delightful? Confusing? Frustrating?

» **Test the front doors.** On a regular basis, try your organization's phone numbers, emails, website addresses, and physical addresses to confirm they're working and that directions (such as physical maps to offices or the options on an automated phone system) make sense.

» **Ensure all kinds of users can get through.** Can a particularly long name fit on your organization's forms? Will your website reject names with accent characters? If you need information about race and ethnicity, can people choose all the options that apply to them? We have a list of these kinds of considerations on our website.

» **Be ethical.** It's okay to create an anonymous account and try your product or service yourself. It's not okay to then post a five-star review.

» **Break down the process of being a customer.** Maybe you can't experience the end-to-end customer experience, but are there parts you *can* experience, like the customer service hotline, the website, sales materials, or enrollment instructions?

» **Recognize when you know too much.** Once you're inside an organization, you can't play the part of an objective outsider, however well-intentioned and creative you are. But no matter how long you've been there, you can always advocate for talking to real people with outside experience.

LOOK BETWEEN THE SILOS

*The Achilles' heel of an organization is the space
between the silos—i.e., between business units,
academic departments, or government agencies—
where broken handoffs or miscommunications
can lead to poor customer experiences or wasteful
repetition. Few people are paying attention or
defending the status quo in these gray areas, making
them ripe for quicker and more well-received
changes.*

One of our favorite tactics is to look between the silos. For Marina, it has never failed to bear fruit in any organization where she's worked, even if she's there for only a few hours. By simply following a process (e.g., a customer transaction) from start to finish, and paying particular attention to places where the process changes hands, you can uncover big wins while triggering fewer bureaucratic antibodies.

Mapping the Refugee Immigration Process

On September 14, 2016, President Obama announced a goal to increase the number of refugees admitted into the United States from 85,000 to 110,000 in the following year. There was just one problem: Homeland Security officials weren't sure they would be able to process that many people that quickly. The process normally took two years from start to finish, and there was less than a year left to meet the deadline.

Determined to find a solution, a small team from the United States Digital Service, a new technology unit in federal government, hopped on planes and flew to refugee processing centers in locations around the world, following individual State Department and Department of Homeland Security immigration officers as they processed refugee case files. The team was initially encouraged to read process manuals and conduct phone-based interviews with field workers in Washington, DC, but they convinced their bosses to let them get out into the field instead. The team was pretty sure that the ways to streamline the process and ensure every one of those 110,000 refugees made it safely into America were not going to be found on a phone call.

The investigators who vet refugees for possible admission into the United States are highly specialized. They're fluent in the local languages of the countries and villages, and they're also hyperlocal historical experts, able to put stories into context and validate very specific narratives. The stakes are high—if they are wrongly suspicious and deny someone, they may be condemning them to suffering and even death; if they are wrongly lenient and let an imposter into the country, they risk harm not only to Americans but also to the reputation of the entire refugee program. These investigators spend the majority of their time in refugee camps and on airplanes.

Perhaps *too much* time on airplanes.

A pattern that the team noticed was that these rare, impossible-to-find experts were often flying *back* to refugee camps more than eight weeks after completing their work there—because they were required to stamp their final documents in the same location where they had conducted the initial interviews, even though the documents were rarely ready for signature before they were ready to move on to the next camp. This meant days of wasted time (and many thousands of wasted taxpayer dollars on airfare) looping back on itineraries when, instead, they could be conducting more interviews in more refugee camps—all because of a signature requirement!

This inefficiency was not written down in any procedure manual, and to many of the seasoned officers, flying back and forth had just become a routine part of their job. But to the fresh eyes of the team that was following them across the silos, it presented an opportunity: digital signature stamps. E-signatures soon replaced wet signatures, and this enormous inefficiency—which, once uncovered, *nobody* defended—was relatively easy to stamp out.

Eighteenth-Century Silos

When Marina was shadowing the process for approving potential foster parents in a particular state, she spent much of the day privately brainstorming how she might convert its all-paper process into an automated, electronic one. But one particular step stumped her for a moment: the request for an applicant's driving record had to be submitted on carbon copy paper.

(If you are not old enough to have used carbon copy paper, it's three thin, stacked colored sheets of paper. You write on the top sheet, and what you write transfers to the two sheets below—if you press down hard enough with your pen.)

Marina innocently asked the case worker she was shadowing: "Why do you have to fill out that carbon sheet for the DMV?"

"Because the people at the DMV live in the 18th century," the worker replied, frustrated.

But Marina had an ace up her sleeve. She could do what that individual case worker was not empowered to do—Marina went over to the DMV and asked them to show her how they processed these records requests on their end.

A friendly DMV employee was happy to show Marina how they fulfilled driving record requests. As the first step in the demonstration, she opened her email to show how requests were received electronically.

"I saw someone send over a carbon copy paper request...where does that play in?" Marina asked.

"Oh, you must have been at child welfare! Those people live in the 18th century. I wish they would just email us the requests instead of using those crazy colored papers."

By hopping across silos, Marina was able to highlight this disconnect and eliminate the dreaded carbon copy paper from *both* departments, which were both happy to immediately replace the cumbersome paper with the electronic form.

Evan Doomes, a recent college graduate who became a Govern for America Fellow at the Louisiana Department of Health, heard Marina tell this story and decided to try this tactic for himself. He wondered why it took hospitals ninety days or more to fix seemingly simple errors on birth certificates—so he watched the process, step by step, across the silos. His journey revealed, among other challenges, that birth certificate errors were disproportionately impacting the Latino community because the state's aging IT systems could not support accent characters or hyphens in names. Armed with insights about how the end-to-end process worked, Evan was able to reduce the turnaround time from over ninety days to an average of just seventeen days, with more improvements on the way.

Bringing Silos Together

One of Marina's most eye-opening discoveries between silos came when she was studying how the veteran disability claims process works. She flew around the country, following real veterans (with their permission) through their paperwork and medical exams, and then watched claims processors evaluate those same veterans' claims.

For context, at the time in 2012, the VA's disability claims backlog was a hot topic. Hundreds of thousands of veterans had been waiting years for their first payments, and they were rightfully frustrated. Congress was constantly looking into the matter, and it was on the front page of national newspapers. The program employed thousands of doctors and claims processors, with a multibillion-dollar budget just for processing claims (not including the benefits payments themselves, which are many more billions of dollars). These silos were *huge*.

Even though the process was demonstrably not working, everyone involved seemed paralyzed, afraid any change could make things worse. Solutions focused on doing more of the status quo, like mandatory overtime. This environment did not exactly foster collaboration or innovation. Marina's ideas were explicitly not welcome when it came to changing either the medical evaluation or the claims processing side. But as she shadowed more veterans, she noticed there wasn't really anybody paying attention to the handoff in the middle. And *boy* was there a lot of opportunity in the middle.

The doctors conducting the disability evaluations told Marina that their evaluations were being read later by *another doctor*. This meant they wrote detailed, multipage reports full of medical jargon. At the same time, they admitted they had no information about the factors used later on to legally decide a disability claim, so to be on the safe side, the examiners included every detail they could.

However, these medical reports didn't go to other doctors—they went to administrative claims processors, who had only five hours of training on medical terminology. These claims processors had clear, strict guidelines for how to determine a disability percentage—so strict, in fact, that their only tool was an on-screen calculator. These poor claims processors had to try to decipher pages of medical jargon in order to pull out the specific details they needed to input into their calculator—details which often weren't in the report at all. In that case, they would have to send the veteran back for another medical exam, which sometimes meant days of travel to their nearest VA hospital.

Marina had no formal authority whatsoever in this process, but she did have some convening power. She invited some of the doctors and the claims processors she had met to get together into one room, and for the first time, had them demonstrate their parts of the process to one another. After the demonstrations, there was understandable outrage—doctors who had spent years carefully crafting medical reports did not appreciate learning that all their work was for nothing. After the anger passed, it seemed impossible to return to business as usual.

With Marina's help, the doctors and claim processors in the room put their heads together and asked: What if we gave the doctor the calculator? Then the examiner could enter the precise medical information needed, while the claims processor could focus on other administrative details. Even better, doctors pointed out that some of the information needed, such as a diagnosis code, didn't even require the veteran to come in for an exam at all—it already existed in their VA health record and could be filled out right away.

This small group of field employees piloted their silo-busting idea together and showed that it was possible to process many kinds of disability claims within *days*, instead of years. (Since this meeting, some kinds of disability decisions have been fully automated, based on existing medical records.) Bringing together siloed teams with a shared goal drove real change in just a few weeks.

HOW CAN I USE THIS?

» **Follow real, specific transactions from start to finish.** You will not learn nearly as much if you only observe isolated steps in a process. Some of the best discoveries are found at the intersection or handoffs between groups. Beware: this tactic doesn't work as well if you simply read process manuals or ask people to describe their work to you. The idea is to shadow real transactions, claims, cases, or people from beginning to end.

» **Be the Queen on the chess board.** Unlike other pieces, the Queen can move forward, backward, *and* diagonally. When you're following a transaction, case, or claim, go *everywhere* it goes: the mail room, the basement, across to another group, etc.

» **Draw the process.** Draw out what you learn on a dry-erase board, large piece of paper, or a digital whiteboarding tool. List completion times, pain points, error rates, volume, duplication, wait times, quotas, capacity measures, and other data elements you encounter—even if they're rough estimates.

» **Show others the process you drew.** There's nothing quite like sitting on the floor with a senior leader and a pile of permanent markers to reveal—and potentially change for good—process inefficiencies. The more one-on-one you can make this, the better, as you'll get more honest feedback and ideas. Be careful though: don't publicly share a process map that hasn't been vetted first.

» **Consider lateral career opportunities in your organization.** A move to a different unit can give you a different perspective on both customer-focused and internal processes. This move could even be very temporary, like covering for a sick colleague in a different division.

» **Walk around.** You never know what you'll overhear, or who you'll meet, simply by walking outside of your own silo.

PLAY THE NEWBIE CARD

Use your newness in an organization or a role to your advantage. Don't be afraid to ask questions about how things work in your institution, which can uncover significant opportunities that your longer-tenured colleagues can't see.

Once you've been at a job for a while, the window to ask basic questions closes. One of the best opportunities you have for shadowing processes, visiting other teams, and getting to ask questions that can unlock significant opportunities is by playing the "newbie" card.

Being a new employee or team member, rather than being a limitation, can be a huge asset—because by being new, you can ask questions and draw connections that more seasoned team members are now either too embarrassed to ask or too entrenched to see.

While it's hard to ask basic questions about your immediate area of expertise after a period of time, you can still employ this tactic with other teams and other organizations. You can always try to get a newer person to ask on your behalf, too. And if you're lucky enough to be a consultant, you should be using this every time you're on a new client site.

The $100 Million Dollar Button

At the VA's Board of Veterans' Appeals, which revisits decisions made about whether veterans are eligible for specific benefits, there was an ongoing battle over individual lawyers' performance standards. The appeals backlog grew higher and higher, with the average appeal taking *seven years* to process. And yet the employee union stood firm that each lawyer should only have to process two appeals per week, insisting that they could not do more. The appeals attorneys were smart and hard-working—none of them were slacking off. Confusingly, it seemed that they really could produce only two appeals each in a week. But why?

As a newcomer to the VA, Presidential Innovation Fellow Robert Sosinski wanted to learn how the appeals process worked, from start to finish. He sat next to attorneys as they processed claims, peppering them with questions about how they made decisions and where they got pieces of information. The process seemed routine enough, and there were certainly hundreds of pages of material to read and carefully consider. But a few days in, he stumbled upon a huge eye-opener: watching an attorney *start* a new appeal.

The average appeal had seven hundred documents—which included many duplicates and many short documents that were typically just a few pages each. The VA had moved to an electronic claims processing system a few years prior, and all the relevant files for an appeal were now scanned into PDFs. To outsiders, this seemed like an efficiency improvement—all files were now electronic, and all in one place.

But to the attorneys, it was an absolute nightmare.

The system did have all seven hundred PDF files in one place—but to access them, an appeals attorney had to *individually* download each PDF, one by one by one, onto their computer. This tedious task took an entire day for every single appeal—making it impossible for an attorney to process more than two in a week, just as they said. In fact, the new electronic process was far worse than when they had a giant stack of paper on their desks. Many attorneys quietly shared that they wished they could go back to paper files, which didn't require days of tedious, mind-numbing downloading.

Robert, being new, was able to ask the obvious question that you likely have already thought of: Why wasn't there a Download All button?

Great question. While we warn later in the book to beware of obvious answers, in this specific instance there was no complicated reason—it was truly that nobody had considered it an option before. The attorneys were not computer programmers, and they had never listed such a feature request in their IT contracting requirements. Within the next year, the Download All button was deployed to all the attorneys and nicknamed "The $100 Million Button" because of the huge cost savings it provided. As of this writing, the average claim processing time is down from seven years to three—a huge win for the VA, for the appeals attorneys, and, most importantly, for veterans with pending appeals. This button was one of a few major changes that helped halve the time. It's an opportunity that probably never would have been uncovered without a new employee having the freedom to ask basic questions about how appeals worked.

Where's the Test for This?

Former Google engineer Carla Geisser shared with us a newbie tactic she uses repeatedly whenever she joins a new development team.

All software engineers know they are supposed to write tests for their code. (Tests automatically run to confirm that software is behaving as you expect; a test might look for the presence of a word in the header of a website or confirm that if you remove an item from your shopping cart, the item is actually removed.) Often, due to time pressure or complexity, engineers neglect to write tests, creating a risk of deploying code with bugs into production. Managers fret about changing the culture around testing, but this is hard to accomplish.

As a new engineer on a team, Carla tries to look at nearly every change and leave only one comment: "Where is the test for this?" This serves as a gentle reminder. Quickly, other engineers figure out that writing a test is going to be faster and a lot less work than trying to argue with Carla. Eventually, on teams that she joins, people start including tests with every change, since they know she will instantly ask this question if they don't.

Use Your Newbie Card to Help Others

Sometimes the newbie questions that are most powerful come from other people at your organization.

Fourth grade teacher Becca A. shared this with us: "I've been the new teacher in a few different districts. Being the newbie on staff often means that your colleagues will ask you to ask questions of the school administration that they don't feel comfortable asking themselves, because as the new person, you can play it off more easily."

HOW CAN I USE THIS?

» **Ask lots of questions.** Whenever you join an organization, department, or team, maximize your time as a newbie to uncover possibilities in their bureaucracy that others cannot access.

» **Show genuine interest.** Asking questions is part of building a relationship and solving problems; it's not a dry academic exercise. Make eye contact, ask follow-ups, and try to take notes in a way that still allows for real conversation.

» **Don't ignore your inner questioner.** Maybe you've been in your role awhile, and you have a question you're hesitating to ask anyone because you think you should already know the answer. Resist the urge to ignore it and find a way to find out— even if you have to enlist a new person or an outside consultant to ask for you.

» **Drink from the firehose.** Jump in the deep end and try to learn as much as you can, in as many places as you can, when you're new to a company, a team, or a project. Keep detailed notes. It won't all make sense at first, but you'll pick up on valuable clues that you can piece together later.

» **Be a nice newbie.** Avoid any temptation to introduce yourself in a way that makes you seem like you're better than the people you're meeting. Be especially careful about highlighting your past employer or experience, especially if it is prestigious or uncommon. As a new person, you don't *really* know much yet—stay humble.

» **Ask questions on behalf of others.** Earn trust and build relationships by playing your newbie card for others, who may feel they have been at the organization too long to ask without embarrassment.

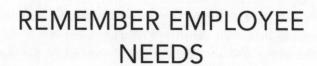

REMEMBER EMPLOYEE NEEDS

Spend time in the field shadowing frontline employees to gather insights about what's really working—and what isn't. Prioritize improving internal processes just as you would end user improvements; use those internal improvements to gain buy-in for other changes you need employees to make that benefit external users.

It's common for new initiatives to fail because existing employees don't embrace them. But it's lazy to blame the employees, when they probably had perfectly good reasons to withhold their support. If you want your bureaucracy hack to succeed, you *must* consider—and win over— the people who will be responsible for implementing it on a day-to-day basis. Part of winning them over is keeping their needs front and center.

Shadow Internal Users in the Field

Just like the TV show *Undercover Boss*—but without a ridiculous disguise—you can head into the field and shadow real workers doing real work. Of all the techniques we've employed in our careers, this is above and beyond the number one generator of ideas and insights for change. You don't need a reality TV show and cameras rolling (in fact, it's probably easier without them) to learn how employees act when the boss isn't looking.

You also don't need to hide who you are—unless you're a restaurant reviewer, we're not advocating for deception and funny wigs. You shouldn't shadow someone with an entourage and demand a reserved parking spot. Show up in a way that shows respect to those you're shadowing, but also gives an air of friendliness and approachability. If you work alongside them and earn their trust, employees will be surprisingly candid with you about which rules or processes are not working or could use improvement.

Some tips for user shadowing include:

- Follow real products, cases, claims, or customers from start to finish. This will give you greater context and highlight gaps at handoffs.

- Have employees narrate as they perform real work—to the extent possible, don't interrupt or guide. You're there to listen and observe.

- Be a real person. Smile, ask questions, and be empathetic.

- Ask them to tell you a mystery. Maybe they always wonder why we ask Question 22, or where Page 7 goes. If at all possible, find the answer to their mystery, and follow up to let them know. In general, "mysteries" are clues to something that needs improvement.

- Make it crystal clear that you aren't there to audit anybody or hunt out errors, especially if you are senior or if you work in headquarters. If you don't, nobody will raise their hand for you to sit by them. We usually address this elephant in the room directly when we initially introduce ourselves. Make sure you mean this—go out of your way to protect anyone you shadow from subsequent punishment, and don't report run of the mill issues or errors. (Do report actual criminal activity or wrongdoing, of course.)

Anthony Lyons, the city manager of Gainesville, Florida, used this bureaucracy-hacking tactic when he rode along with building inspectors for a day. He joined as they drove all over town, all day long, only to be faced with grumpy customers who missed an entire day of work so they could be home during their specified window (described as "sometime today" in their appointment notice). When he asked the inspectors about their jobs, employees said they didn't understand why they couldn't use remote video to do routine inspections like those for hot water heaters, which would both alleviate the need to drive all over town *and* give residents a precise inspection time.

Anthony didn't understand why they couldn't, either. After confirming it wasn't actually against any rules, he greenlit the change. Today, most building inspections in Gainesville are completed over Skype. (Thanks to our friends Hana Schank and Sara Hudson for this story, from their book *The Government Fix*.)

Another example of shadowing and listening to city workers comes from Bob Stone, a former federal employee during the Clinton administration. Bob offered his services to Los Angeles Mayor Eric Garcetti for $1 per year to serve as a "bureaucracy buster." Again and again, he went out into the field and shadowed city employees to find and solve inefficiencies. He saw firefighters filing piles of paperwork to get their annual allotment of two pairs of pants, which then arrived in one bulk order that had to be delivered all over the city. In response, he successfully proposed letting firefighters order pants shipped directly to their homes. Later, he went on-site to learn about fire truck water pressure gauges, which were constantly breaking and being replaced at the cost of $2,000 a pop. But a mechanically inclined employee showed Bob how to repair them in just a few minutes for about $2, leading to $100,000 in annual savings and eliminating months-long repair timelines.

Make Smart Trades—and Trade-offs

Pitching a new process that improves outcomes for customers but adds ten cumbersome chores to an already overwhelmed clerical staff is a tough sell. But you can often find a happy medium. For example, you could fix two employee pain points in exchange for adding one new task that would make a real difference for customers. You also want to be careful about taking *too* much off someone's plate, lest they think you are taking away their job.

Part of making smart trades involves understanding what motivates particular employees you want to influence. (We have a whole other chapter on that.) Spend genuine time with them and immerse yourself in their work and world to understand where you can make compromises or agreements that are win-win for everyone. You can also ask people directly what they'd consider a fair trade for your ask.

In most cases, it makes the most sense to roll out internal changes slowly, building trust and leveraging existing change management mechanisms over time. Big bang changes are pretty much guaranteed disasters. But sometimes you'll have the chance to package a bunch of changes all at once, as part of a bigger shift that's happening anyway. One such opportunity is when your organization adopts a new IT system—with staff learning a brand-new interface *anyway*, you can make a *lot* of changes to wording, forms, requirements, and more all at once.

Consider Both Sides of the Coin

Prioritizing employee needs doesn't always mean weighing them against customer needs—there are also times when the primary trade-off is the needs of some employees weighed against the needs of other employees.

This tension is common when it comes to the seemingly simple question of what software employees can use on their work computers. If you don't work in IT, you may be frustrated that you can't use the browser of your choosing, for example. You could probably make a strong case that you could be more productive if your organization removed these restrictions.

But if you are the IT team that supports employee computers, the idea of letting everyone use any version of any browser is a *nightmare*. Every support call will take longer, as the support team first has to determine which browser the caller is using. They'll have to stay on top of a wider variety of security patches and known bugs, and they'll feel less prepared to support their users.

Marina faced this exact trade-off at the VA. The compromise she brokered proposed that the IT team would support any Web browser that's used by at least 10 percent of visitors to the VA website (which is a simple metric to track using Google Analytics). This gave VA employees a choice of browsers that were in common usage, while giving the IT team a finite and manageable set of browsers to support.

Leverage Existing Change Management

Every bureaucracy changes *some* things, *some* of the time. Yours might even have an entire change management team. When you need internal employees to make a change, make it as easy as possible by delivering your change through familiar channels. This might be a memo, a monthly webinar, an email newsletter, or a standing meeting— whatever it is, avoid the temptation to skirt the usual way your organization disseminates updates, and instead use it to your advantage.

We've seen cases in which a change-maker, having been immersed in their idea for months or years, believes their change is "so simple" or "so small" that employees will just adopt it overnight, and that they don't need any corresponding training or communications. This is wrong. Imagine the greatest number of demos, instructional memos, examples, or training you could possibly need—and then *add more*. If you want your fellow employees to change their behavior, you'll have to do the hard work to make it easy for them to learn (and do) things the new way.

Making the Case to Invest in Employee Needs

Your ideas to make employees' lives easier may get pushback under the guise that time and resources should be focused on customers, not internal users. The most successful counterarguments will vary based on what your organization values most, but some ideas include:

- **Employee satisfaction scores.** Some companies care about making "Best Place to Work" lists (even if it's in a local newspaper or magazine), while others track—and care about— employee satisfaction.

- **Employee retention rates.** Is this something being measured, or that senior executives are concerned about?

- **Hiring challenges.** The flipside of retention rates: if you know a team is unable to meet their recruiting or hiring goals, you may be able to get them to care more about retention (and therefore more about the employee experience).

HOW CAN I USE THIS?

» **Shadow employees in the field.** Ask them to show you how they really work and share their ideas for improvements. As you build rapport, they'll share more and more.

» **Find mutually beneficial compromises.** If you're expecting someone to take on more work to help you achieve your goals, you'll need to find a way to give them back something they value, too.

» **Consider the impact your proposed changes will have on internal employees.** Just because one set of employees will be positively impacted by a change doesn't mean a different group of employees won't be negatively impacted. Planning for this up front can avoid unexpected resistance later.

» **Leverage the standard change management process.** Don't go around it or mistakenly believe that your changes are so obvious or so simple that nobody needs advance notice or training to adopt them.

» **Make the case to invest in employee needs.** Use the logic that makes the most sense for your organization, focusing on metrics such as retention rates and employee satisfaction scores.

BEWARE OF RED TEAMS
AND PROBLEM LISTS

You don't always have to chop with the
sword of truth. You can point with it too.

—ANNE LAMOTT

---

*Avoid the temptation to make and share a laundry
list of problems. You might gain some short-term
attention for your insights, but you'll alienate too
many people in the process. Worse, if you incorrectly
characterize a problem, you might find yourself on
the hook for having to solve it. Instead, focus your
efforts on creating and testing solutions to problems.*

In Henrik Ibsen's *An Enemy of the People*, Dr. Stockmann lives in a
town whose economy revolves around sick tourists coming to spend
the summer to bask in the town's water supply, which allegedly has
healing properties. The doctor suspects that the water is poisonous, and
he sends away for tests that confirm his suspicions. Proof in hand, he
naively believes that once the town officials—including his brother, the
mayor—learn the truth, they will shut down the bathing water—their
main source of income—to remove the contaminants.

But the locals—primarily the Chairman of the Householders' Association—know better. The Chairman warns that "officials are not generally very ready to act on proposals that come from other people" and cautions the doctor to keep his discovery to himself. Dr. Stockmann tells the town the truth anyway, and he is promptly rewarded for his honesty by being fired, evicted, and shunned.

It's *so* tempting to make lists of everything that's wrong in your environment. This can be especially true when you're new, and you (wrongly) believe that you are the first person to discover inefficiencies, gaps, and other issues. But lists of problems without context, and especially without practical proposed solutions, can cause much more harm than good.

Marina learned this lesson in a particularly hard way. When she worked at the White House, she traveled all over the country to different hospitals and offices to compile a laundry list of challenges with the way the US Department of Veterans Affairs processed disability claims. In the short term, her behavior was rewarded: she got a captive audience of senior White House officials who literally applauded her presentation in the West Wing's Roosevelt Room. Eventually, the White House did what it always does with a list of problems—it sent the list to the VA for a formal response.

Except, by the time it sent the list, Marina had become the chief technology officer of the VA—and she found *herself* responsible for responding to the very list of ninety-six issues she had written! It was easy enough to make the list of problems, but explaining how she was going to solve each and every one of them—with decades of processes, old computer systems, and complicated rules—was beyond challenging.

These kinds of problem lists can take many forms, such as:

- Audits

- Red teams

- Strike teams

- Third-party assessments

- Inquiries

- Investigations

Regardless of what you call it, this kind of list doesn't get people poised for change and improvement; it makes them *defensive*. That's not a productive starting place for getting buy-in for your ideas and projects.

What can you do when you start tracking a list of issues in your head? Write them down—but keep that list to yourself, and use it as a starting point for identifying practical solutions for your environment. You probably can't solve all, or even most, of the challenges you've identified, but you can definitely pick one or two to start working on.

There's also a more productive, yet fast, method called a discovery sprint. This involves immersing yourself in a situation to understand it from every angle, generally for no more than one or two weeks. These discovery sprints usually result in a report that contains a healthy balance of identified challenges and proposed (but not confirmed) solutions. We have more information on discovery sprints on our website.

Our advice is to avoid making and airing laundry lists of problems—not to keep silent about *every* problem. If you see something that's causing harm, you should definitely sound an alarm, even if you don't personally know how to solve it. And sometimes highlighting *one* problem in the right environment can generate productive brainstorming about how to make it better. But an endless list of problems alone will get you more of a reputation as a complainer than as a problem solver in your organization.

When You Have to Investigate

What if you *have* to make a list of problems because your role requires you to participate in an investigation or an audit? We have some tips:

- Try to get to a root cause analysis whenever possible (by following our other tactics, like talking to real people and understanding why). An inaccurate problem list can leave behind a legacy of confusion that makes it harder for anyone else to actually solve the core problem.

- Avoid the temptation to list every single last thing you find; consider your mandate, the context, and your audience, and refine accordingly.

- A corollary to the above is that there might be good strategic reasons to include *other* issues in your report. Perhaps you can pair a very challenging, intrinsic problem with another solution that's ready to go, giving an overeager audience something productive to do as a next step.

- Consider how you can frame your report to get the necessary resources or attention to people who may have been trying to sound the alarm and generate traction already, but who were not yet successful.

- If possible, share your findings with the people who will be most affected by them and obtain their feedback *before* publication. This can be a delicate balance, but it at least gives them the chance to prepare for your findings and to correct factual errors.

We highly recommend the book *The Field Guide to Understanding 'Human Error'* by Sidney Dekker for detailed guidance on how to conduct a bureaucracy-shifting, human-centered investigation.

HOW CAN I USE THIS?

» **Don't make a public list of problems.** If you want to keep a private list of challenges to spark ideas for solutions, that's certainly fine. But nobody likes seeing their process or their office in a list of things that are bad or wrong.

» **Try a discovery sprint.** This two-week process productively surfaces potential solutions alongside problems. See our website for resources.

» **Focus on solutions.** Anyone can point out problems. If you want to hack your bureaucracy, focus on *solving* problems, however small your solutions may be at first.

LEARN YOUR ORG

FIGURE OUT THE REAL ORG CHART

Relationships, knowledge, and power aren't captured by traditional org charts. Making your own map of who knows what, who controls what resources, and who is in cahoots with whom can help you strategically map out who to include, in what order, on your schemes.

Every time you need something from colleagues in your bureaucracy—feedback on a draft, funds for a prototype, a change in policy, a meeting with a key decision maker—there is a strategic way to go about getting it. Create your own personal stakeholder map, so you can map out who to go to, and in what order, to get things done faster and more effectively.

Unlikely Sources of Power

In writing this book, we asked colleagues for stories of stakeholders who ultimately had serious sway over outcomes, despite their unassuming titles on the official org chart. A few of the most memorable include:

- A second-generation coal executive was struggling to find his own footing in the shadow of his famous father, for whom the town (and half the townspeople) was named. He knew that the company had to make significant changes to survive, but the rank and file were skeptical of the severity of the problem. But he noticed a shift in employee resistance after a midlevel member of the accounting team joined the weekly executive transformation meetings. It turned out that this quiet accountant also organized the company poker games—and he had been slowly but steadily passing the word about the company's impending financial trouble every Wednesday night. As a trusted truth teller, the accountant was ultimately the one able to persuade the workforce to make the needed changes for the company's survival.

- At one government agency, a whistleblower—someone who reports alleged wrongdoing to outside parties—was causing his boss a lot of stress. Simultaneously, this boss was launching a high-stakes digital transformation effort. Recognizing the influence this whistleblower had on their peers, the boss took a risk and included the whistleblower on the core team, now making him directly responsible for many decisions. Taking his newfound power seriously, the former whistleblower became an active team member, and encouraged other whistleblowers to work on implementing solutions and *not* on bringing their dirty laundry to the press.

- A family-owned manufacturing company that employed the majority of a small town's residents was struggling financially. It needed employees to work overtime in order to stay afloat, but the workforce was reticent. What persuaded them? The town preacher, who also had a night shift at the plant. He used his Sunday sermons to bring the community together to save its main source of economic development.

What to Include on Your Stakeholder Map

A formal org chart, listing who reports to whom, is *not* a stakeholder map. An effective map has more than just names, titles, and departments. You'll want to include the following:

- Who controls information flows? Examples include:

  * invitations for decision-making meetings;
  * the CEO's reading materials for her next plane trip; or
  * senior executive calendars.

- What incentives drive key resource gatekeepers? What do they want?

- Who hates change? Who is hungry for it?

- Who energizes others? Who is known as a naysayer?

- Who has time or resources available? Who is over capacity?

- Who is in your karass already? Whom do you *want* to be in your karass? (A karass is an informal collection of aligned individuals—a term coined by author Kurt Vonnegut in *Cat's Cradle*. We'll talk more about this in our chapter "Cultivate the Karass.")

- Who is openly against your project? How about privately?

- Who used to work together?

- Who reports to whom? (The formal org chart is not useless—it's just one data point.)

- What unique or unexpected skills do people have? Who has hidden technical talent?

Using Your Map

We make and consult mental stakeholder maps on nearly every project we're on. (Though we will deny this if you ask to see it!) Every time you're trying to solve a problem—and even sometimes just to refresh your strategic thinking—you should consult your map with questions like:

- Who should I talk to, in what order?

- Who did I forget to include?

- Who is going to be opposed, and why? Are there incentives I can create or control to win them over? Are there other people (such as a friend or a direct report) I could enlist first, to strategize on how to win over the opposition?

Keep Your Map to Yourself

Under no circumstances should you share your stakeholder map with other people. The more detail you add over time, the more sensitive it becomes. This is your personal, strategic map for getting things done in your organization. We suggest keeping it on paper somewhere private (not on a dry-erase board or in a digital tool you could share accidentally).

Just because your map is personal doesn't mean you can't or shouldn't strategically share information from it with others. If a teammate comes to you for help, you can consult your map for ideas, and then pass those ideas along. You can let a teammate know that Susan in marketing is uncomfortable with Excel (so they should send over a summary document instead of a spreadsheet), or that fifteen years ago she *wrote* the policy they're trying to change, or that she loves burritos. We just don't suggest sharing the entire map itself with anyone. (Furthermore, other people in your organization may have *different* mappings of the same people, based on their own relationships, history, and needs.)

Sometimes a team trying to solve a problem may find it helpful to construct a map based on the combined experiences of its members. Together, you might have more paths forward than you would alone. But you should be *very* careful about what you say or write down in a group environment. You may still want to overlay your own perspective afterward (e.g., back-channeling a draft to a key person who would be upset if they weren't looped in early, but with whom other teammates don't have the same relationship as you do).

HOW CAN I USE THIS?

» **Forget hierarchy.** You should always listen to and solicit ideas from all corners of the organization, regardless of whether someone is "below" you on an organizational chart.

» **Don't forget your own place on the official org chart.** You shouldn't consider the hierarchy immovable when you're seeking input and allies, but you should also always assume other people know your specific role in the hierarchy, and respect those boundaries. Don't bust in on meetings where you weren't invited, misuse titles, or go "around" a leader, however well-intentioned.

» **Keep asking who else you should meet next.** Whether you're talking to a supporter or a skeptic, ask at the end of a meeting who else you should speak with. This is a great way to further flesh out your map.

» **Keep your stakeholder map private.** Few things will take you down faster than a leak of your list of allies and frenemies. In many cases, you'll want a *mental* map of how some people work together and you should never write it down at all.

» **Get new teammates up to speed on how the organization really works.** Share information with them that they can't find in their onboarding manual, like someone's past role on another team, or an executive's preference for visuals over written summaries.

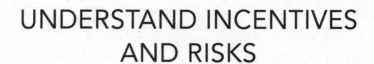

UNDERSTAND INCENTIVES
AND RISKS

Bureaucracy is a construction designed to
maximize the distance between a
decision-maker and the risks of the decision.

—NASSIM TALEB

---

*Everyone in your organization operates within a
framework of incentives and risks. If you want a
coworker to do something differently, you need
to understand what's stopping them from making
that change today. Where possible, change their
incentives to make doing what you want them to do
the lowest-risk, highest-reward path.*

When you are bureaucracy hacking, it's important to understand
the explicit incentives and risk frameworks in your organization.
If you are trying to get the attention of the VP of sales during the last
week of the quarter when she is trying to hit her numbers, you aren't
likely to get much of her attention unless your project *helps* hit those
numbers. But if you can help her close the quarter successfully, you'll
have a much better chance of getting her help later.

Similarly, you may need something that seems so low-risk and inconsequential that you'd barely give it a second thought, but from the perspective of the person you need it *from*, it's actually incredibly risky and frightening. Understanding and mitigating their fears *up front* will help save you (and them) a lot of headaches and lost time.

Identify Incentives

Incentives can influence individual behavior, and the impact can be felt across entire teams, departments, and organizations. In the context of bureaucracy hacking, we are using a broad definition of incentives, which includes a range of economic, social, and moral inducements that motivate human behavior.

Some incentives to consider include:

- Recognition or reputation

- Security

- Convenience or comfort

- Self-perception (being seen as in the know, smart, etc.)

- Desire to learn or demonstrate expertise

- Desire to help others

- Networking opportunities

- Achieving a greater good or purpose

- Loyalty

- Saving time or money

- Earning money or other benefits

- Being first (or not being first)

- Being in the news (or staying out of the news)

- Obeying the law (or changing it)

- Meeting contract or grant requirements

- Meeting stated goals (such as timeliness, customer service satisfaction scores, Six Sigma, etc.)

How can you find out what your coworkers' incentives are? Ask them. People are usually quite clear on what they're after if you engage them in a friendly conversation. Try to keep them talking; sometimes people are internally clear about what they're after, but they're hesitant or embarrassed to admit it for whatever reason. Other times, a conversation can help them uncover their true fears or desires. Asking interested follow-up questions like "Tell me more..." can uncover deeper layers of the incentive onion.

In addition to trying to figure out the incentives of your coworkers, also consider *how people work*. If Marsha in accounting always sends spreadsheets, send her your pitch in a spreadsheet. If Miguel likes to socialize, get his take on your new idea over coffee. Make it as easy as possible for them to absorb your thoughts and to work with you. Just as students have different learning styles, your coworkers have different working styles—and process new ideas differently.

Once, while visiting an office in Michigan, Marina caught sight of a sticky note on a security guard's desk: "Be the best security guard in the world." A moment earlier she had been annoyed with him for enforcing the rules and not letting her in a few minutes before the building's official opening time. But after she saw the note, she softened: he was driven by, and derived his self-confidence from, being a good security guard—*not* by shirking the rules for random guests. If she wanted him on her team, she needed to play by his rules.

Identify How People See Risk

Understanding the incentives and motivation of your colleagues is only half the picture; you also need to understand how they see risk. An activity that is completely common and normal in one organization or team could be seen as extremely risky in another.

We are often consulted on digital transformation projects in private companies and government agencies. Again and again, when we hear visions of using cutting-edge technologies and entirely new ways of working, we cringe because these plans completely forget that the future that seems so desirable to executives can be downright terrifying to the current team on the ground.

If someone has spent decades of their career perfecting a skill, like reviewing applications or keeping a server running, and you then propose doing it in a completely new way that renders them a beginner again, the risk to their reputation and career probably means they will fight your progress. Marina sometimes likens this to being told that, starting tomorrow, she has to conduct her entire job in Portuguese. If this happened, no matter what the rationale, she would kick and scream because she can't speak Portuguese and would have to spend a long time learning it before she could get any work done. Realistically, she might *never* return to her previous productivity levels.

This is known as the local rationality principle—we each make the best decisions and choices we can, given the environment in which we individually operate. Our local rationality may be very different from yours, even in the same situation.

Perceived risks might include:

- Losing their job

- Losing resources like budgets or headcount

- Not being employable elsewhere

- Being seen as inexperienced or having to start over

- Having to take on extra work or responsibilities

- Not meeting their exact performance standards

- Being ostracized by peers

- Getting negative feedback from a peer or manager

- Being associated with a failure

Shoulder All the Risk

We haven't seen a lot of success in trying to persuade other people to take on risk, but we *have* gotten lots of traction by instead absorbing risk ourselves. If someone objects to signing a form or having their name on a committee, try putting your name there instead.

You can also use your stakeholder map to determine if there might be someone else in the organization with a different framework who might actually be *incentivized* to work with you.

An advanced move is to actually *change* the risk. Let's say that a quality assurance tester won't sign off on your new prototype because it doesn't allow them to check box 23 on the old form. You're not going to have any luck trying to persuade them to improperly check the box or to ignore the box. But you might be able to get a new version of the form published that removes or modifies box 23 so that it no longer stands in your way.

Rohan Bhobe, cofounder of Nava, shares this helpful approach:

A tactic we've used successfully and repeatedly is changing the risk calculus. We're not trying to eliminate a risk-based mentality— instead, we're trying to create a situation where individuals begin to perceive the status quo as a riskier way of operating than the 'new' way. For example, after we helped rescue HealthCare.gov, we were able to successfully advocate for the agency to adopt more iterative software methods, because project after project demonstrated that this approach could provide 10x value at 1/10th the cost relative to the status quo. It became much more difficult to justify the status quo in the face of that math. The risk of 'sticking out' in the bureaucracy was still the mentality, but we got the changes through because people perceived the new way as less risky than the old way.

Beware of the Cobra Effect

Economist Horst Siebert coined the term "cobra effect" to describe perverse system incentives, based on a true story from Delhi, India. (It's also known as Goodhart's Law: "When a measure becomes a target, it ceases to be a good measure.") The city was overrun with dangerous cobra snakes, and the local government sought to solve this problem by paying for every dead cobra someone brought in. But instead of diminishing the cobra population, this incentive scheme caused an explosion in the cobra population—because people started *breeding* cobras to earn the incentive payments.

If you've heard about the harms caused by stop-and-frisk policing in New York City, you're familiar with a decades-long story about perverse incentives. But you may not know that at the root of this story was one well-meaning transit cop with a genuinely good bureaucracy hack that eventually took on a harmful life of its own.

Jack Maple, a low-level transit police officer known for his three-piece suits and wing-tipped shoes, was always focused on learning the rules and using them to his advantage. He hated being restricted to the subways as a transit cop, and so he used a loophole—that he *was* allowed aboveground for his lunch hour—to make daily arrests in Times Square. This meant he spent the rest of the day at the office booking the criminal instead of returning to the transit beat. He later used a similar tactic when his superiors retaliated against him and reassigned him two hours away to the Bronx; he would simply make an arrest during his commute into the office. He reportedly never spent a single day in the Bronx.

Crime at that time in New York City was overwhelming, and Jack had an idea: he and his colleagues would draw the entire New York subway system on their office walls (430 stations in all) and use it to map out the types of crimes that were occurring and when they happened. He printed out the complete list of crimes on a dot-matrix printer.

Visualized in this manner, certain themes became immediately apparent. Almost all purse snatchings happened at the same three stations; meanwhile, the pickpockets seemed to move along a particular subway route over the course of the day. By concentrating cops on these high-crime areas and times, Jack's map was able to have an astounding impact, lowering crime dramatically in a very short period of time. This map later became the computer program CompStat (short for Computer Statistics), used by many major police departments across the country.

The initial premise of the program—to use data to catch real criminals and stop crime—was noble, and it worked, at least initially. But after crime in New York had gone down for twenty-five years straight, it got harder to keep driving it lower. Allegedly, then mayor Rudy

Giuliani demanded action: specifically, if he couldn't take credit for a further-reduced crime rate, then he wanted credit for *more arrests*. So the New York Police Department began assigning quotas—a specific performance incentive—to cops for arrests and summonses. In a lawsuit years later, police officers testified that they would often drive around together in a van, trying to come up with any reason to issue someone a summons (such as blocking a sidewalk or loitering) to meet their quotas. Worse, at one point, arrest quotas were assigned based on crime reports—so if there was a robbery near a park and the victim reported the thief had been a young Black male, officers were given quotas to arrest young Black males near the park. This caused unforgivable harm and trauma to multiple generations of people of color in New York City.

The misuse of CompStat created another perverse incentive: it encouraged police officers to *downgrade* actual crimes. This allowed them to achieve the goal of "less crime" at the margins, when one or two incidents materially changed their percentage rates. As more and more cops downgraded actual crimes, they artificially lowered the bar for their successors, who subsequently had to use more and more creative accounting to keep their own crime rates down.

This story is important because it's all too easy to believe that *your* project will not eventually cause harm—but it very well may. In fact, it *probably* will. As you create incentives for colleagues to meet certain key performance indicators with the best of intentions, it's critical to consider the downstream effects over time. If you want an outcome and create incentives and track metrics to get it, you might spur a lot of unintended behavior.

One way to defend against this future is to make sure you're including a diverse set of end users or colleagues in your planning and prototyping, and that you open your metrics and incentives for feedback. For example, at the VA, a well-intentioned team at headquarters set a requirement for every state to reduce their percentage of homeless veterans. They announced this initiative with great fanfare but failed to ask any local leaders for feedback first. North Dakota pointed out that in December it had zero homeless veterans in the survey (because it was too cold to survive outdoors), yet it was being marked as a failure for not *reducing* the number of homeless veterans.

The Bureau of Labor Statistics published a report explicitly outlining the incentives that employers have for underreporting workplace injuries, including decreased odds of being inspected, lower workers' compensation rates, a positive public reputation, and safety bonus payments. Wells Fargo faced billions in fines and civil suits after its incentives-based program drove employees to open over two million fake bank accounts (that charged real customers real fees) to meet quotas. These stories happen all the time.

Amir Shevat, who has been a product manager at companies like Slack, Twitch, and Twitter, suggests this test to protect against the cobra effect: "Assuming I'm an evil Product Manager, what would I do to achieve this Key Performance Indicator or goal?"

The Innovator's Dilemma

We would be remiss in talking about frameworks for incentives and risks in an organization without mentioning the most famous research on this topic, conducted by the late Harvard professor Clayton Christensen: *The Innovator's Dilemma*. In it, Christensen encourages organizations that want to enable innovative new ways of working to create separate units that operate under explicit, different rules. If you're in a position to create a new unit within your organization, we certainly encourage you to do so—but as an individual bureaucracy hacker, you may have better luck pitching this down the line, after accumulating sufficient political capital and a karass to make up the new team.

HOW CAN I USE THIS?

» **Ask coworkers about their incentives and risks.** People are usually aware of their concerns, but they may not name them without prompting. For example, someone might reject a form because you left a section blank, and when pressed can probably tell you all about their colleague who was once reprimanded in a meeting for approving the form with a missing section—and that *they* have no interest in being yelled at.

» **Take on risk for others where you can.** Sign the form, put your name on a RACI matrix (a project management chart that assigns roles for each task: Responsible, Accountable,

Consulted, or Informed), or otherwise formally indicate that if shit is going to hit the fan, it's going to hit *you*.

» **Defend against perverse incentives.** Ask yourself Amir's question: "Assuming I'm an evil Product Manager, what would I do to achieve this Key Performance Indicator or goal?" Then put measures in place to disincentivize bad behavior.

» **Learn what behavior your organization finds most risky. Eliminate or change those risks.** For example, someone responsible for signing off on paperwork will probably never accept blank or missing responses because they will be penalized later if audited. In this case, you may need to update the paperwork itself.

KNOW THE CONSEQUENCES

Learn the rules like a pro, so you can
break them like an artist.

—PABLO PICASSO

---

*Know the consequences for breaking rules or not
following existing processes. On one extreme is
breaking the law and facing fines or imprisonment;
on the other hand, if the worst that can happen is
that you don't meet a performance goal next quarter,
it might be a risk you're willing and able to take.*

As you explore the depths of your bureaucracy, you'll also want to find out *what happens* if you deviate from the established norms. Will you go to prison? That's probably a sign you should not get too close to the bright line. Will you enrage the administrative assistant who approves your travel? That might *feel* like prison every few weeks—but perhaps that's a risk you're willing to take. Are you not sure what will happen? That's worth investigating *before* you make your next move.

Constraints can unleash creativity. Understanding the boundaries, and what happens if you cross them, can help you design solutions that work within your current environment *and* achieve your intended outcomes.

The Loop Loophole

Tens of thousands of people with diabetes (including Marina) are walking around connected to hacked insulin pumps. These devices, which are not officially available or supported commercially anywhere, read a person's blood sugar every five minutes and automatically adjust insulin delivery up or down accordingly. With the right settings, and coupled with a low-carb lifestyle, this means people with type 1 diabetes can achieve normal, non-diabetic blood sugars, which can help them prevent (and even reverse) complications and live longer.

The FDA clearance to officially design such a system takes years and costs millions of dollars. This community of insulin pump hackers—who refer to themselves as Loopers, for their closed-loop systems—had no patience for the FDA's bureaucracy; in fact, their motto is "We Are Not Waiting."

Loopers come together freely over the internet to share and improve code, swap devices, and troubleshoot. And the FDA can't do anything about it because this community understands one specific rule very well: while you can face federal prosecution and imprisonment if you hack *someone else's body*, you can hack *your own body* all you want.

When you read the directions for how to start Looping, they are very careful to stay on the other side of this line. For example, you must download and install the code yourself; it is not available in any app store, and community members are highly discouraged from building and installing the code for another person. (Luckily for the community, volunteer Katie DiSimone sweats the small stuff—her documentation is very detailed, so even a non-techie can follow along and get it going on their own.)

The Loop community ultimately wants this technology in the hands of every person with diabetes who wants it, without the hassle of learning the Apple programming environment or having to troubleshoot every time their mobile phone updates automatically. But at the beginning, there didn't seem to be any path to FDA clearance. Instead, the community focused on everything it *could* do without breaking the rules—which was a lot!

In 2013, Howard Look saw an opening. He became CEO of a small nonprofit called Tidepool, which sought to make it easier for people with diabetes, healthcare providers, and researchers to access, compile, and analyze diabetes data. If all the Loopers would voluntarily contribute their data, and he could make it easy to analyze that data trove, perhaps he could collaborate with a clinical research team to conduct a study to show the safety and benefits of Looping. The amount of data from Loopers is *incredible* relative to any previous diabetes studies because the devices record every user's blood sugar and insulin level every five minutes, which adds up to 288 data points per day. Multiply this by the number of Loopers over six to twelve months, and all of a sudden this volunteer-led effort could generate more data than all other closed-loop studies combined. This, he theorized, could be a persuasive, data-driven argument for the FDA.

The FDA agreed and has taken an admirable stance on the use of real-world evidence in clinical studies; in fact, they encouraged Tidepool to submit its existing evidence before the study even enrolled its first member. It took a few years of meetings and paperwork, but this volunteer data pool became the Loop Observational Study, coordinated by the JAEB Center for Health Research, which ultimately demonstrated that the do-it-yourself system and algorithm are safe and effective. Tidepool—after making a few modifications to Loop to fit some specific, additional FDA rules—was able to submit for official approval for the Loop system in late 2020. Taking into account pandemic-induced delays at the agency, Tidepool is expecting official FDA approval of Tidepool Loop in 2022.

Finding Opportunities Within Restrictions

The best way to find the consequences for going against the grain is to understand the root reason your organization does (or does not) do something, or the reason behind someone else's trepidation or refusal to help you. The repercussions may be spelled out in the law or a rule, or a colleague may be able to explain them to you ("Jane tried that once ten years ago, and she was never seen again").

Even if what you're trying to do *seems* like it is against a policy, reading the source document or consulting with a knowledgeable expert can create opportunities to move ahead, like with Loop. Another example of this is a close read of one of our least favorite laws: the Paperwork Reduction Act.

The Paperwork Reduction Act of 1995 is a relatively obscure law in the US federal government. Outside of government, you are unlikely to have heard of it. When you're inside, it's one of the first obstacles change agents hit. In short, this law restricts what questions the government can ask the public (such as on a form to apply for benefits). It was written long before widespread consumer use of the internet and requires that any proposed updates to "information collections" (a fancy way to say forms) be published in the *Federal Register* for at least three months before the changes can go live.

Not reading the letter of this law caused many people in government to falsely believe that the PRA forbids user research (like the interviews with high school students we recount in "Talk to Real People") without a ninety-day notice. When we served in federal government, it was a common myth that watching users try prototypes or asking citizens about their experiences with government services was illegal under the PRA.

But our White House colleague Erie Meyer—a fierce consumer protection advocate and current chief technologist of the Consumer Financial Protection Bureau—read the law, and she knew the ground truth. The Paperwork Reduction Act defines the word *information* as well as what is *not* information. And right there in black and white, the exceptions list includes:

> Facts or opinions obtained through direct observation by an employee or agent of the sponsoring agency or through non-standardized oral communication in connection with such direct observations.

Unfortunately, the exact letter of the law was not widely known in government. To combat this misperception, Erie, an incredible bureaucracy hacker, got the agency in charge of enforcing the Paperwork Reduction Act (the Office of Management and Budget) to publish a memo *encouraging* other agencies to conduct user research, citing her close read of the law.

Don't Be a Bull in a China Shop

It is an unfortunate belief of many people who want to change a bureaucracy that the best approach is to "blow it up" or "break things." (This also tends to be a hallmark of start-up culture.) Don't do it.

Intentionally breaking or bending rules with full knowledge is one thing. Ignoring them entirely, or not bothering to learn about the consequences in the first place, is at your peril. We assure you that someone *else* in your bureaucracy has read every last page of the policy and will use it to shut you down at the first opportunity. Even if you don't wind up facing serious consequences, that's a hard reputational hit to come back from, and may very well permanently set you back. Your failure will also make it that much harder for anyone else to succeed in your stead.

Our advice includes respecting *processes* in addition to hard rules, including approval processes for communications (e.g., a clearance process for publishing a blog post), budget allocations, and technology purchasing. You can influence their outcomes and you can leverage the processes to your advantage, but you should *not* skip them. You can, however, choose the easier of two competing processes if your idea qualifies. We've found that sometimes there is a process that will take many months or even years to complete, while there is a lighter weight alternative (perhaps for an experiment or for a modest scale) that might take only weeks.

HOW CAN I USE THIS?

» **Understand the consequences for breaking a rule.** They might be written down clearly, or you might have to ask someone. Don't accept the first answer you hear; find ground truth by getting real examples of when the consequence has happened, or what the policy says.

» **Look for ways to change the rule itself.** This is one of the best ways to codify change in a bureaucracy, even if it can take a while. Before you propose a *new* rule, though, be confident (through user research, prototypes, and sweating the details) that your new change isn't going to introduce new problems.

» **Design a solution that works within the current rules.** When you read the letter of the law, you may be surprised at the flexibility you have to get things done with a few careful considerations.

» **Don't break a rule without understanding the consequences.** It's one thing to make an active choice to bend or break a rule, but it's an amateur (and highly ineffective) move to break rules that you didn't know existed.

UNDERSTAND WHY

The difficulty does not lie in
finding new ideas, but in escaping the
long-outdated belief in old ones.

—JEFFREY FRY

---

*Getting to the root reason behind a particular
practice is often the key to changing it. It's possible
the original rule, policy, or law gives you much more
flexibility than people think—and sometimes that
original reason may not even apply anymore! Asking
why repeatedly and tying current practices back to
specific reasons makes it clear what needs to change,
and what may not need to change at all.*

You should always question "water cooler rules"—the informal
guidelines that everyone seems to know—that you come across in
your organization, to understand their origin and purpose. Often, you'll
find that they are no longer relevant or that they are based on requirements from other parts of the organization that no longer exist. This is
sometimes known as Chesterton's fence: don't take down a fence until
you understand why someone put it up. Even if the rule is real and has a

good rationale behind it, reading it may reveal that you have more flexibility than you originally thought.

Ask the Five Whys

A 2001 edition of Canadian *Reader's Digest* shared the following mystery:

> When my friend Dale opens a can, she always turns it upside down to open it from the bottom. One day her young son asked her why. "I don't really know," she said. "My mom always did it that way." She decided to call her mom and ask.
>
> "When we brought the cans up from the cellar, the tops were always dusty," her mother explained. "I couldn't be bothered to clean them, so I turned them upside down and opened the bottom."

In his book about cancer, *Malignant*, Vinay Prasad tells a similar story about how doctors measure the size of tumors. In 1970, sixteen oncologists sat at a table and tried to sort marbles using calipers. Despite all the technology and machinery developed since then, *this* continues to be the definition of tumor growth today: "the amount of change in a marble that can be reliably discriminated by two oncologists measuring through foam rubber with a caliper."

Bureaucracies are fraught with so-called water cooler rules. People do things because they've always done them that way, because their predecessor taught them to do them that way, and so on. By following a process with fresh eyes, you can often uncover—and stamp out or replace—these practices with relatively little resistance.

One technique, which originates from Toyota's production system, is to ask *why* repeatedly—at least five times in a row—to get to a root cause. Not every problem takes five *why* questions, or has a single root cause, but we've found it to be an effective method.

Our friend Matthew Weaver (known to his colleagues as simply "Weaver"), an intense engineer who once slept in an RV outside Google for a year and is now Marina's business partner at Layer Aleph, wrote an entertaining case study tracing the requirement to use a certain type of enterprise software in the US Department of Defense. The software, called an enterprise service bus, was outdated, and this requirement created a ton of unnecessary expense and work. Weaver kept asking why, tracing the requirement to the US Air Force, which pointed to the US Department of Defense, which pointed to the Office of Management and Budget, which pointed back to the council of CIOs across the federal government, creating a full circle.

The moral of the story is not just to be careful about unnecessarily codifying practices into rules (especially in technology, where best practices can change rapidly), but also how bureaucracies can diffuse decision-making responsibility, sometimes comically, in a full circle.

The Loaner Loophole

Our friend and master bureaucracy hacker Carl Malamud recounts overcoming an amusing *why* in his book *10 Rules for Radicals*. Carl was an early pioneer of open government. Among his many projects, he wanted all government-produced videos (like the first walk on the moon) to be on the internet for free—a concept we now take for granted, thanks in large part to him. At the time, in 2007, the only way to access videos produced with taxpayer dollars was to mail a check for $55 to a small, obscure agency called the National Technical Information Service (NTIS) to get a VHS tape mailed back to you.

Carl's first idea was to fundraise, thinking that if he could buy each VHS tape *once*, digitize it, and then post it on YouTube, he could slowly but surely make the entire library freely available. His fundraising website had cheeky calls to action, like "Be the last person to buy this tape!" But nobody donated.

Frustrated, Carl sent a memo to the NTIS, explaining his goals. To his surprise, he got a call back—explaining that the NTIS team was very much on board with his goal of making the content widely available, but that the law required they "recover their costs." Labor, shipping, packaging materials, and blank tapes quickly added up to the $55+ purchase price.

Now understanding the *why*, Carl proposed an alternative that fully followed the law: What if he just *borrowed* the tapes and covered the postage? To sweeten the deal, Carl also offered to send back a hard drive with the digitized video when he returned the VHS tapes, which helped the agency achieve the digitization wishes for which they had no budget. That worked—and soon he had an operation called FedFlix that was scanning boxes of government videotapes at a time. Carl posted hundreds of government-produced videos to the internet for everyone to see—a win-win situation, all because Carl discovered the nature of the constraints under which NTIS was operating.

Making Friendlier Websites

Have you ever encountered a government website that screams, **"THIS U.S. GOVERNMENT SYSTEM IS FOR AUTHORIZED USE ONLY! THIS SYSTEM IS SUBJECT TO MONITORING. INDIVIDUALS FOUND PERFORMING UNAUTHORIZED ACTIVITIES MAY BE SUBJECT TO DISCIPLINARY ACTION INCLUDING CRIMINAL PROSECUTION."** in bold and all caps? It's intimidating to some people, causing them to doubt their interaction with the government. In fact, this language is so frightening that it stops some people from even using government websites at all, despite needing information and benefits.

You might assume that it's some sort of federal law—and indeed, it seems most people working on the more than 7,000 .gov websites assume this too, because they've all copied and pasted the same sentences, verbatim.

Except, it's not. When Bret Mogilefsky joined the federal government after a career designing classic computer games like *Secret of Monkey Island* and *Grim Fandango*, he really wanted to get rid of this scary, intimidating notice. Bret researched the reason for it and found the answer: a standard written by the National Institute of Standards and Technology (NIST) called control AC-8. This rule *does* say that information systems need to make it clear to users that they are accessing a US government system—but it says nothing at all about *how* to do this.

Armed with the rule itself, Bret was able to put up instead a user-friendly sentence, with no capital letters or bold font, on his team's site (cloud.gov) in a small yet visible banner. This was one of many steps he took in making government websites more accessible and authoritative while complying with the well-meaning letter of NIST guidelines.

HOW CAN I USE THIS?

» **Question water cooler rules.** Seek to understand the unwritten rules and customs in your workplace, and their origins. Sometimes they are rooted in precedent, myths, or misunderstandings.

» **Ask *why* five times.** This technique can uncover the root cause behind many issues because the first or second answer often doesn't give you the full picture.

» **Defend against becoming a future water cooler rule.** Cite your reason where possible. For example, in Washington State, the foster home inspection checklist lists the applicable state law next to each checkbox. This makes it harder (though not impossible!) for the form to deviate too far from the actual law.

TRY THE NORMAL WAY FIRST

Before declaring that a process is broken and looking for ways around it, try it first. Your firsthand experience will help you gather real data about why and where the process isn't working. Armed with the nuances of what a truly effective new process could look like, you'll have more credibility to convince others that you can design a new way of doing things.

Learn the Rules—and Use Them to Your Advantage

Once all the senior executives from various federal agencies present—the Office of Personnel Management, the Office of Management and Budget, and the United States Digital Service, among others—had taken their seats, VA deputy secretary Sloan Gibson got up and locked the boardroom doors. As a no-nonsense West Point graduate, former Army infantry officer, and ex-CEO, Sloan meant business.

"Nobody is leaving here until we figure this out," he declared.

The problem? It had been nearly two years since the federal government had started trying to hire a technologist onto Marina's team—and despite having some of the most qualified software engineers on the planet ready to come and serve, and the attention of leaders all the way up to President Obama, human resources still hadn't cleared a legal path for them to begin work.

Many well-intentioned people advised Marina to pursue a shortcut.

Hire the technologists as janitors; make the head of human resources force their team to approve the hires; or hire an outside contractor who could do the hiring. But this is not how bureaucracies work. Even if she could somehow persuade multiple senior officials to break the rules—and why would they risk their jobs and reputations so she could hire a few people?—this would work exactly *once* before she got caught.

Millions of pages of Inspector General reports can attest that when a government bureaucracy finds a broken rule, like Medusa it grows three more rules in its place. To make it so the government could consistently hire technologists, Marina was going to have to understand exactly how hiring worked; exactly what barriers were stopping the new hires; and then go through the slow and painful process of questioning or changing the rules themselves.

Marina diligently followed the traditional government hiring process step by step, bringing senior leaders along with her by CC'ing them on emails and sending regular progress reports. Interestingly, most of these leaders had never been exposed to the weeds of how the hiring process worked, despite in some cases having hundreds of thousands of employees underneath them.

Demonstrating stumbling blocks proved quite effective: for example, the selection process rejected top technical talent from corporations like Google and Facebook (who had explicitly applied to help Marina's test) in favor of University of Phoenix PhDs who couldn't write a line of code. Why? They were rejected at the resume review stage, where well-meaning frontline human resources staff—who had no technical experience—tried their best to *guess* which resumes were qualified and which were not. They saw "PhD" and thought "expert" without realizing that these candidates had absolutely no coding experience.

Marina complaining that "nobody she knew" looked for jobs on the official government hiring website, USA Jobs, also fell on deaf ears. After all, hundreds of people *were* applying. But once she had definitively demonstrated that adhering to the letter of hiring policy couldn't accomplish the agreed-upon goal, human resources was much more willing to consider changing decades-old policies.

By carefully studying the current process, Marina was able to identify the exact steps and policies that needed modifying, instead of following her temptation to "blow up" hiring and create a new process. (Blowing things up comes with the inherent danger of introducing a slew of unanticipated new problems in its place.) In the end, some of the barriers turned out to be water cooler rules. For example, many in HR believed that subject matter experts were not allowed to conduct resume reviews, leaving novice HR professionals to try to sift through the pile of resumes (hence the University of Phoenix PhD preferences). But now, knowing that "rule" was never real in the first place, Marina could propose a *real* rule for the VA that experts *had* to be interviewed by other, similar kinds of experts. This simple change had far-reaching effects: today, this is how the federal government hires tens of thousands of employees, all the way up to VA medical center directors.

Mobile Meat

A group of farmers on Lopez Island in Washington State was fed up with adhering to regulations. The requirement to use a USDA-approved slaughterhouse meant they had to ship their cows, pigs, and sheep hundreds of miles away for processing. This was not only prohibitively expensive, but it caused the animals unnecessary suffering—and all those trucks were not exactly environmentally friendly, either.

Reading the letter of the USDA law, the farmers—who banded together as the Island Grown Farmers Cooperative—conceived of the idea of a *mobile* abattoir (slaughterhouse) that would meet all of the existing regulations, including some complicated ones, like having a dedicated bathroom for the USDA inspector. Instead of spending years and significant money lobbying to try to change the rules, they invested their time and resources into making the first-ever compliant mobile unit, which looks like a trailer. By making sure they followed every rule to the letter, the Island Grown Farmers Cooperative was able to gain USDA approval. Today, the farmers can share one regulation mobile unit across their farms, eliminating the cost and stress of transport. The idea has inspired others; licensed mobile abattoirs have sprung up around the country.

Hacking a Holiday

In 2020, Stanford students Sean Casey, Jonathan Lipman, and Nik Marda had an idea: they wanted Stanford to declare Election Day a holiday, permanently canceling classes and extracurriculars to encourage students to vote and become more politically informed. They called their proposal "Democracy Day."

The students didn't give their proposal high odds of success, assuming that the academic bureaucracy valued class time too heavily, and also would just generally resist change. After all, it's not every day a new holiday comes along.

But instead of giving up, they sweated the details and followed the university process to the letter. They sent a proposal to the student government, the Associated Students of Stanford University, where it became a bill. They wrote newspaper articles in support and encouraged student and faculty supporters to write op-eds, too. They dutifully followed the nearly year-long process, and patiently worked with the two subcommittees that the bureaucracy tasked with studying the issue. They worked through details like make-up class time and any impact this day off could have on the college's accreditation requirements.

Finally, the day came for the formal vote. It wasn't unanimous, but the proposal passed. Democracy Day is now a formal Stanford University holiday, all thanks to a few undergraduate students trying the normal way first.

Testing the Waters

When he first joined the Department of Homeland Security Digital Service team, David Koh was told by developers at the department that it was impossible for them to gain read access to the production database (which would show when real users, who were applying for visas, experienced errors). Before he raised a red flag to his boss (the US deputy chief information officer) and caused a commotion, David decided to make sure: he messaged the IT approvals team asking if he and the developers could get read access. They replied that he should fill out a particular form. He filled out the form—and, after a few follow-up emails, a couple weeks later he successfully got access.

David made copies of the form and shared them with the existing development team, including instructions on where to send it. Other team members filled out the forms—and a few weeks later they got access, too! Once the team saw that this "impossible" process actually worked, they even included the approval form into their standard onboarding process for new engineers. While longtime employees had grown so accustomed to a dysfunctional bureaucracy that they just assumed a (presumably) once-broken process would stay broken forever, a fresh attempt at the normal approval process proved successful— no escalation necessary.

HOW CAN I USE THIS?

» **Try the normal way first.** Even if it's obvious to you that an existing process won't work, bureaucracies don't respond to your opinion or your mounting frustration. After all, from the perspective of the people currently doing the process, it's been working for decades. You must prove it.

» **Follow existing processes exactly.** This helps you identify exactly what changes need making, instead of complaining without details that a process is broken or should be eliminated. Include detailed timelines instead of complaining a process is slow. Documenting that you tried and failed can be important proof to executives in a bureaucracy. At each pain or failure point, collaboratively seek help from the existing team to fix it. This can reveal options that you missed and gain your colleagues' participation in brainstorming solutions.

RELAX FIXED CONSTRAINTS

In a bureaucracy, it's easy to see the status quo as unmovable, akin to laws of physics, rather than just the result of human inaction. Question assumptions about which constraints are really fixed, and see if you can develop a sense of shared agency with others.

As a former presidential speechwriter for Bill Clinton, Josh Gottheimer knew the drill. It was quicker and simpler to meet off campus. Nick's tiny office on the fourth floor of the Eisenhower Executive Office Building, with multiple people crammed into it, was not conducive to meetings. So Nick, his colleague Kumar Garg, and Josh met at Caribou Coffee on the corner of 17th and Pennsylvania, just across the street from the White House campus. Sitting at one of the few outside tables, the group enjoyed the pleasant weather during a beautiful fall day in 2012—but the conversation soon became heated.

As someone who had served in a past White House, and was a few years older than Nick and Kumar, after hearing their proposal, Josh didn't hold back: "Rockefeller will never go for it. His people would go nuts if they even caught wind of the idea." Josh was certain that this was a wild idea by idealistic young White House policy staffers out of their lane.

Josh was worked up about what Nick and Kumar were floating: lifting the E-Rate cap at the FCC. At the time, Josh was the senior advisor to the FCC chairman—essentially the senior political advisor—and Senator Jay Rockefeller was arguably the most important voice at the time in Congress on FCC matters. Rockefeller's committee oversaw the FCC and its E-Rate program, which subsidized connections to schools through surcharges on business and household telephone service. Raising the cap, which means everyone in the country would pay a few cents more for telephone service, would give the FCC the funds to invest in delivering broadband internet to elementary schools. At that time, low connection speeds were depriving millions of students of the opportunity to take advantage of everything the internet had to offer, including a burgeoning universe of apps and services designed specifically for educational purposes.

Nick wondered if the FCC could unilaterally raise the surcharge and use the additional revenues to invest in broadband capacity for schools, using funds for Wi-Fi and fiber-optic construction. Gigs for Kids, he would later call it on an internal one-pager. But Josh wasn't having any of it—he thought it was totally politically unfeasible and lectured Nick and Kumar about the way DC "really" works.

But getting yelled at by Josh Gottheimer wasn't enough to deter Nick and Kumar. Nick brought the idea up with his colleague, Tom Power, the staffer in charge of telecommunications policy. Tom was a longtime telecommunications lawyer, wickedly funny, and totally unpretentious; the *Washington Post* ran an article about him serving as a temporary bartender in a friend's Georgetown bar during the 2013 government shutdown, refusing to take tips. Tom was intrigued by the idea. Kumar inquired with Michael Steffen, a friend in the FCC who worked closely with Josh. Michael sounded skeptical about the idea but promised to look into it. A few days later, Michael called Kumar back and told him that maybe, just maybe, this could work.

You'll get a lot of nos in bureaucracy hacking, and Nick and Kumar were used to them. Inspired by the FCC slowly warming to the idea, they tried to get the idea into the 2013 State of the Union and failed. But it kicked off an interagency policy process—expertly run by Tom Power—which gained momentum as various government agencies competed to provide policy ideas to help enhance digital learning. Soon after, in June 2013, President Obama announced the ConnectED initiative to promote digital learning in schools. The flagship action of his announcement was the FCC reforming E-Rate to fund broadband in schools, increasing speeds up to one hundred times or more.

As the senior political advisor to the FCC chairman, Josh had been treating Rockefeller's previous opposition to changing the program as a *fixed constraint*. Not knowing much about the Hill—and a bit naive about how Congress really works—Nick respected Josh's political savviness, but also wasn't convinced that Rockefeller was unmovable. And sure enough, it turned out that Rockefeller's people, who had been previously adamant that E-Rate wasn't to be touched, were actually open to considering the reform proposal. (As one of the major forces behind school funding in the original Telecommunications Act of 1996, Senator Rockefeller was a fierce advocate of school broadband, so it was somewhat ironic that his office, which was very protective of his signature program, became seen as a political obstacle to reform.) The limits of FCC actions weren't really as fixed as they thought—they were actually changeable.

In your organization, you probably see many things as a fixed constraint: the boss would never approve this; your company always does it this way; customers or partners always act this way. Ask yourself: What is truly fixed? Why is that so?

Try this as a thought experiment: What would be possible if you assume that the previous constraint is actually changeable? And what if you can persuade others to relax constraints that they think are fixed?

Our mentor Tom Kalil talks about developing shared agency with colleagues to expand their sense of what is possible, using psychologist Albert Bandura's definition of agency as "the human capability to influence...the course of events by one's actions." Tom observes:

> The particular dimension of agency that I have experienced is a sense that **there are more aspects of the status quo that are potentially changeable as opposed to being fixed.** These are the elements of the status quo that are attributable to human action or inaction, as opposed to the laws of physics...Sometimes when I am talking to an individual, a team or a community, it will become clear to me that there is some aspect of the status quo that they view as fixed, and I view as potentially changeable. It might make sense for me to explain why I believe the status quo is changeable, and **what are the steps we could take together in the service of achieving a shared goal.**

Nick and Kumar were able to turn an idea into a presidential initiative due to several concurrent forces—including masterful outside pressure from Evan Marwell, head of the EducationSuperhighway, a nonprofit specifically designed to advocate for expanding broadband to schools. Once the policy process gathered momentum in 2013, there were dozens of dedicated people across the White House, FCC, and Department of Education that made it into a successful presidential launch. Post-announcement, it took the sustained efforts of an FCC determined to make these reforms, started under Chairman Julius Genachowski and then implemented under Chairman Tom Wheeler and Acting Chair Mignon Clyburn. But it all started by convincing Josh and colleagues in the FCC to challenge their notions of what was a fixed constraint.

The push to bring broadband to schools to accommodate digital learning succeeded; according to EducationSuperhighway, the percentage of classrooms with usable broadband connections jumped from 10 percent in 2013 to an astounding 99.6 percent in 2020. "We closed the digital divide in America's classrooms in just seven years," said Evan Marwell. "Thanks to the leadership of the Obama-era White House and FCC, we've given every student equal access to educational opportunity through the power of digital learning."

Josh's ability to reconsider fixed constraints and see opportunity continued post FCC—he went on to get elected as a congressman from New Jersey, and famously stood up to Nancy Pelosi in 2021 as one of the leaders of the moderate wing of House Democrats.

HOW CAN I USE THIS?

» **Expand people's views about what is changeable.** Encourage coworkers to challenge their assumptions about what really is fixed. Ask them why, and what circumstances would make them believe that the constraint is movable.

» **Develop a sense of shared agency—a joint belief in your own and your colleagues' abilities to influence the course**

of events through your actions. Describe what success might look like and discuss the actions you each might take to achieve a shared goal.

» **Raise the aspirations of others.** Sometimes the constraints people feel are related to their own career trajectory and what is possible. In the words of economist Tyler Cowen: "At critical moments in time, you can raise the aspirations of other people significantly, especially when they are relatively young, simply by suggesting they do something better or more ambitious than what they might have in mind. It costs you relatively little to do this, but the benefit to them, and to the broader world, may be enormous. This is in fact one of the most valuable things you can do with your time and with your life."

BEWARE
THE OBVIOUS ANSWER

When it comes to long-standing problems in large organizations, solutions can appear obvious, especially to outsiders or newcomers. But it's rarely that simple.

After Marina hired the first few private-sector technologists onto her team at the US Department of Veterans Affairs, she drew a chart on her wall, predicting how each subsequent hire would react to the problem of the disability claims backlog. At the time, over 600,000 veterans were waiting an average of 2.5 years to receive a decision on their disability rating, which determines how much the VA will pay them in benefits.

The chart correctly predicted the following:

- On their first day, based only on what they had seen in the media, every new hire would suggest that the solution was to move the disability claim processing onto servers in the cloud, to make it faster.

- In their first few weeks, they would gather data to back up their hypothesis: the cloud would save five minutes per claim, and there were 600,000 claims, so this would save twenty-four years of time! Surely that would solve the backlog!

- After shadowing claims processors and learning how the process really works, by the six-month mark these employees would have a completely different perspective. Claims adjudicators processed no more than two claims per day—and saving ten minutes per day didn't result in anything besides a slightly more leisurely lunch break. Cloud computing might help the VA solve other challenges, but it was *not* a way to end a backlog.

This reflex to pour resources into a solution—an obvious answer—is something we see often. For example, when COVID-related unemployment claims began to climb in California in 2020, the state moved quickly to hire thousands of new claims processors and call center agents. Many other states made similar moves. This seemed like the obvious first step: more humans could attack a backlog of unemployment claims faster, right?

However, this solution was absolutely the *wrong* one. New employees now vastly outnumbered experienced ones, who had to spend all their time training new people instead of processing claims themselves. This meant that instead of thousands of *extra* hands, there were now almost *no* hands processing claims.

When the State of California analyzed call center data, it became clear that the new agents could answer fewer than 1 percent of incoming calls; the rest of the time, Californians waited on hold for hours just to be told, when they finally spoke with a live person, that they didn't know how to help. This was an objectively worse outcome.

In the face of this realization, the call center was shut down *entirely* and all experienced employees were refocused to full-time claims processing. If the State of California had been more wary of the "obvious" answer, they could have avoided the lost productivity—not to mention the bad publicity from shutting down a call center it had just stood up.

How to React to a Seemingly Simple Problem

Few things will garner you more enemies inside a bureaucracy than the word *just*. You are playing with fire if you find yourself saying:

- "*Just* change the org chart."

- "*Just* make an app."

- "*Just* change the policy."

Odds are extremely high that the thing you're proposing they "just" do has been tried before, is a lot harder than it sounds, and/or won't actually solve the problem at all.

A large technology company once pitched Marina on using artificial intelligence to solve foster care placements. The machine learning algorithms would analyze data about foster children and foster parents and produce optimal matches. This sounds like a great solution to reducing the number of placement moves a child in foster care experiences—until you realize (a) the original placement matching system was literally a box of index cards, and (b) there were far fewer foster homes than children in need of homes, so there was not enough flex in the system for optimal matching to work.

The next time you encounter a problem and think the solution is to "just" do X, keep that initial reaction to yourself. Even if your research leads you to believe it *is* a viable approach, leave the word *just* out of your pitch. We also suggest leaving out phrases that highlight your "otherness," such as touting that you are new or "fresh" and therefore smarter than those who came before you.

Instead, you'll want to:

- talk to others about the problem, asking what's been done about it already;

- learn about the problem in detail: follow our advice in other chapters to shadow processes, look between silos, talk to real people, and understand root causes; and

- informally run your preliminary ideas by trusted colleagues for feedback.

Get a History Lesson

While outsiders do bring a fresh perspective and occasionally notice an overlooked opportunity, it's a lot more likely that many people have tried to figure out the answer long before you. And they probably failed.

Marina learned this lesson early at the VA. She was invited to a large meeting with representatives from every corner of the department to consider a "brand new" idea: What if the VA had one database (instead of dozens of them) with a veteran's basic information, like their address and phone number? Then, if a veteran moved, they would need to update their contact information just once, instead of having to interact separately with each business unit within the department. Everyone was excited by this "new" idea.

Afterward, Bonnie Miranda, the head of the executive secretariat, invited Marina to come by her office. There, Bonnie showed her a shelf of eighteen thick binders—each one from a *different* initiative to create a consolidated veteran database, from the past three decades. All eighteen had failed. Somehow, everyone at the meeting except for Bonnie had no idea that this had ever been tried before, much less eighteen times.

Thanks to Bonnie's archival work, the newest team was able to understand why the past attempts had failed. The nineteenth time was the charm: informed by the many lessons of the past, veterans were finally able to update their address in one place in 2018. Among other challenges, prior efforts all tried to include every line of business in the address update all at once; this new, successful approach incrementally folded in one line of business at a time, allowing the team to gain traction and solve technical issues early and often.

Similar examples abound: in 2021, the Biden administration set new customer service goals for federal agencies, touting the goal of a single website and phone number for interacting with the government. But James Pinkerton, a White House staffer under Reagan and George W. Bush, had promoted this same idea as early as 1991 (and others likely had done the same before him).

Understanding the history of a "new" idea isn't just useful for avoiding past mistakes; you might also uncover people involved in the past efforts who are willing to try again. They might be a little cautious or cynical, but if they gain enough confidence that the environment is more accommodating, or believe that certain structural obstacles have become less formidable, they can be powerful allies.

HOW CAN I USE THIS?

» **Beware of solutions that seem too easy.** In an organization of any complexity, the likelihood that you are the first one to discover and propose an obvious solution is low. Before blazing on the scene as a know-it-all, seek to learn what others have tried first. Likely, there *is* an answer—it's just more complicated than you first thought.

» **Don't discount easy solutions without some research.** We suggest you be *wary* of easy answers, not dismissive of them. Sometimes the best solution really can be a modest form change or practice shift.

» **Keep early solution ideas to yourself.** It's possible you're right, sure...but there's no harm in doing some sleuthing first. Talk to others to learn about the history of the problem and who tried what solutions already. Use techniques like looking between the silos and asking *why* repeatedly to suss out details.

» **Find the person who had your idea first.** Even if they aren't willing to actively help you, they might be willing to explain what they tried, what worked, and what did not.

» **Don't say "just."** Just don't.

PITCH
THE SOLUTION

WRITE A ONE-PAGER

Writing is more than a vehicle for communicating ideas. It's a tool for crystallizing ideas. Writing exposes gaps in your knowledge and logic. It pushes you to articulate assumptions and consider counterarguments.

—ADAM GRANT

Talk is cheap. Write down your idea on a single page to clarify your thinking and message.

One of our favorite pieces of advice to anyone looking to make change in an organization: write a one-pager. Nick used to tell Marina this so often when we worked together in the White House that to this day she has written a one-pager for basically every idea or project she has had since (and she still sends them to Nick for feedback). Lest you think one-pagers are beneath you, British general Bernard Montgomery, the ground commander under Supreme Allied Commander General Dwight D. Eisenhower, wrote the plan for the D-Day invasion *on a single page.*

It sounds simple, but sit down and try it: Can you write something that a busy executive could skim and get the gist of in sixty seconds? Can you write something devoid of jargon? Can you make it compelling and interesting—without overdramatizing? Do you have a specific example that has a real person, with a mini-narrative? Is there an authoritative fact or statistic that proves your point?

But more than all of that, as Nick likes to say to his Harvard students: Would your parents be able to read it and understand it? In other words, have you put in the hard work to make your one-pager clear and compelling to non-experts?

What Can a One-Pager Do for Me?

Writing a one-pager can help in several ways:

First, it helps crystallize your thinking. You may realize that you don't have as sharp of a description of your initiative as you thought, or that you need to better understand (or triple-check) a particular example that supports your case. You don't have room for many examples in a single page, so you need the one you choose to be the most compelling. When you put the words on the page, it's harder to hide mushy ideas or faulty logic. The questions that your idea raises—Why now? Who else has bought in? What proof points are there that this idea will work?—should seem more obvious when you read it.

Second, it forces you to write clearly for multiple audiences, including non-experts. Your one-pager is not just for your boss, and your boss's boss, but also for others in your organization who could be helpful to your plan—not to mention those who might veto it, or at least make your life difficult. Maybe you're also writing for external stakeholders or partners that would be able to support your initiative. If you write something that is broadly accessible—i.e., that a non-expert could read and understand—you maximize the reuse potential of the one-pager. And since bureaucracies often require a *lot* of consultation about new ideas, you'll spend more of your time having conversations and building trust with people if you don't have to write each one a custom document. Ideally, you'll tailor your pitch for each person you are trying to persuade to support your idea, or at least vary the emphasis depending on the audience. But a one-pager saves you time when you're initially socializing your idea.

Third, you'll never know when you might need it, and who it might get shared with. How information flows in a large organization is a fascinating topic in its own right, and we're sure it could fill an entire book.

As a thought experiment, imagine getting access to every email, Slack message, text message, direct message, and other communication channel inside your company; what would analyzing those communications tell you about how things get done? A well-written one-pager has the potential to be forwarded well beyond your control, taking on a life of its own.

Fourth, having a well-written one-pager makes it much easier for others to advocate for you. Rather than following up after a phone or in-person conversation with just an email, you can send a personal message with the one-pager as an attachment or a link. Then they can forward it to their boss or to their team, with their own brief commentary. This helps others become your ally.

A single page is just long enough to explain the problem, outline your idea, give examples, and propose tangible next steps. There is tremendous power in the forced brevity. Every additional page you add to a document decreases the chance someone is going to read it.

There are variations on this idea: create a single-page website, a five-slide presentation, or a sixty-second video. If you can send someone a website, it can be a useful way to show that you have thought enough about your idea to make it public. Having a hyperlink that you can send people means the idea can travel easily—because anyone can forward the link.

How a Memo Changed Monday Night Football

In 1960, twenty-nine-year-old Roone Arledge had an entry-level job scheduling film crews to cover boxing matches for ABC—and an idea. An idea that would transform American sports forever. Roone wrote his idea down in a memo, which he allegedly composed in one sitting, over a beer.

Roone noticed that when the major networks filmed a football game, they focused only on the game itself. They never aired much of what we take for granted in televised sports today: commentary, the fans, the scoop about local rivalries, cheerleaders, or even halftime shows. By leaving all this content out, Roone argued, the audience couldn't build relationships with other teams—and audiences caring about sports beyond their local team was the key to tapping a huge new viewership.

"Heretofore, television has done a remarkable job taking the game to the viewer—now we are going to take the viewer to the game," Roone declared. His memo included details like a recommendation that camera operators go out into the stands, interview fans, and take in the stadium from multiple angles to make at-home viewers feel like they were actually there.

Roone began his career as a crew member, but with passion and a well-written memo, his initiative and vision led to him eventually becoming the head of ABC Sports.

What makes a compelling one-pager?

1. **A simple title.** The reader should be able to "get it" with just a glance. Consider introducing the name of your initiative in the title.

2. **The BLUF.** Put your conclusion at the top, known as the bottom line up front (BLUF).

3. **Description of the issue.** Why does anyone care? You might be living a particular challenge, but does anyone else in your organization think it is a significant problem?

4. **An anecdote or statistic (or both) that illustrates the problem.** What examples do you have to convince your reader that this matters?

5. **Proposed change.** What is the change you desire?

6. **Concrete next steps.** Specifically, who do you propose to do what, in what time frame? The next steps might seem small compared with the overall proposed solution, but it's better to start with concrete, measurable actions.

7. **It's actually one page.** We've all played with margins, fonts, and point size to make more words fit on the page; but the idea here is to genuinely limit yourself to one page with one-inch margins and a legible font set no smaller than 10 point. Ideally, it's 1.5 line spaced for readability. There is a lot of value in several-page memos, but the discipline a one-pager creates is powerful.

HOW CAN I USE THIS?

» **Write a one-pager.** Concisely describe your idea on a single page. Assume the reader has zero knowledge or context.

» **Test your one-pager with a colleague.** Ask a colleague or friend whose opinion you trust for critical feedback.

» **Share your one-pager with different audiences.** Ask them what questions it raises and if it is compelling enough for them to share with others. The test: if they gave it to other colleagues, especially people who lacked context, would it convince that colleague that it's a promising idea, too?

THINK OF THE END AT
THE BEGINNING

Be specific about what the future you envision looks like by doing things like writing the launch press release or mocking up potential media coverage. Use this future state vision to drive your day-to-day planning.

"Think of the end at the beginning" is a variation on the classic idea of visualizing success. In the White House, at least for us policy staffers, success meant a presidential-level launch of an initiative or a new policy change, with a clear press release and good media coverage.

One particularly valuable exercise that our friend Kumar would suggest when someone wanted to start a new initiative: first, write the press release and fact sheet, and then write a fictitious news article covering the launch. This forced the staffer to be specific about what they ultimately wanted to accomplish, and how they hoped others would see it.

Writing the news article was often the hardest part—it forced us to imagine how a skeptical press would cover the launch. It also made us strip out jargon and explain outcomes simply.

We didn't know it then, but it turns out that Amazon has a similar exercise: the press release (PR) and frequently asked questions (FAQ) process (or PR/FAQ). Amazon product managers use it to consider the customer perspective on potential new product launches.

As longtime Amazon executives Colin Bryar and Bill Carr explain in their book *Working Backwards*, a press release needs to describe the hypothetical new product in a way that encapsulates the main benefits:

"If the press release doesn't describe a product that is meaningfully better (faster, easier, cheaper) than what is already out there, or results in some stepwise change in customer experience, then it isn't worth building."

The second part of Amazon's required written narrative, the FAQ, has two sections: answers to questions that customers might ask about the product, and answers to questions that internal Amazon executives might ask. According to Bryar and Carr, a single team might write ten drafts and meet with senior leaders five times or more to refine these final artifacts.

Amazon's iterative development of a narrative document—grounded foremost in the question of what the customer cares about, using market and internal data—is one way Amazon makes decisions about where to commit resources. This is a tactic that you can use to great effect in your organization, too.

Both Kumar's and Amazon's exercises take the idea of visualizing success, and expand it in four important dimensions:

First, both exercises include writing down the future version of success. As we talk about in other chapters in this book, simply writing things down can be an important bureaucracy-hacking tactic.

Second, both processes include workshopping the document with colleagues for feedback. Running your draft by teammates, and incorporating their feedback, strengthens a document's clarity and accuracy. It also builds awareness of your idea, and as you receive comments, it can help build consensus and support.

Third, both use the framework of a press release, which requires clear facts and a story that is new and exciting enough to garner attention. Kumar's exercise goes one step further, including a hypothetical news article based on the press release, outlining the new, specific, and measurable steps that everyone is taking, and the exciting outcome of those steps.

Finally, both are explicitly trying to get at the perspective of the end user. Ultimately, Amazon is trying to determine whether customers actually care—and the White House wants to know if an idea matters to the American people. The customer lens sharpens this focus.

You can easily borrow these techniques. Write down what success looks like at launch and share with teammates for feedback. Imagine your desired future state through the eyes of a skeptical press and discriminating customers. Author a press release and write a news coverage describing your successful launch. Then, use these documents to inform your planning process and next steps.

HOW CAN I USE THIS?

» **Visualize yourself at the end.** Visualization isn't just for high-performance athletes. If you are going to spend weeks, months, or even years on an initiative, doesn't it make sense to increase your chances of reaching your goal by trying a short visualization exercise? Find some quiet time, close your eyes, and imagine yourself and your feelings if the future you're imagining materializes.

» **Write a narrative document—such as a press release, FAQ, and news article—announcing your successful project.** Be specific about why it's a success. Include as much context as necessary for an unfamiliar reader. Make sure the "so what" shines through. Share it with colleagues to get feedback and improve it.

» **Ask others about what success means to them.** Even when discussing the same initiative, you and your colleagues might have very different versions of success. Schedule time to get your colleagues' input on what constitutes a win in their eyes.

SET YOUR NORTH STAR

He that rules by mind is like the north star, steady
in his seat, whilst the stars all bend to him.

—CONFUCIUS

*A compelling vision of the future that is both
inspiring and broadly accessible makes it easier to
get others across your organization to join forces
with you. That vision, when written down and
widely shared, can inspire and drive change in your
bureaucracy.*

Early in Marina's tenure at the VA, she developed a "North Star" plan for what a "21st Century VA" could be: a single website where a veteran could apply for every benefit in one place; a single customer service call center; and the elimination of claims backlogs, among other features. It was one of her most successful early moves. Each point in her North Star pitch was just a few sentences, without a lot of detail, but it gave readers enough of an idea that they wanted to be part of the future it described. (You can see Marina's original plan on our website.) Creating a simple and compelling vision—a North Star—is a play she has successfully replicated in child welfare, unemployment insurance, and with many private companies. A shared written vision can be a powerful motivator.

It might take many years to achieve your North Star vision, and that's okay. When Marina wrote the "21st Century VA" vision, it seemed virtually impossible to ever achieve from her vantage point; when she left four years later, her team had accomplished all but two items in it. A North Star helps keep you focused and on track even in very dark times.

Why a North Star?

Bureaucracies fall in love with the details and entirely miss the destination. They pour all their efforts into making comprehensive, multiyear plans in lieu of starting to make any *actual* changes and improvements, or asking how the world will be any different after its plan is complete.

This can be beyond frustrating when you see obvious improvements right in front of you—improvements that are endlessly put on hold in favor of the bigger plan. But here's the trick: rather than trying to *sidestep* that bigger picture, you can provide your organization with the big North Star vision it craves.

Bureaucracies spread decision-making power across departments and often require buy-in from numerous executives. Across so many disparate groups and departments, it can be hard to align thousands or hundreds of thousands of employees toward a shared goal. A succinct but compelling North Star vision helps communicate a distinct future direction across a range of senior and mid-level executives in a bureaucracy.

Paradoxically, large organizations often reject smaller or short-term ideas as "not big enough" or "not moonshots"—even though these organizations demonstrably fail to achieve their enormous visions and would be better off with many smaller wins. The key is to find the right balance between laying out a vision that will inspire others to support your goals, while leaving enough flexibility that you can get started with pilots and progress quickly.

Finally, an inspiring North Star vision can cause subtle but widespread behavior changes across your organization thanks to a concept known as cognitive dissonance. Psychologist Leon Festinger coined the term to describe the deep discomfort people feel when their actions are not aligned with their beliefs. Cognitive dissonance is so uncomfortable that it generally prompts people to change either their actions or their beliefs to align accordingly. If most employees believe they are coming to work to achieve a mission, and you can tweak that mission even a little bit with your North Star, then you may find a lot of employees start to shift their behaviors to match the new mission.

What Makes a Good North Star?

A compelling North Star should:

- Focus on what's possible and the positive, not on what's wrong. In other words, lay out what the future *could be*, not what the future *won't* be.

- Be inspirational. A North Star isn't a small step change—it's a *big* change for the better.

- Balance the right amount of detail to paint a picture without being overly prescriptive. This is known as construal level theory. If your pitch is too short-term, your audience will get caught up in questions about the details.

- Look visually compelling (see our next chapter on the power of visual design).

HOW CAN I USE THIS?

» **Develop a North Star.** You can capture it on sticky notes, a dry-erase board, a digital whiteboard, or plain paper at first. If you close your eyes, what do you imagine your organization or cause being like in the future? Who is benefiting from that future? How would you describe those benefits?

» **Share it with colleagues for feedback.** Asking for and incorporating feedback helps generate a shared ownership of the North Star vision.

USE THE POWER OF
VISUAL DESIGN

*Make your ideas stand out with written proposals
printed on heavy stock, professional-looking
presentations, and visually compelling prototypes.
Even the most formal of reports can benefit from
professional design elements.*

Make Your Documents Visually Compelling

An often overlooked bureaucracy-hacking tactic is to make just about anything you write visually compelling. Beautiful design is persuasive. A captivating layout or even a distinct font can catch people's attention and get them to read your report sooner or more thoroughly. Google's artificial intelligence team found that users develop opinions within seventeen *milliseconds* of looking at a proposal.

Marina had the help of her team members, Mollie Ruskin and Danny Chapman, in transforming her ho-hum draft of her North Star, "The 21st Century VA," into a document that looked professionally designed. Marina then spent $2,000 of her own money printing copies of the plan on heavy, glossy paper at Kinkos. The shiny blue booklet helped compel busy, overcommitted senior VA leaders to read and stay engaged with her proposal, and it really stood out against the stacks of white papers set in double-spaced Times New Roman that her pitch was competing against for attention.

Compelling design has even helped change the face of entire

countries. In 2016, a group of architects in Bratislava, the capital of Slovenia, set out to transform everything from their public spaces to their elections. The result was Plan Bratislava, which was so gorgeous it was even featured in *Monocle* magazine, a lifestyle and design brand. When is the last time you heard of a government document being highlighted in a design magazine? The solid underlying points of the plan, coupled with a persuasive and engaging visual design, helped usher in a new mayor and a chance at a more effective democracy.

Design Everything

It's not just North Stars that can benefit from a strong visual design. When Marina applied to be one of the first Presidential Innovation Fellows, she swapped out her boring Microsoft Word resume for a $3 template she bought online. The design was blue and said "I'm Marina" in large letters at the top. The reviewers still remember her resume almost a decade later, out of the more than six hundred in the pile, because of its pop of color. While she also had to be qualified for the job, the document's design helped ensure her resume was at least read and considered.

In his book *Thinking, Fast and Slow*, psychologist Daniel Kahneman suggests using high-quality paper and bright colors to attract people's System 2 brain, which makes automatic positive associations between the visuals and the ideas being portrayed. (Within reason—the effect doesn't hold up if your resume or plan is bad.)

You don't necessarily need to hire graphic designers to make your pitch stand out: new Web-based services make it a lot easier to create beautiful documents these days. In fact, we used one to design our proposal for this very book!

HOW CAN I USE THIS?

» **Make your next proposal stand out visually.** Visit our website for marketplaces for affordable, beautiful templates. Even printing on bright or heavier paper can make an otherwise routine report stand out.

» **Include relevant photos.** If you're making a pitch to change the experiences of real humans, show those humans front and center. (Make sure you have their permission, though.) This applies to any other relevant photos (screenshots, product designs, etc.) Even a few stock photos can liven up a written document.

» **Don't go overboard.** We're suggesting you want to stand out thanks to professional, thoughtful visual elements. Don't overload presentations with photos, too many colors, or off-topic material like cartoons. These can easily distract from the content of your pitch.

» **Be mindful of accessibility.** Use color-blind–friendly color palettes and image captions so your entire audience can experience your presentation.

CONSULT A THESAURUS

In your organization, specific words have connotations based on years of history. Choose your words carefully to find the ones that maximize what you're trying to accomplish while minimizing baggage.

Words matter. You might discover that in your organization, calling a small bug in a new software application a "defect" triggers a lengthy "defect" documentation process and a ding on the project report card, but referring to it as a "revision" escapes all that overhead. In child welfare, a "best practice" requires a multiyear research study published in a specific clearinghouse, so Marina calls her recommendations "promising practices" instead. And when Fitts and Jones set out in 1947 to study what factors contributed to plane crashes, they intentionally used the term "experiences" instead of "failures" in their research, to encourage participants to focus on root causes and not attribute everything to the catch-all "pilot error."

Consider the team of employees at GE who were trying to design a new type of refrigerator, as told in Eric Ries's *The Startup Way*. They successfully built sixty refrigerators, intending to have real customers try them out in their homes for a couple of months to give feedback. Just before shipping, compliance stopped them, insisting that they needed to submit the fridges to a "hinge test"—a test that took three months and would cost $500,000. But when the team lead, Mahan, said the magic words—this was "only a test"—they were able to skip the hinge step and move directly to in-home testing.

Using a thesaurus—or more specifically, leaving *out* a word—was one of the keys to Earthbound Farm creating the organic salad market. In its early days, the company was nothing more than a stand on the side of the road run by two people who hand-washed and bagged organic lettuce. A Costco store expressed interest in carrying their lettuce, but only if they *didn't* call it organic. Instead of putting up a fight, they agreed, selling organic lettuce without the organic label. Today, Earthbound Farm is worth over $600 million, and the popularity of their salad blends eventually gave them the standing to add "organic" back on the packaging.

You want to find and use the words that help you get things done, and avoid loaded words. You can also use words to add a bit of magic—like the Digital Service at the Department of Homeland Security naming a regular conference room the Situation Room to add energy to their meetings.

Find the Shibboleths

Bureaucracies have their own cultures and almost always varied subcultures. Language—choice of words, jargon—is a key signaling aspect of all cultures. Most people are familiar with the TLA—three-letter acronym—phenomenon of government bureaucracies, but language reveals details of the organization in ways beyond that.

When spelunking a bureaucracy and finding yourself in the various rooms with a smattering of people who are unclear about who you are and what opportunity (or threat) you represent, careful observation and use of language can be invaluable. Looking for the shibboleths—the words that those perceived to be insiders or those in the know use—can be a powerful way of dampening the bureaucratic immune system from rejecting you out of hand. Careful listening and adoption of the right words can also demonstrate respect and openness; as a corollary, ignoring language cues and forcing one's own jargon and terms of art can alienate people unnecessarily.

Dave Guarino spent six years overhauling the experience of enrolling in the food stamp (SNAP) program in California, building GetCalFresh. org at the nonprofit Code for America. In California, the food stamp program is not administered by the state, but rather by fifty-eight different counties—ranging from the tiny Alpine County in the Sierra Nevada to Los Angeles County, with a population of about ten million. A lesson learned very early in working there was that each county had its own terms of art—even when, broadly speaking, they seemed to be the same things. One county would refer to their frontline staff as "eligibility workers," while another would say "case workers." Yet another might say "eligibility specialists" or "eligibility technicians" or "CalFresh workers."

For his purposes, and from his role within the system, these differences were not significant. But adopting the language that a particular bureaucratic culture chose to use showed both a respect for the specifics of the agency as well as prevented allergic reactions to "outsiders who don't get it."

In that same project, Dave and his team found another shibboleth. Years earlier, there had been a vaguely similar attempt at simplifying the food stamp application experience to what Dave and his team were trying. In that prior case, a tax preparer had added an option for someone to quickly screen and apply for related benefits if they looked like they were income-eligible, after they filed their taxes. Despite the good intentions of this effort, agencies had a very rough time with how it was executed: many started receiving a massive volume of faxed applications with virtually no notice. It made it very hard for agencies to successfully process the applications and get people benefits. Many left the experience traumatized and suspicious of talk that sounded anything like "simplified applications."

But in that real challenge was also a hidden shibboleth. In the first meeting with a new county, the team tried out starting with: "Remember that bad fax experience a few years ago?" Often the reaction would be immediate, with people physically expressing their negative memories, saying something like: "Oh my gosh, yes—that was such a nightmare!" The team would reply: "Great; we're here to make sure that doesn't happen again." Shoulders would ease and the conversation would move forward a little bit lighter. Speaking to something that was very much an internal experience on the agency side—and signaling that, even as outsiders, they understood the potential pitfalls—made rightfully cautious administrators more open, with the knowledge that these folks were not all that naive about the risks involved.

Make It an Acronym

It wouldn't be a bureaucracy if every project wasn't eventually shortened to an acronym or an abbreviation. Thinking about your project's acronym up front can help you choose a fitting, confident name, instead of being held to whatever shorthand your organization eventually comes up with.

Marina once failed to name an application she was building at the VA in time. When a well-meaning IT specialist had to fill out a required "project name" box, she put in "Clinician User Interface"—and that name stuck. This was not only highly generic, as the VA had thousands of clinician user interfaces, but when people tried to pronounce "CUI," it came out "cooey"—which sounded childish.

In a better example, a team at US Customs and Immigration Service charged with building an auditing tool for the existing background check system (called ELIS) wanted a name that projected confidence and was easy to remember. They worked backward from the acronym VERIFI to come up with the name "Validation of ELIS Risk and Fraud Information."

Naming a New Concept

The Nature Conservancy's mission is simple: it buys land so that it can protect it. But as the nonprofit began to analyze the amount of land that needed conserving in California, they were bowled over by the numbers: 40 percent of the entire state! How could they buy 40 percent of California?

As recounted in *Made to Stick*, Chip Heath's class of Stanford students first tried to break down this problem with math. The students proposed raising money to buy 2 percent of the state each year, which is two million acres. But this was still way too big a goal—donors could not visualize two million acres. And while it's overwhelming to think about two million acres, it's simultaneously not much of a rallying cry to get people to care about a measly 2 percent. It therefore proved very difficult to fundraise against the goal of "two million acres."

But here's what *did* work: making up a new concept, called a landscape. The first landscape was an area of brown hills outside Silicon Valley. It was not visually appealing, but the Nature Conservancy believed it was one of the most important areas to protect. They carved out a 1.5 million acre area they dubbed the Mount Hamilton Wilderness, which gave potential donors a concrete idea to get behind preserving. The name was made up; the idea of a landscape was made up; and yet it was exactly the right size of an *idea* to fundraise against. Suddenly, large corporations and Silicon Valley tech companies were proclaiming their dedication to protecting "the Mount Hamilton Wilderness" and the Nature Conservancy met its fundraising goals in the very first year.

How to Find the Right Words

If only bureaucracies came with glossaries! But it's up to you to make your own glossary for your organization. Some places to gather intel include:

- Strategic plans: How do they refer to problems? Planned projects?

- Goals: What are the objectives of your organization and how are they measured (KPIs, OKRs, MBOs)?

- Progress or progress reports or dashboards: What do they count (e.g., bugs, days, people, dollars, social media mentions, articles)?

- Peers' presentations and proposals: What terms do they use to describe their initiatives and goals?

There are also going to be terms that aren't necessarily problematic, but that you still shouldn't use in order to avoid confusion. These tend to be more obvious over time, but if you're new, listen carefully for them. One particular thing to listen for: Does your organization use a generic term to mean a specific thing?

Finally, you should avoid casual historical references or comparisons unless you're quite sure you understand them, as we learned earlier in Dave's food stamp story. Once, when pitching the idea of a "one stop shop" for veterans to apply for all their benefits in one place, Marina was deeply confused by the angry reaction she got from her audience of fellow senior executives. One even stormed out of her presentation! It was only *months* later that someone clued her in that an offhand reference she made to "VAMROC"—a joint health and benefits building that the VA had in the 1980s—had done her in. Yes, VAMROC was a "one stop shop," but it was also fraught with political tensions and history. Merely mentioning the term didn't add clarity—it caused her audience to tune out the rest of her pitch.

Common Loaded Terms

Here are some terms that may be problematic; make sure you know what they mean in your organization:

Agile	Modernization
Best practices	Next generation
Champion	Pilot
Development	Plan
Error/Bug/Defect	Playbook
Exit	Project
Hold each other accountable	Start
Innovation	Test
Iterate/Iteration	Toolkit
Lightweight	Transformation
Minimum viable product (MVP)	Usability

HOW CAN I USE THIS?

» **Make a glossary.** Keep a list of terms and their connotations in your specific organization, especially those that can help you skip unnecessary paperwork or scrutiny in an aboveboard way.

» **Make it an acronym.** Bureaucracies love shortening project names; plan ahead with a project name that creates a descriptive, memorable acronym.

» **Use synonyms.** Don't waste energy trying to redefine a word that has a negative connotation or lots of baggage—pick a new word!

» **Don't play buzzword bingo.** Use plain language that makes sense to your audience.

SHOW THE HARD NUMBERS

> Facts are facts and will not disappear on account of your likes.
>
> —JAWAHARLAL NEHRU

Showing real numbers that contrast with the way most people in a bureaucracy currently perceive reality—especially data that they have not seen before—can be a powerful catalyst for change.

Challenge the Status Quo with Data

Dr. Lucia Coulter had become disillusioned with being a physician in the UK, particularly after reading a statistic that an individual doctor saves only about six lives over the entire course of their career. She wanted to impact more than six people—and a charitable club she had joined in college sparked an idea. She wanted to protect children around the world from the harmful effects of lead poisoning.

Challenged to think about how she could make an outsized impact in just six months, Dr. Coulter designed a small pilot study. One of the main sources of lead poisoning in children is lead paint. She flew to the country of Malawi, teamed up with a graduate student from the

University of Malawi, bought a bunch of paint, and analyzed it for lead content. Her tests showed really high levels of lead.

"This was an invisible problem in Malawi before our study. Lead paint has been banned for over 50 years in most high-income countries, like the United Kingdom and the United States, so it was simply not on the radar of the Malawi government officials," Dr. Coulter recounts.

Persuading a government to implement new regulations practically overnight is unheard of—but thanks to her never-before-seen data, Malawi implemented lead paint regulations mere months after her first presentation. Malawi now monitors paint for lead levels and is updating its existing paint standards to include lead limits.

This data collection exercise also helped her narrow her focus. She ran a similar experiment in Botswana, but didn't find a lead paint problem there. This was because Botswana imports almost all its paint from South Africa, which had implemented lead paint regulations a decade earlier.

Crunch Your Own Data

Dave Feldman is not a doctor, but that hasn't stopped him from making a big dent in the way the medical world thinks about cholesterol.

Conventional wisdom, which Dave is proving wrong, is that there are two types of cholesterol: HDL (often called "good" cholesterol) and LDL (often called "bad" cholesterol). It's also widely thought that cholesterol numbers change slowly over time—not overnight.

In 2015, Dave started a low-carbohydrate diet to lose a few pounds. He felt great, was never hungry, and his pants fit again. But his doctor chided him, pointing to his cholesterol number: 329, a level traditionally considered dangerously high.

Dave didn't feel close to death; in fact, he felt better than ever. He began to read up on cholesterol. As an engineer who specialized in networking computers together, he thought he saw a similar pattern in the way that our body's lipid system worked. And this gave him an idea for an experiment.

Live on Twitter, he had his cholesterol measured: 367. He then proceeded to eat nothing but white Wonder Bread—a diet that absolutely no one would consider healthy—for the next week. Every day, he had his cholesterol measured at a lab.

At the end of that week, his total cholesterol was "perfect": 195.

How could this be? Dave's live data collection challenged many established beliefs: that cholesterol can't change on a daily basis, and that it's directly correlated to a healthy diet (since one of the worst imaginable diets produced an "ideal" result, and in only a matter of days).

Dave's self-experimentation inspired thousands of others to try it themselves, with the same results. He has since written a book, *The Cholesterol Code*, and founded a nonprofit called the Citizen Science Foundation to raise money for an official clinical trial to formally challenge how medical science thinks about cholesterol in relation to health.

It will be years before we know the results of a full-fledged research trial, but Dave's story highlights that small, individual, data-driven experiments might reveal interesting insights that you will want to study further, whether that's via a clinical trial or another statistically significant type of research.

Decarceration Through Data

Showing the numbers has also been a key strategy for bureaucracy hackers working on criminal justice reform.

In Virginia, there were many anecdotal stories of people being sent to jail for failing to pay court fines and costs. But rumors don't sway systems, so nothing much happened—until Ben Schoenfeld, a software developer with an interest in government, began requesting copies of Virginia's court records in order to publish them on the internet. Anyone can request government records in the United States using a process called a FOIA (Freedom of Information Act) request at the national level, and open or public records requests at the state and local levels.

Ben turned these scanned paper records into spreadsheets that any interested party could download and analyze. Jonathan Black, an attorney in Virginia, together with the Legal Aid Justice Center, utilized Ben's spreadsheets in their class action suit against the state, where they argued that a law that automatically suspended driver's licenses for failure to pay fines and costs, which led to incarceration, was unconstitutional. They also used this data to lobby the Virginia legislature and governor to ultimately repeal the law.

Ben's spreadsheets uncovered some shocking numbers that economist Steven Peterson presented to the court: in Virginia alone, over one million people had their driver's licenses suspended for unpaid fines. Thirty thousand people had served a total of 750,000 days in jail between 2015 and 2018, for an average of twenty-five days each, simply for being too poor to pay fines between $700 and $2,000. This was a horrible injustice to hundreds of thousands of people who were already struggling financially. Even if you are not persuaded by the moral argument, putting people in jail, where they cannot earn any money, does not seem like an effective way to get them to pay up.

After seeing the presentation of this data, the presiding judge used his authority to stop the automatic suspension of licenses for failure to pay fines and costs, and to immediately reinstate the named plaintiffs' licenses. This ruling led to the Virginia legislature passing a bill that reinstated all previously suspended licenses and allowed individuals previously convicted, like Samantha Nicholson—a single mother facing over 180 days in jail—to avoid jail time.

Clementine Jacoby has also been using data to successfully hack state prison bureaucracies. Like Marina, Clementine followed an unusual career path—she started out as a circus performer, then worked at Google as a product manager. She founded Recidiviz, a nonprofit focused on decarceration, when she was just twenty-six, with early funding from Schmidt Futures.

In contrast to the absence of lead paint data, US corrections data exists and is typically robust, but it's *messy*—often fragmented across many siloed databases, which makes it hard for decision makers (the people running prisons and probation and parole systems) to see what's working. Clementine's team at Recidiviz connects and standardizes these fragmented data systems so insights can be harnessed for real-time decision-making. Money, time, and political capital are poured into criminal justice reform, and in the modern reform movement, there is a good deal of alignment; people all across the political spectrum agree that there's opportunity to reduce incarceration without negatively impacting public safety. However, there is a resource-intensive debate on how to do so. Recidiviz focuses on helping practitioners and policymakers answer those questions with data.

As their first move, Recidiviz uses data to identify people who are eligible to get off supervision. A person on probation or parole may need to do ten things to be discharged: complete treatment, have stable employment, et cetera. The criteria for discharge are burdensome for the client to complete, and, unfortunately, also time consuming and manual for busy parole officers to track, leading to a lag between eligibility and recommendation for discharge. By crunching the numbers, Recidiviz helps leaders identify hundreds of people who can immediately get off supervision and move on with their lives. This not only helps people who are already succeeding continue to succeed, but it also means that there's more time and resources to help the people who are struggling.

Next, Recidiviz uses data to make more advanced arguments, like helping leaders understand which vocational programs lead to stable employment; which treatment programs help people get out of prison and stay out; which policies are having their intended impact; and which ones aren't. To settle debate on legislative action, Recidiviz models the five-year projected impact of proposed bills on the incarcerated population, supervision population, community, and budget. For example, Recidiviz projected that ending federal prison sentences for marijuana offenses would reduce the federal prison population by 2,807 over five years and save the federal government $578 million, injecting evidence into the decriminalization debate. Recidiviz is accelerating the rate of reform by making existing data usable, visible, and digestible, affirming the role of data and evidence in catalyzing change.

HOW CAN I USE THIS?

» **Find a Minimum Viable Measurement.** Whether it's lead paint on store shelves, or your own cholesterol numbers, is there something you can start measuring right away to give you a clue about problems or potential solutions?

» **Check the facts.** If you have a hunch that a claim is incorrect—like the idea that Malawi had no lead paint—investigate it! Trust your skepticism and get the data.

» **Replace adjectives with data.** This is one of Amazon's "rules of writing."

» **Run the numbers.** You don't necessarily need to be a data scientist or math whiz to use this tactic; your organization might have numbers in old spreadsheets or even PDF files that have never been analyzed before. Sometimes in big organizations you can even find *existing* data reports that were previously forgotten or never elevated.

» **Figure out what metrics matter.** Depending on who you need to convince, you may choose different measures. Focusing on cost and spending data when your audience is actually concerned about schedule and quality risks losing your argument.

» **Show your numbers in a compelling way.** Few people will take the time to learn how to interact with a complicated dashboard; even fewer will crunch numbers on their own. Make simple graphics or charts to make your point clear and obvious.

» **Start small.** You can't ban all lead paint in the world, or decarcerate every deserving person in prison at once. Use your data to help find the least controversial areas where you can make a data-driven argument for change.

TAILOR YOUR PITCH

Align your idea with your organization's strategy, goals, and priorities. Reframe your messages in the context of what your audiences and organization care about most.

Every bureaucracy has goals it says it wants to achieve. You can get more traction for your own initiatives by showing how your projects fit into your organization's existing vision. This kind of strategic reframing can get you more money, visibility, responsibility, and team members, without needing to change much of your underlying plan.

Aligning your project to your organization's strategy isn't necessarily a one-time task. You might frame your project one way for the CFO, another way for your boss, and a third way to an outside consultant. You should tailor your pitch, proposal, or interaction to stress what is important to your current audience.

What does this mean in practice? It might include:

- **Word choice:** Use the same words that are used in the corporate mission statement or organization-wide goals.

- **Focus:** If your project saves money *and* improves employee morale, focus on saving money with the CFO's office, and focus on the employee morale when pitching to peers.

- **Outcome statements:** Highlight the outcomes that match your audience's interests, rather than a laundry list of benefits. Or consider a new outcome statement altogether.

Examples of Tailoring Your Pitch

Here are three examples of reframing a project to win support from a given audience:

1. When the Trump transition team began taking informational meetings shortly after the 2016 election, presumably to decide which Obama-era projects to continue and which ones to can, they announced up front that they valued data-driven and business-savvy proposals. Some teams in government, distraught by the election results, declined to meet altogether. But the team at the VA working on a unified customer experience for veterans saw this as an opportunity to frame their vision as one that would save millions of dollars and improve VA's customer satisfaction scores. They were sure to define customer satisfaction using the common business measure Net Promoter Score (NPS), which is a measure of how likely a customer is to recommend you to others. This pitch went so well that not only did the Trump administration declare it a key initiative (one of the very few Obama initiatives embraced by the Trump administration), but one of the original meeting attendees went on to become the agency's next chief veteran experience officer.

2. The Global Maritime Forum is an international nonprofit dedicated to shaping the future of global seaborne trade. A key aspect of their mission is decarbonizing international shipping. Their team recognized capital (loans) as a key lever in getting large shipping vessel operators to change course, by getting the companies *financing* these large ships to require greener practices as part of their loan agreements. At the time, Citi, one of the largest banks financing these vessels, had just launched a $500 billion Environmental Finance Goal. By making the connection between financing and shipping emissions, Citi learned that their shipping vessel financing was *not* aligned to their wider environmental goals. Citi, along with DNB and Societe Generale, two other large banks, now lead a drafting group together with the nonprofit and ultimately signed on to a public commitment to support maritime decarbonization through transparent emissions data collection. This is now

an international effort, cleverly named the Poseidon Principles, with twenty-seven leading banks and export credit agencies signed on. (This is also an example of using public commitments, another bureaucracy-hacking technique we discuss later in the book.)

3. The 2014 Veterans Choice Act made new funding available for reducing the physical footprint of VA facilities. While this was not a goal Marina particularly cared about, she *did* care a lot about making it easier for veterans to renew their prescriptions online and get them delivered via mail. By framing her online pharmacy proposal as aligned with this new funding—honestly arguing that an online pharmacy would reduce the space needed for pharmacy waiting rooms in every hospital—she was able to secure desperately needed funds from an unexpected source.

Pitching the First White House Science Fair

Kumar Garg faced an uphill challenge: How was he going to persuade the risk-averse and busy White House communications team to let a horde of kids stampede through the hallways for the first-ever White House Science Fair—a new idea he had just come up with to anchor a big push on STEM education?

Kumar had a few advantages. He had worked and volunteered on multiple presidential campaigns, and therefore understood how political people thought about ideas. And since it was early in the Obama administration, there were fewer people actually in the White House, which meant fewer layers of approval.

Although he was a recent Yale Law School graduate turned policy staffer, Kumar knew his audience: communications professionals think about how an event looks on TV and in pictures. He decided to pitch it visually, using photos of kids to show "what the President would see."

He also knew he had to show a credible plan for how he would recruit a diverse set of kid scientists and engineers, using existing connections his team had with science fairs, clubs, and national competitions. As part of his pitch, he included a brief but concrete recruitment plan. Communications staffers also care about local press, and they could immediately see the value of having kids from many different states attend.

Emphasizing the visual appeal of young scientists with 3D printers and robots showing their inventions to President Obama, instead of focusing on the opportunity to release substantive science policy announcements (which is what most policy staffers would emphasize), Kumar made the science fair idea appealing, easy to understand, and credible under short deadlines.

By calling the event the "White House Science Fair," Kumar planted the seed that if it was successful, it could repeat every year—providing an opportunity to highlight science education and announce new STEM policy work on an annual basis.

In fact, Kumar eventually developed a reputation for being the policy staffer who brought pictures to the meetings where the policy councils would compete for presidential events—and he was often the staffer who got the event.

Why was the White House Science Fair pitch successful, and what lessons can you take from it?

- **Simplicity.** Without even seeing Kumar's pitch, it's easy to understand the idea of a White House Science Fair. It's not a complicated explanation. You don't have to know anything about science or science policy.

- **Compelling.** The idea of President Obama playing around with kids and teen scientists and inventors evokes a positive emotional response.

- **Specific.** This was not a multiyear series of science fairs across the country, but rather one event taking place on a single day.

Where to Find Alignment

Consider these areas and functions of your organization when you think about aligning your project with your organization:

- **Company-wide strategic goals or mission statements:** Can you show how your initiative aligns with big picture priorities and goals? Or can you make a case that *not* supporting your idea is counter to the mission?

- **Budget requests:** How are budget decisions made? Can you align your intended outcomes in a way that increases your likelihood of getting funding?

- **Procurements:** Do you have a contract (or is your company trying to win a contract) that calls for specific values, strategies, or outcomes?

- **External consultants:** Is there a team of management consultants looking for cost savings or new market opportunities? How can you make your project compelling for them to highlight in their recommendations?

- **Solicitations for employee ideas:** What's the criteria for selecting winning ideas? How can you pitch your idea in that frame?

- **Audits and compliance:** Was there a recent finding of a gap or deficiency that you could help address?

Don't Shift Too Much

We're not telling you to bend the truth, to take on a bunch of responsibilities outside the scope of your original project, or try to align to *every* strategic priority and budget goal. Few projects really hit every note. If you stretch *too* much, you run the risk of spreading your resources too thin or diverging too far from your original goal. You might also annoy and alienate people who will see right through you. This tactic is much more about *reframing* your project to match an existing framework, rather than *redefining* what you're trying to do or how you're going to do it.

Before you share your newly aligned pitch, ask yourself:

- Does this add scope to my project?

- Does this change my goal or metrics?

- Will I really be able to deliver on this new framing?

- Might I now be beholden to new requirements or oversight that could impede my progress?

HOW CAN I USE THIS?

» **Brainstorm different ways to tailor your pitch.** Emphasize the message, goals, and metrics to match what your audience cares most about.

» **Look for existing strategies and initiatives with which to align yourself.** These might be long-standing company values, annual strategic goals, or brand-new employee innovation competitions.

» **Use known analogs.** Kumar also used a sales technique familiar in Hollywood ("Rocky meets Star Wars") and venture capital ("Uber meets prescription drugs")—pitching with known analogs as shorthand. Imagining a science fair at the White House was self-evident at the outset and didn't require a long explanation.

» **Name your idea.** A White House Science Fair isn't a real science fair with entrants, judges, and prizes, but it was easy to visualize a science fair–like event in the White House residence.

» **Pitch with visuals.** Kumar used pictures of kid scientists with robots to help White House communications professionals visualize a White House science fair. Whether you are pitching in a document, slide deck, or a video, remember that seeing an example is golden.

» **Don't bend over backward.** You want to align yourself, not confine yourself, in your pursuit of support and resources.

DO THE WORK OUTSIDE
THE MEETING

*Do the hard work before and after a meeting to
make sure that nothing unscripted or spontaneous
happens. This work includes sharing materials
ahead of time, having one-on-one conversations
with key participants, and prepping allies with
helpful talking points and questions to ask.*

Kumar Garg, one of the greatest bureaucracy hackers we know, used to say: "I don't go to meetings. Why would I waste my time?" For most White House staffers, meetings dominated the schedule, with calendars double- and even triple-booked. And yet here was Kumar insisting that he didn't go to meetings—and he mostly meant it. He knew that meetings (especially large ones) are not actually where decisions get made; that happens elsewhere.

As our good friend and bureaucracy hacker Mina Hsiang reminds us, good pre-meeting and post-meeting work is important—precisely because the *actual* meeting is a good place to cement or create momentum. A meeting with many participants is where everyone can see the enthusiasm of an executive for a specific initiative or project—and can see others moving to remove roadblocks. Witnessing senior executives champion your idea and peers commit to help, in person, can be a powerful signal to your colleagues, especially those skeptical or indifferent. But you don't want to just hope to get lucky and have that kind of catalytic meeting; you have to do the hard work before and after.

This may conflict with how you usually think about meetings: as places to show a presentation, make your case, and win over hearts and minds. Those activities are key to getting buy-in and support for your ideas—but we're telling you that the place to do them is *not* in meetings. The real work happens *outside* the meetings—mostly before, but sometimes after. When you embrace this, you can change the outcomes in your favor.

Making Things Happen Outside a Meeting

Formal meetings, where a committee or group is making an important decision, are almost always predictable—it's all about whether you did enough research to learn the script ahead of time. A key to bureaucracy hacking is to understand who is making the decisions and who is influential in that process, and then spending time with them *before* the meeting happens.

Some questions to ask yourself well before a meeting:

- **Who is attending?** Do you know everybody? Is there an opportunity for a brief coffee or a warm introduction beforehand, so you're a familiar face to everyone when the meeting starts?

- **How will each person vote?** You should always know this before going in.

- **How many votes do I need?** It's nice to get a unanimous decision, but it might not be necessary.

- **Who influences the decision makers?** This is when your stakeholder map comes in handy.

- **How can I reinforce my supporters?** Recognize them; thank them or their team members for the support; or find ways to subtly remind them why they're supporting. Arm them with facts or materials to back up their stance. Don't ignore your supporters and spend all your attention on trying to change detractors' votes.

- **How can I learn how people I don't know will vote?** Consult your stakeholder map to figure out who you know who might know. You can also just ask them!

- **How can I enable my supporters to support each other?** This can exponentially increase the number of positive comments happening among the group, beyond just you and each person.

- **How can I persuade neutral parties?** Consider their motivations and how they perceive risks. Provide materials and opportunities for them to ask about questions and concerns in a safe, one-on-one environment—few people will be comfortable asking once the meeting starts.

- **How might I shift the opinions of detractors?** At the very least, you should consider stabbing them in the chest so they know how you'll disagree. (See the chapter "Stab People in the Chest.")

- **Who else is doing this pre-meeting work?** If your opponent is also reading this book, you'll need to factor in their actions—maybe you'll need to get pre-meetings even earlier, or spend some political capital on intel.

- **What's the read-ahead process?** Similar to how voter information pamphlets explain candidates and ballots, you'll want to influence how your issue is being framed in these materials. Don't assume someone else will do your story justice.

- **Who "owns the paper"?** Have you addressed their questions and do they know your priorities? This might have a different answer for who owns the paper ahead of the meeting (e.g., agenda, pre-reads) and who owns the paper after the meeting (e.g., notes and agreed-upon next steps).

- **What is the scheduled agenda?** You might be able to make small administrative tweaks that help your cause. For example, if votes are always taken in alphabetical order by last name, and you know Ashley Adams is always going to say no, you could suggest the meeting moderator randomize the order of each vote. This way, Ashley doesn't always get to set the tone just because her last name starts with "A."

- **Is there a Q&A portion?** You *always* want to orchestrate these with planted questions that can help raise issues you know or suspect people have, but are too embarrassed to ask, or that help raise points you were otherwise unable to make. (You also want to avoid fifteen minutes of dead silence when you have so many key people's attention!) Tag people ahead of time to ask specific questions in an in-person meeting; in a virtual meeting, you can provide these questions in private messages, making it easier for participants to post them in the group chat.

This is a lot of work at first, but as you develop these skills and relationships, orchestrating a meeting behind the scenes gets easier and easier.

When You Want Something to Happen in a Meeting

Our advice so far has assumed a meeting where *something* will in fact be formalized in a meeting, such as a vote or decision, but that the work that goes into that something happens outside the meeting.

In other cases, like a homeowners association meeting, it's possible for years of meetings to transpire where truly nothing happens. If this is the rut you find yourself in, you can use the techniques in this chapter (along with others) to drive to a decision meeting, such as by adding a vote to a standing agenda, or creating or joining a committee. For example, if you regularly attend a meeting that lacks structure and breaks down into whatever attendees want to talk about that day, you could start drafting and distributing an agenda, or appoint yourself timekeeper.

It's easy to rag on recurring meetings that never accomplish anything, but indecision can be deadly. In 2021, a twelve-story Florida condominium building collapsed, killing ninety-eight residents. An investigation found years of meeting minutes where condominium owners complained that they had discussed building repairs for years, and never gotten anywhere. The board president sent a letter complaining of this lack of progress just months before the disaster. We don't want to criticize her in the wake of such a tragedy, but it should seem obvious in retrospect that sending out a complaint letter was clearly *not* an effective way to get the building repaired. With nearly 400,000 condo owners associations in the United States, there are many more tragedies waiting to happen if no one steps up in the bureaucracies closest to home.

Guard Your Calendar

Kumar may not have needed to go to many meetings because he trusted his colleagues to go in his place, but if you're just starting to make a name for yourself in your organization, you'll probably need to attend at least *some*. Consider them an investigative opportunity: you can see who speaks up, who sides with whom, what sort of materials individual stakeholders use (e.g., does your manager prefer slides, a memo, or an extemporaneous speech?), and what the general flow and agenda is of most meetings.

But as you get to know the rhythm of your bureaucracy, and as your own responsibilities increase, you'll need to be more judicious about what meetings you attend, or you will easily find yourself in meetings all day long—*where nothing is happening.*

HOW CAN I USE THIS?

» **Focus on the decision-making process before the meeting.** All decisions and announcements should be orchestrated ahead of time. Is there a written agenda? Get on it. Is there a vote? Find out ahead of time how each person is voting, and what's influencing their decision. Share your materials early and often for feedback. If there's going to be a contentious issue or competing priorities, get time with key executives to hear your pitch one-on-one beforehand.

» **Leverage the post-meeting process.** The National Security Council (NSC) is one of the more structured places we've been exposed to—they have a written SoC (Statement of Conclusion) that comes out after every meeting. A staffer writes up the conversation, what has been agreed to, and who has agreed to what action (called "due outs"). Knowing the NSC staffer who was drafting the SoC was an important way to influence the agreed-upon next steps. More modern meeting culture may have notes being written collaboratively in real time, where there isn't a time lag and a chance for interpretation post-meeting. Regardless, if you can understand how the decisions in a meeting get documented and formalized, you can influence the resulting content.

» **Guard your time.** Review your calendar regularly to ask why you're attending specific meetings (in particular, recurring meetings). You might even try color-coding meetings by goal. A meeting that was once a critical way to get face time with a key stakeholder may be totally useless once you've established a working relationship with that person.

SELL, BABY, SELL

*Gaining buy-in and resources for your idea is
ultimately a sales job. Recognizing this, and learning
the fine art of enterprise sales, can help your
bureaucracy hacking gain traction.*

Bureaucracy Hacking Is Sales

If you are trying to make a change in a large organization, you're selling, whether you realize it or not. You might not have direct experience
in sales, but you should think of yourself as a full-fledged salesperson
inside your organization. One in nine people in the United States are
technically in sales professions, but as best-selling author Daniel Pink
writes in *To Sell Is Human*, "We're all in sales now."

You might ask: What exactly am I selling as a bureaucracy hacker? It
turns out: quite a lot.

You are selling a vision of an improved version of the world—one
that your project or change will bring about. You are also selling other
coworkers on joining your team (a sales genre better known as recruiting). Even if all you need is a simple approval or a bit of help from
another group, you are selling the idea that people should be turning
their attention to you and your project, over all other alternatives.

But your sales job doesn't stop there. You are probably also selling
for funding, budget, and other resources for your project. And since
there are likely various decision gates, you are probably selling for permission, approvals, and, sometimes, for forgiveness.

At a higher level, and especially to executives, you are selling that your project matters—that your idea, if implemented successfully, will achieve value, measured in more revenue, customers, donations, or users. That it will open up new markets or expand the opportunities for your organization. Or that it will cut costs, streamline operations, or improve efficiency. Ultimately, you are selling value with measurable impact—aligned to executive goals and objectives.

Plenty of projects *could* have an impact if they are successful. A harder and more interesting question: Why *your* project and not another one? Finally, you are also answering the question: Why now? Why can't your idea wait until later? You are selling urgency.

Bureaucracy Hacking as Enterprise Sales—on Your Own Enterprise

In the business world, enterprise sales means selling to large organizations, like Fortune 500 corporations. It also generally means a consultative sale, where salespeople engage with multiple people across an organization over months, sometimes even years, culminating in a signed agreement committing to pay for goods or services. Enterprise selling is a structured process with multiple sequential steps, including mapping out decision makers, learning their goals and incentives, making sure they are heard and understood, aligning your vision to fit into their vision, and securing their commitment of resources and action.

Sound familiar? Bureaucracy hacking has a lot in common with enterprise sales—and you can use some of the same tactics of top enterprise salespeople for your own benefit.

Great enterprise salespeople are good listeners, so they can learn what really matters to their prospective customers. Rather than initially pushing their product or service, talented salespeople focus on listening to their prospects describe a problem that they are experts in. If the problem can be solved with the salesperson's product or service, then of course she is going to explore a match. But if the prospect's problem can't or shouldn't be solved that way, or if there isn't sufficient need or budget right now, then an experienced salesperson will gracefully move on.

If a prospective customer has sufficient need, budget, and urgency, in sales lingo, the customer is "qualified." Properly qualifying opportunities—and not spending too much time with customers that aren't likely to buy—is the hallmark of enterprise sales.

Similarly, "discovery" is a key tactic in bureaucracy hacking. Listening to other people in your organization and understanding their motivations is essentially a discovery process. When you find colleagues that care about the same issue that you are passionate about, you are "qualifying" them. You'll invest more time with them—by incorporating their feedback, helping them accomplish their goals, etc.—just the same way an enterprise sales rep will invest more time in qualified opportunities. Your time is precious, and you want to focus it on building mutually valuable relationships.

A well-run enterprise sales process is structured into a series of steps, with more leads and opportunities at the top of the funnel, and only a relative few that make it through all the stages to become customers. To move to the next stage, the customer has to show affirmative interest and buying behavior. The same is true as you look for allies in your organization. Not everyone is going to be excited to help you; some are going to sound interested but won't commit; and still others will commit but won't actually deliver. But if you apply objective gating criteria, and prioritize which people you'll partner with on your project based on their actual behavior and actions, you'll identify your true allies who will have your back, especially in challenging times. Together, you'll be able to make changes bigger than any one of you could make individually.

Finally, great enterprise salespeople know how to get customers to talk about where they are, where they want to go, and what impedes progress—and then position their solution to help close that gap. Not every idea you have is going to be focused on a problem of strategic significance, but for those that do, position your initiative as addressing real problems that haven't been fixed yet, just like an expert salesperson.

If you are one of those people who says, "I would never do sales," consider our friend Kumar Garg's line: "Sales is the terminal job in all professions; CEOs sell, and university presidents sell. It is the one thing you can't give away as you become more senior."

HOW CAN I USE THIS?

» **Listen.** Empathy and listening are hallmarks of great salespeople. Take the time to practice your listening skills. Instead of waiting to talk, ask questions that demonstrate empathy, humility, and curiosity.

» **Research.** Know your audience. Leverage available public and private data services to learn about current and annual organizational goals and objectives. Review contacts' LinkedIn profiles for individual background and common connections.

» **Practice.** Get good at your pitch, at various levels of detail (a sentence, an elevator pitch, and a seven-minute pitch).

» **Develop and use a structured process.** Keep track of your conversations, with introductions at the top of your funnel. Invest more time in allies you have "qualified."

» **Learn from sales experts.** If you work in a large company, befriend your sales executives. If you work at a university or nonprofit, chat up your development officers (the people who ask wealthy people or foundations for donations). Find the effective salespeople in your organization and learn from them.

START SMALL AND
BUILD MOMENTUM

FIND YOUR PAPERCLIP

Do what you can, with what you have,
from where you are.

—TEDDY ROOSEVELT

*No matter where you sit in a bureaucracy, it can
feel like you don't have enough resources under
your control to accomplish your goals. You might
be surprised at what you can accomplish when you
trade with others for what you need.*

The Unobtainable Dry-Erase Board

A lack of resources is a surprisingly common problem in a large organization, no matter how many millions or billions of dollars and thousands or millions of people it may have overall. Budgets and headcounts are often determined well in advance, making them seem impossible to allocate to a new idea or initiative.

When Marina began as the chief technology officer of the US Department of Veterans Affairs, she was told by the VA chief of staff that her job was "to redefine the art of the possible as to how America cares for its veterans." To tackle this mission at the country's largest civilian agency, with over 330,000 employees, she was given a budget of exactly $0 and exactly zero employees. To make matters worse, while signing her human resources paperwork, Marina learned that her presumed title at the VA, "Chief Technology Officer," didn't really exist. On paper, she was a "Senior Advisor to the Secretary."

Lest you think Marina had particularly powerful qualifications to overcome these limitations, consider: on paper, she had just turned twenty-eight years old, never finished college, and never served in the military. Marina had approximately zero typical characteristics for success in the famously hierarchical and military culture of the VA. But she knew she had to try.

One of our favorite true stories is "One Red Paperclip," where Kyle MacDonald blogged about a series of fourteen successive barters that began with a single red paperclip and ended with him owning a *house*. While Marina had no budget, she *had* inherited a drawer of paperclips (and Post-Its) from her desk's previous owner, and she thought a lot about Kyle's blog in her first few weeks. Unsure exactly where to dive in, she read as much as she could about previous successful innovations at the VA and began sticking ideas on her wall with her Post-Its.

A key fact about Marina—she *loves* dry-erase boards. In the portion of her official bio where people often reference pets and loved ones, she called out her dry-erase board collection. Aspiring to turn her wall of Post-Its into a dry-erase den, she hunted for a spare whiteboard in the building. In her hunt she found a closet full of unused barcode scanners, and a lifetime supply of three-ring binders, but no whiteboards.

After politely asking around as to how she might get one, Marina learned that her annual $100 office supply allotment was not enough to purchase even *one* board from the official government supplier. Bringing in her own was not allowed either, as hanging it herself would be an OSHA violation! (The Occupational Safety and Health Administration allowed only trained personnel to hang objects on walls, to prevent risk of injury.)

The First Paperclip Trade

Just as Marina was about to throw up her hands at this seemingly Sisyphean task, one of the executive secretaries popped her head in Marina's office to inquire if she had seen "Green Pack 82." Marina hadn't—but "Green Pack 82" was about to become her red paperclip.

At the VA, official correspondence to the agency—such as letters from members of Congress—went into green folders known as green packs. Despite the fact that we live in the age of email and electronic signatures, each *paper* folder physically moved around the building as relevant parties made changes or signed off on the agency response, which was eventually cleanly retyped and sent back. But in the twelve-story office building that was the VA headquarters, the executive secretariat (the group responsible for managing correspondence and internal paper flow) was forever hunting down green folders by walking from office to office. Eager to make herself useful, Marina asked some questions about how the folder process worked—and didn't work—and created a simple app she dubbed FolderFinder to keep track of the folders.

Marina returned to the supply closet and passed out those abandoned barcode scanners to every green pack recipient. Each folder was now printed with a barcode on it, and when a folder arrived on someone's desk, they simply scanned the barcode, and the app logged its location. Now the central team could easily find any folder—no more hunting around the building!

Even better, Marina had unwittingly become a trusted problem-solver to the most important group of people in any building: the secretaries. Amusingly, instead of keeping the name FolderFinder, the secretaries called the app M-BOOP—M for Marina, and BOOP for the sound the barcode scanners made.

Marina's first paperclip trade—swapping surplus bar scanners and a home-built tracking app for the goodwill of the secretaries—wasn't what she was hired to do, but it was something practical she could do given her situation. And it helped her make friends in very powerful places.

Trade #2

Marina saw so many opportunities to improve the lives of veterans and VA employees alike, and wanted to get others excited about the possibilities, too. She cobbled together a group of like-minded colleagues and spent two days in a borrowed room, brainstorming what "the art of the possible" could be.

They thought about what the future could look like, asking: What if veterans could use one website, instead of the over 1,500 the VA had at the time? What if a disability claim could be processed instantly, instead of taking over a year? What if the VA could tell you all the benefits for which you are eligible, instantly, instead of veterans having to figure it all out themselves? What if you could schedule medical appointments online, like in most private healthcare systems? The walls quickly filled with ideas on Post-Its.

The ideas kept flowing, and Marina and her colleagues captured them in a beautiful blue booklet that two colleagues designed, called "The 21st Century VA." Determined to get her plan read by other VA senior executives, Marina spent $2,000 of her own money printing the booklets on glossy paper at Kinkos. With the help of new executive secretariat friends, she scheduled a one-on-one with every senior official to give them a copy of the booklet and ask for their feedback on the ideas.

As they saw their edits and feedback incorporated into the "21st Century VA" plan, the executives Marina consulted started to feel they were part of the vision. They strategically helped place the plan in the weekend reading material for a key audience: Marina's boss, Secretary Eric Shinseki. A four-star general who served multiple tours in Vietnam, and former chief of staff of the Army, Secretary Shinseki was a man who understood, and was determined to change, the largest of bureaucracies. He was also a former college English professor and avid reader. After reading her proposal, Secretary Shinseki found the ideas persuasive enough that he offered to increase Marina's headcount from zero to two senior-level employee slots. Another trade up!

Trade #3

It would take more than two years for the first official hire on her new team to actually walk in the door, but Marina didn't know that then. The HealthCare.gov crisis, when the new website for President Obama's signature initiative for Americans to sign up for health coverage was down for *weeks*, hit just two months after she joined the VA, and it gravely underscored the lack of technologists inside the government. (In fact, a large part of the holdup in hiring for her first two positions was that there was not yet an approved position description for a modern technologist in government, and she had to write one!) It also made the White House extremely leery of launching anything else on the internet, which at this point had been around for forty years.

As luck would have it, the VA was slated to launch the next big website under President Obama: the GI Bill Comparison Tool, the first-ever tool for veterans to compare their GI Bill education benefits against different colleges and vocational programs. Without such a tool, many veterans were unknowingly missing out on thousands of dollars in higher education benefits. The VA had spent a year and over a million dollars building it.

And—surprise!—it didn't work, either.

A week before it was supposed to launch, the original GI Bill Comparison Tool failed to stay up if more than eight people used it. As a result, Marina received a phone call from Deputy Undersecretary Curt Coy. Curt was a no-nonsense retired Navy surface warfare officer who made no secret of the fact that he had completely lost faith in IT. He heard a rumor from his secretary that Marina was a whiz with barcodes—maybe she could do something to save the tool?

This was Marina's chance.

While Marina had no formal employees at that point, the VA did have three Presidential Innovation Fellows—technologists and entrepreneurs doing a temporary fellowship in government—with whom she was able to work closely. Tom Black was a Web developer and a veteran himself; Ben Willman was an experienced engineer and manager; and Mollie Ruskin was a talented user researcher and designer who had designed Marina's "21st Century VA" pitch. The team also adopted Emily Tavoulareas, a technologist who had recently come to government from the private sector to help VA leadership reimagine how veterans engaged with the VA online.

The informal team of five rallied and reviewed the code, quickly concluding it had to be rebuilt from scratch. So that's what they did.

A week later, Marina found herself on another phone call, swearing to White House officials on her nonexistent firstborn that this revamped tool would stay up just fine if President Obama highlighted it in a speech.

And it did.

Fixing the GI Bill Comparison Tool was another paperclip trade. Building on her reputation as a scrappy technologist and using her relationships with the executive secretaries, Marina gained the opportunity to work on—and save!—a high-profile presidential initiative.

Trading Up

The VA was often on the front page of the newspaper in those days and never for anything good. Having the first successful website launch in the wake of HealthCare.gov was something the agency was very proud of, and Marina had earned a *lot* of trust—political capital—from that success. But her political capital mainly came from the fact that she was making *other* senior VA officials look good—and that collectively the VA was starting to show White House officials, however modestly, that it could actually deliver good news.

This success led to Marina being invited to a meeting for a new cross-agency initiative focused on consolidating employment-related federal websites for veterans. The VA alone was spending more than $27 million per year for duplicative employment websites—and there were even more at the departments of Defense and Labor, as well as the Small Business Administration. Instead of awarding one large contract to subsume all the others, Marina suggested that the VA might want to back up and understand the problem better. Did veterans even want to use a government resume tool or job search engine, given the wealth of private sector options?

Marina thought the VA could save millions of dollars by instead creating a very basic site to test out which features were actually useful to veterans. She wrote up a plan for a pilot that would cost just $3,000, having recently learned this was the maximum amount she could put on a government charge card, which was the only source of funds available to her. She still had no staff.

Once again, Marina leaned on her informal network, including Presidential Innovation Fellows, to not only help build the new site, but also to move content from the old sites so they could be shut down and unspent funds recouped. They had over a thousand pages of content to copy over, one by one, before the previous contract ended, and they were running out of time. In a particular moment of desperation, Marina and her team taught web page coding to some security guards to help them meet the deadline. The guards joined the team on their lunch hours for tutorials, then formatted web pages on borrowed laptops in-between admitting visitors. (Those guards have all since moved on to work full-time in the IT field.) This mighty army of secretaries and security guards was unexpected, yet formidable.

A few months later, after many grueling late nights and long week-ends of coding and demos, and many difficult meetings, Marina watched bleary-eyed as Michelle Obama and Dr. Jill Biden announced the launch of the Veterans Employment Center at the anniversary cele-bration of Joining Forces, a White House initiative created to promote economic opportunities for veterans and their families. A few days later, Marina was given permission to use a portion of the funds she had helped save—$3 million—for her first budget.

The Ultimate Trade

These successive paperclip trades gave Marina chances to get closer to her original goal. The credibility of launching the GI Bill Compar-ison Tool led to her getting the opportunity to launch the Veterans Employment Center—and the success of that website helped get funds for Marina to get closer to the goals in the "21st Century VA" plan she had originally envisioned. In stories we recount in the rest of this book, Marina's successful trades grew her headcount to seventy-five and helped her team create a legacy of successful flagship projects at the VA. Marina's paperclips really added up.

But her shining achievement came in her last year at the VA. Once Marina started to be seen as a trusted technical resource, she was invited to serve on a number of committees, including one where she met Board of Veterans' Appeals executives Lee Becker and Barbara Morton. Lee and Barbara were two of the most dedicated civil servants Marina had ever met, and since she was a new political appointee, it may not have seemed like they had a lot in common at first. However, it quickly became apparent that they shared the same vision for what the VA could become. Marina partnered with them to embed a team (using some of her new headcount) inside the Board—a part of the VA that historically got very little in the way of IT budget or headcount—that carefully studied the appeals process, ulti-mately shaving *seven years* off the average processing time with a new set of processes and technology tools collectively known as Caseflow. Barbara later went on to become the chief veteran experience officer of the VA.

To celebrate the launch of Caseflow, Barbara and Lee rode the Metro across DC to Marina's office for the best paperclip trade yet: as thanks for sharing her headcount with them, they presented her with her very own VA-approved dry-erase board.

HOW CAN I USE THIS?

» **Develop genuine relationships with more people at work, in groups outside of yours.** For example, get to know colleagues in security, janitorial, procurement, administration, legal, and accounting. If you're going to be a successful change agent, you don't want to alienate or disrespect anyone.

» **Consider your "paperclip" options.** Perhaps you can plan a flawless event, wrangle a complicated Excel spreadsheet, write an inspiring speech, or help a colleague on a project that's important to them. Others are much more likely to help you if you help them first.

» **Start from where you are.** Look around your current environment, relationships, and resources to find one tangible improvement you can make happen from where you are—and build momentum from there. Even in the most senior positions, you may not be able to—and indeed may not want to—start out with a huge new initiative.

ACT "AS IF"

Bring your idea to life by acting as if it's already reality, even if it's not quite there yet.

In the European folk story of stone soup, a weary traveler comes to a village looking for a meal. The villagers are unwilling to share their food, so he fills up an empty pot, adds water from a local stream, drops in a large stone, and places it over a fire. When asked by a curious villager what he is doing, the traveler says that he is making delicious stone soup, and that he would be happy to share, although he just needs a little bit of garnish to improve the flavor. The curious villager contributes a few carrots. Another villager walks by, asks about the pot, hears about the promising soup, and is persuaded to donate some onions. More villagers walk by, each interested in partaking of the soup, and are persuaded to add potatoes, cabbages, and even meat. After simmering the individual ingredients together to make a tasty broth, the traveler removes the inedible stone, and everyone, villagers and traveler alike, shares a delicious pot of soup.

This story, which varies by European country—the inedible stone removed at the end can also be a button, nail, axe, hammer, or piece of wood—is fundamentally about strangers persuading the locals to share. Sharing benefits everyone who contributes, as the moral of the story goes. But we also see the story as a classic tale of entrepreneurship, where the protagonist created something from nothing; or more precisely, he created something using a lot of different resources that weren't under his control. By painting a vision of a delicious soup, the traveler convinces villagers of a future state—even though he starts with just a rock and water.

Stone soup is essentially a bureaucracy hack of "acting as if" the soup will exist. By convincing the first villager that an amazingly delicious soup is on the way, the traveler gets a few carrots donated. More important than the actual flavor profile of carrots, however tasty they may be, is the social proof the traveler gains—someone from inside the *trusted circle* of the village now believes that the soup is actually going to come to fruition. This makes it much easier for the next villager to believe the soup will exist and contribute their ingredient, and so on.

You can make stone soup in your organization. This bureaucracy hack works especially well if your organization exhibits diffuse decision-making authority, where few or no people can globally say no to an initiative. In that kind of environment, one particular executive might be able to deny their support for your idea in their particular business unit or group, but they don't have the power to say that your initiative can't exist anywhere *else* in the entire organization. If that distributed dynamic exists in your company or organization, then getting just one executive to say yes—ideally with some modest skin in the game—provides social proof (the proverbial carrot) that can help you build momentum and ask others to contribute resources. As you build momentum—adding team members, gaining resources, developing prototypes, and showing value to customers or coworkers—the fact that you originally had nothing will quickly recede into memory.

The Green Button Initiative

Nick is a particular fan of the stone soup tactic; he used it in the White House to get many presidential initiatives off the ground. For a new staffer in the several-thousand-person bureaucracy of the White House, sitting atop the several-million-person executive branch, creating a new initiative is a multisided challenge: you must convince White House colleagues, federal agencies, and outside stakeholders that your new initiative is not only worthy, but also has sufficient support and momentum.

When Nick came to the White House from the FCC, he wanted to take a policy idea he had been working on—getting Americans access to their own energy consumption data in easy-to-use formats, to promote energy efficiency and innovation—to become a real thing. But he had no budget, staff, or authority.

While saving on energy bills is a pocketbook issue, energy data portability is a wonky subject for the West Wing. Further, utilities are the definition of risk-averse bureaucracies. Using the bully pulpit of the White House to highlight electric utilities that voluntarily agreed to make energy data available to consumers in a standard format (called the Green Button) was hardly the stuff the West Wing gets excited about...unless Nick could show them that the soup was already being made.

Locking the CIOs of three largest California investor-owned electric utilities in a room together with Nick's irrepressible boss at the time (US Chief Technology Officer Aneesh Chopra), with plenty of staff work ahead of the meeting, secured a public commitment from those three utilities to make data available back to their customers. Aneesh initially framed it as a ninety-day challenge, with only two of the three utilities actually making the deadline, but those results showed colleagues in the White House that this idea—challenging highly regulated utilities to volunteer to make energy data available to consumers—was not as crazy as it sounded.

Nick and Aneesh were able to include the California utilities who were committing to this action in various White House blogs and fact sheets about energy efficiency. This served as social proof to utilities in other states that the Green Button was a standard that was being adopted. Ultimately, through a combination of White House–branded events, individual conversations with utility executives, and working closely with both state regulators (who oversee utilities and their IT systems) and energy efficiency entrepreneurs (who were building new apps and services), Nick and his team were able to build enough momentum to convince dozens of utilities, representing over sixty million households, to commit to making energy data more accessible for their customers. (The technique of getting third parties to make voluntary public commitments is discussed further in the chapter "Get Public Commitments.")

Utilities and their regulators don't exactly move fast—hence the need for a White House initiative to catalyze action—but as of 2020, the initiative, now called Green Button Connect, is being deployed by numerous utilities across the country. According to Michael Murray, the president of the Mission:data Coalition, a leading advocate for the adoption of the Green Button Connect nationwide, "of the approximately 90 million electric smart meters in the U.S., over 36 million currently have, or will soon have, portable data via the GBC standard." In California, for example, Green Button Connect is how customers share their data with third-party companies that curtail energy demand when the grid is near capacity. During a recent heat wave, these "demand response" companies delivered hundreds of megawatts to the grid, quite literally keeping the lights on for millions of Americans.

HOW CAN I USE THIS?

» **Offer to brief people across the organization.** Part of making stone soup is everyone in the village believing that the soup will exist. If you take the time to brief various groups about your project, and reinforce your vision with various tailored documents, the repetition will breed familiarity, and possibly even a sense of inevitability.

» **Ask for feedback instead of permission.** Most people aren't going to be the first villager to give you carrots, but many will opine on their favorite flavor of soup or how to best make a soup. Ask for feedback on your project, acting as if it is going to happen and you want advice on the *best* way for it to happen. If people provide useful feedback, incorporate it into your project, thanking them for their contributions. Even if they haven't given permission or resources, you can mention their input to other groups to build social capital.

» **Keep a list of who else is on board and use it as you discuss your initiative.** Getting a respected member of the organization to support your project makes it that much easier for the next person to support you. But don't overstate anyone's level of support—they will find out.

DELIVERY IS THE STRATEGY

The secret of getting ahead is
getting started.

—MARK TWAIN

Plans and pitches can be effective bureaucracy-hacking tactics—but if you really want to drive progress toward your goals, start delivering on those plans. Even a seemingly small project, like improving a tracking spreadsheet for an internal team, can put you years ahead of where you'd be if you spend all your energy describing what you're going to do one day.

Start Small

Ask yourself: What is the smallest increment of change I might be able to deliver right now?

A small successful change can accrue a lot of goodwill and political capital that you can then invest in bigger projects. And if your small change didn't make a difference, that's okay—it's easy to quietly undo and try something else.

Some examples of pint-sized innovations that made big impacts in big bureaucracies:

- In the UK, teams of consultants were focused on how to increase tax revenue. While they were busy writing white papers, an enterprising clerk who had read the book *Nudge* (about behavioral science interventions) added a single sentence to tax collection notices: "The great majority of people in your local area with a debt like yours have paid it by now." This one line brought in over £210 million in new revenue that year alone.

- In Rhode Island, red tape and lack of technology were keeping the foster parent licensing team from processing hundreds of families in a timely manner—hundreds of families that they needed to take kids *right now*. While larger-scale transformation efforts were underway, the licensing team couldn't wait any longer. They creatively announced a Recruitment Weekend, where every family awaiting licensing could come and complete all their remaining steps in under three days. They had stations for fingerprinting, tuberculosis screening, fire safety, and other requirements, as well as every required training class available all weekend long. By Monday, nearly two hundred families had completed application packets. And as a bonus, many of those families became friendly with one other, creating an informal support and peer network that ultimately increased the retention rate of these families, too.

- In Australia, the New South Wales Department of Education got three times as many newly graduated teachers to apply to work in rural areas in 2017 simply by sending them prefilled applications inviting them to apply, instead of waiting for them to take the initiative to download and send in the application forms.

The Unappreciated Power of Internal Visibility

Many of the bureaucracy-busting projects we've seen succeed start in the same place: with the oft-neglected spreadsheet, made more visible inside the organization.

Roman had a problem. As an engineer at NASA's Jet Propulsion Laboratory (JPL), he realized that to design and build the Mars Perseverance Rover, he needed to know what parts were available in inventory in their manufacturing department. But since NASA JPL is a research facility and not a high-volume manufacturer, there wasn't a way to know what parts were available for building.

Instead, Roman literally had to "check the shelf" to see what was in stock. The US space program is so much more impressive than when we last went to the moon, but inventory systems haven't exactly been a priority.

Determined to fix this, Roman researched and bought a Web-based collaboration platform called Smartsheet. He began using it to schedule and track the 2,700 mechanical parts and 17,500 machining operations moving across 18 departments and 12 buildings.

By tracking inventory in real time, NASA's JPL was able to make resource decisions more effectively, and keep senior management up to date about the status of the Rover build—even amidst changes in the supply chain and internal design changes.

When Rebecca Wilhelm joined the City of Detroit as a project manager and business analytics specialist, most requests stemming from litigation or Freedom of Information Act requests were handled through email. Attorneys couldn't always tell who was responsible for a particular request or how long it had been in process. "We had a lot of issues with department communications," shares Rebecca. "If you'd been at the city for a long time, you had a leg up because you had made connections with people in different departments; you could call your friend that you've known for 15 years to get you information needed for a lawsuit. But we had no way of tracking our requests; there was no official point of contact and no procedure. So we wanted to improve efficiency and communication with departments."

Using Smartsheet, Rebecca created a simple form for people to input litigation requests, instead of sending them through email. The form spit into a shared spreadsheet, where everyone had visibility into who owned each request, and its status. This new process halved the time it took to respond to requests. As an added bonus, the form made sure that every request had all the required information—something that email can't do.

*   *   *

In Syracuse, New York, city residents were fed up with traffic jams caused by multiple construction crews simultaneously blocking busy streets. Adria Finch was an employee on the city development council who wanted to solve this problem, but she had no budget or technical resources to do so. She was able to solve the problem with a shared spreadsheet, where a dedicated employee listed all construction projects in one place to prevent traffic-inducing conflicts. Our friends Hana Schank and Sara Hudson share more about this story in their book *The Government Fix*.

Paradoxically, collaborative spreadsheets also helped Seattle Children's Hospital adopt cutting-edge technology. The hospital has a program to 3D print realistic anatomical models that its surgeons can use to plan out complex surgeries. Surgeons were struggling to convey the details they needed in these models, and the 3D printers had trouble keeping track of very specific requirements. Enter: a spreadsheet! Seth Friedman, PhD, the manager of innovation imaging and simulation modeling at the hospital, moved both surgeons and modelers to a shared spreadsheet for inputting, refining, and tracking requests for surgeries. Now, thanks to the improved trust and relationships with top surgeons, Seth has political capital to spend on expanding the use of 3D modeling throughout the hospital.

Show, Don't Tell

In 2005, Barry Marshall and Robin Warren won a Nobel Prize for their discovery that stomach ulcers are caused by the bacteria *H. pylori*. But when they first uncovered this in 1982, the medical bureaucracy would not listen to them. Not only were they in Australia, which is not generally known for making medical breakthroughs, but they were also still in medical school—and therefore written off as not "real" doctors.

What got the medical establishment to listen? After trying the usual routes—including trying to publish their research, only to be rejected by every single journal—Barry decided to take matters into his own hands. He went to the *Medical Journal of Australia* and had them perform a gastric biopsy to confirm he did *not* have an ulcer. Then, in front of them, he drank *H. pylori*—and, over the next two weeks, documented the development of an ulcer. This demonstration persuaded them to publish his findings—though it still took another ten years for this knowledge to be widely accepted.

Delivering Solutions for Ebola

In 2014, when the Ebola outbreak began in Liberia, Steve VanRoekel—then the chief innovation officer of the US Agency for International Development—started soliciting solutions from every tech company and smart person he could think of. Their ideas, like building a mobile app, drones, data standardization, and social media monitoring, "were all bad," he recounts. Among other problems with sitting around a table brainstorming in DC while a deadly outbreak ravaged a continent away: the well-meaning participants didn't seem to grok that Liberia had very limited cell phone and internet access.

Steve knew then that there was only one thing to do: get on a plane and go to Liberia.

On the ground, faced with real Liberians and real Ebola cases, delivery wasn't just the strategy—it was the key to survival. Steve and his team paired with local experts to develop a communications plan that could reach the maximum number of people quickly, which ended up mimicking a lot of social media tactics, only in the offline world: posting jokes on physical walls, hosting in-person town halls, and disseminating pamphlets via motorcycle. Being there in person also made them realize that ineffective personal protective equipment was a big, and dangerous, point of failure, so they focused their efforts on flying in experts who rapidly prototyped new and better suits. Not only did the suits prevent the spread of Ebola, but they also allowed patients to see their doctors smile.

Familiar with another bureaucracy-hacking tactic—giving away the credit—Steve highlights that while he and his team were able to help here and there, ultimately, "West Africans solved this crisis, not me." Steve, like just about every person we interviewed for this book, gave away credit or included more teammates in the telling of the story.

Don't Aim for Culture Change

Changing an organization's culture is a byproduct of changing what and how it delivers, not a useful goal in and of itself. "Culture change" efforts through motivational seminars, employee comment boxes, or lip-service incentives don't work, because no one gets excited about changing culture. It's also an amorphous idea that is challenging to measure.

In our experience, you change culture by making progress with your signature initiatives while simultaneously changing the incentives and frameworks in which people operate. In other words: deliver real change, and the culture change will follow.

HOW CAN I USE THIS?

» **Start.** As the saying goes, the best time to plant a tree was thirty years ago. The second-best time to plant a tree is today. You can always use what you learn in a future planning process.

» **Make it tangible.** Maybe you don't need to drink bacteria, but you could show real users or employees benefiting from your new tool, or invite decision makers to experience it firsthand.

» **Start with a spreadsheet.** You may not be able to *completely* solve a problem with a spreadsheet, but we've seen many big problems solved by starting with a well-organized spreadsheet. If you need to collaborate with others or add light automation (such as Web-based forms), swap out Microsoft Excel for Smartsheet.

GO SECOND

The more established the bureaucracy, the less likely it wants to be the first one to try a new process or adopt a new technique. Going first is often seen as risky and prone to errors or failure. Find or create precedents to make it seem like your organization is going second to create powerful peer pressure while mitigating risk.

A risk-averse organization is not motivated by the idea of being first out of the gate; in fact, the exact opposite is usually true.

The title of this chapter comes from a conversation Marina had with a state child welfare official who candidly told her: "I don't want to go first. I want to go second." This person supported making changes and improvements for their foster kids, but also understood their political reality: the environment tolerated almost no risk, where risk was defined as "anything new."

Rather than try to argue or insist that some of her proposed changes were low-risk and high-reward enough to try even without precedent, Marina took this requirement to heart. She currently runs a multistate child welfare project based largely on this premise: finding ways to help foster care systems avoid going first, and then using positive peer pressure to get as many as possible to go second all at once.

Show You're Not First

For Marina's foster care working group, she publishes public dashboards to track specific practices of states: do they ask new foster children if they have adults they might be able to live with (a good practice); do they require grandparents to get tuberculosis tests in order to foster their grandchildren (a bad practice, however well-intentioned); do they require foster parent applications to be notarized (a bad practice that creates unnecessary friction); and so on.

If a state follows the good practice, they get a dot. If they don't, no dot. If you see you're missing a dot, you can click through and get materials (forms, practice manuals, etc.) to copy from states that have already adopted the practice.

These dashboards can generate a lot of change very quickly, because they offer tangible evidence that not only would your state *not* be sticking its neck out as the first one to try a practice, but actually, your state is *behind*—dozens of other states may have their dots filled in before yours.

Such a dashboard may not already exist for your measure, but you can do research to create one. Ask around the office, or search your corporate intranet (and the internet) to find out who may have already done the thing you're trying to do. Cast a wide net across your organization. This is also a useful technique for finding out if someone tried *and failed*, which is worth learning about, too.

What If No One's Gone First?

You have a few approaches, depending on your situation:

First, you can look more widely for comparable analogs that could, without squinting very hard, count as someone else going first. We suggest using the Sinatra Test. In his song "New York, New York," Sinatra sings: "If I can make it there, I'm gonna make it anywhere."

What is the New York equivalent—the most demanding environment you can imagine—in your situation? Did the federal government do it? (We find these examples to be most persuasive across industries.) Did your competitor do it? Did a major supplier or donor do it? Did a school or agency in another state do it? Don't restrict your scope to just your immediate geography or organization (though you should look there *first*).

Second—and this can be a lot of work, but may be worth it—you can help someone else do it first. Maybe you have a colleague in another department or agency who has been noodling on the same challenge, but they have a more favorable incentive and risk environment in which to get it done.

If you really can't find another example, don't despair—we've gotten very risk-averse orgs to go first, plenty of times. It will just require using other tactics in this book to get to yes.

HOW CAN I USE THIS?

» **Find a precedent.** Your idea might be novel for your organization, but there are likely *components* of it that have been done before. Are there competitors or analogs that you can point to as precedents?

» **Use positive peer pressure.** Your organization might not want to be first, but it may not want to be *behind*, either. How can you use a chart or list to drive action?

» **Help someone else go first.** Then follow in their footsteps in your own team or org.

GIVE REAL DEMOS

Once a decision maker interacts with a real working demo or prototype, you've changed the bar for the game—subsequent presentations with smoke and mirrors won't cut it. When you provide real, interactive demonstrations of your future vision, you make it that much harder for your competitors to win out.

This tactic is short and sweet: you can change—and raise—the bar on how your organization thinks about and treats pilot projects by hosting *real* demonstrations of your progress, as often as you can. This way, when a competing project or opposing force comes along, they'll *also* have to give a demonstration—a quick elevator pitch or one-pager, however compelling, will no longer be enough.

It's not just about beating out the competition; immersive demos are simply much more compelling at winning over customers and colleagues, as well as for getting useful feedback, compared with mere conceptual descriptions. When you describe a new internal process or new feature for customers, it's easy for people to have different interpretations. But when they actually see and experience it for themselves, it lessens the chance for misunderstandings.

There are many technology tools you can use to build interactive demos without needing to know how to code. (We have some suggestions on our website.) But a demo doesn't have to mean a technology demo on a computer at all. It can also mean:

- setting up a demonstration store or office area;

- mocking up forms or other paperwork;

- acting out a customer or employee scenario; or

- producing a physical model, perhaps 3D printed.

If your demo is hard to show live, you could also record it and share the video. We also encourage you to record (with permission!) potential customers, employees, or other users trying out your prototypes—both for your team to gain feedback, and to build social proof for your solutions as you develop them.

HOW CAN I USE THIS?

» **Design real demos.** Record (with permission) actual customers or end users trying your demonstration. Make the recordings available for peers and colleagues, and invite senior leadership and decision makers to watch, too.

» **Build digital demos with no-code tools.** Drawing a prototype by hand is fine early on, but over time a polished interactive demo will be way more impressive. There are a myriad of low-cost, easy-to-use tools that let you design websites, forms, mobile apps, and other interfaces without needing to know how to code.

PILOT IS THE PASSWORD

Show a prototype of your idea and get feedback
from the actual customers or the people impacted,
in order to convince your organization to explore it
further.

A tactic for launching your new product, initiative, or campaign is to describe the effort as an "experiment" or as being "in beta." Framing your idea as a beta test is a time-honored way of getting started in almost any large organization.

Before an idea is live, your colleagues can come up with a million reasons why it won't work, why it presents too much risk, or why customers or employees won't respond. But once you have data and testimonials showing you are on the right track, your idea can gain a lot more traction and support, a lot faster.

Prove Your Boss Wrong

Greg Linden was an early Amazon employee who invented the concept of algorithm-based product recommendations—a feature most of us think of as synonymous with Amazon itself. But his original boss *forbade* him to work on the feature, believing that distracting customers with additional items would keep them from checking out. Luckily for Greg, Amazon's culture encouraged data-driven pilots. Defying his boss, Greg submitted a pilot for the cart recommendations, and the feature performed so well that it was adopted immediately—and has since been copied by every major e-commerce website.

Greg was able to convince Amazon to make a significant change to the most critical part of its infrastructure (the shopping cart) by showing data that the company was actually *losing* money by not adopting his new idea. He took his experiment (an algorithm to suggest additional products) and was able to show—with real customer data—that *not* scaling his idea would be far worse for Amazon, financially.

Bureaucracies, almost by definition, are risk-averse. Large organizations have processes to defeat bad ideas and properly resource promising ones—but sometimes good ideas can't get through the gauntlet of objections. Well-meaning colleagues might raise concerns, constraints, and trade-offs to consider. A lawyer might raise a legal issue; a marketing or communications executive might worry about reputation; or a financial executive will note that this activity wasn't explicitly budgeted for. It's uncanny how many obstacles you'll encounter that are straight from the CIA sabotage manual we shared in this book's introduction.

Instead of seeing your colleagues as saboteurs, we suggest viewing them as constructive critics, or tough-love mentors. Thank people for their concerns and criticisms. Get them to explain the details of their objections, where people have gotten tripped up in the past, and most critically—what they think would mitigate their particular concerns. Part of hacking a bureaucracy is navigating objections, and handling them in ways that convert critics into champions.

But a bureaucracy can be endless in its reluctance, and it can feel like you are pushing boulders uphill. If you can bring positive customer testimonials and customer behavior data to an issue, like Amazon's Greg Linden, you are far more likely to win the argument. Greg took it one step further and made the argument that *not* changing was *more* risky and costly to Amazon.

Pilots in Unlikely Places

"And one more thing—please don't write swear words on the walls."

Bryon Kroger was running the morning standup meeting at Kessel Run, the Air Force's internal start-up designed to build new software better. Standups are quick, informational meetings common in tech culture where participants literally all stand, to encourage brevity. They include status updates, quick introductions, and mundane reminders—in this case, the reminder to not write curse words on the glass walls.

Located in a WeWork in a downtown Boston skyscraper, full of young people casually dressed in t-shirts and jeans, Kessel Run felt like any other software start-up. This was especially true the first couple of years, when they shared glass walls with other tenants. An employee from one of those other companies had complained to WeWork management about the colorful language they could read (even written backward) through the glass.

Kessel Run was cofounded by Colonel Enrique Oti, a fast-talking cyber operations and China expert who had commanded an intelligence support squadron processing images from U-2 planes. Enrique had first-hand experience working in an Air Operations Center (AOC), the primary planning, tasking, and air traffic control system for the Air Force. Enrique knew how out-of-date the Air Force's software had become, especially in contrast to the fast-growing software companies he hung out with at Stanford during a mid-career fellowship.

After Stanford, Enrique joined a new Silicon Valley innovation unit designed to help the Defense Department find and buy new commercial technology. But instead of helping buy technology, Enrique wanted to show the Air Force what a reimagined AOC could look like. Part of his motivation was his own crummy past experience with software that he thought wasn't that good, especially compared with what the commercial world had available. But another reason was that the Air Force wasn't exactly inspiring him with its vision of the future.

During the fall of 2015, the Air Force released its Future Operating Concept to describe greater operational agility twenty years in the future (2035). It was shockingly unambitious to Enrique. "When you read it, there was nothing futuristic about it. It sounded like things that half of Silicon Valley was already doing," Enrique reminisced to us about the strategy. It was the Air Force's vision of "what the future looked like—only it looked like the present."

Despite not having a background in software, Enrique knew that it was possible to provide much better results than what the Defense Department was getting from their large contractors. So he pitched the idea of a demonstration project as "a beta test" to the CIO of the Air Force, Lieutenant General Bill Bender, who thought it was an interesting idea and gave him $100,000 to get started. Enrique hired a consultancy to help him interview airmen and brainstorm the components of a new AOC. The results of the exercise—called a design sprint—were promising enough that Enrique wanted to actually build it.

His new boss, Raj Shah, was skeptical. Raj, an F16 pilot and former cybersecurity entrepreneur, reminded Enrique that their mission as the new Defense Innovation Unit Experimental (DIUx) was to find and buy new commercial technology in Silicon Valley, not to actually build it. But Enrique was persistent.

Raj relented but insisted that Enrique run this new effort like a start-up and get mentoring from experienced venture capitalists and entrepreneurs. Frankly, Raj didn't think that Enrique would succeed, but he was willing to let him try, giving him a few months of runway and a modest amount of resources to see what he could do.

Enrique was a couple months into his pilot project when he got an urgent call from Raj, who was in Qatar, traveling with the Defense Innovation Board chaired by Google chairman Eric Schmidt. The Defense Innovation Board, a group of outside innovation expert advisors to the Defense Department, was visiting the Air Force's Combined Air Operations Center at the Al Udeid Air Base, which oversees and coordinates flight operations in over twenty Mideast countries. While the airmen used dozens of software applications in the course of their jobs, not everything was done with computers. Schmidt was flabbergasted when he came across complicated work being done on a decidedly less-high-tech tool: a whiteboard.

It turns out that airmen were planning and scheduling the refueling tankers by hand, on an oversized dry-erase board covered in magnets, laminated disks, and handwritten notes. As they planned military missions for the coming days, pilots determined where and when they would need to refuel. They literally marked on the board where and when they were going to be, and the planners then figured out where to send the refueling tankers (the massive planes that refuel the fighter jets and bombers midair). This handwritten information was then manually fed back into the AOC, which hadn't seen a meaningful technical upgrade in twenty years.

At the time, the Air Force was engaged in an offensive against the so-called Islamic State forces in Mosul, Iraq. During the Defense Innovation Board visit, the Air Operations Center commander, Lieutenant General Jeffrey Harrigian, was asked about his biggest concern. He gave a shocking answer: "I don't want them to erase my whiteboard."

On that late night phone call, Raj explained to Enrique what they saw and asked: Instead of building a demonstration of the entire AOC, could he build a small but real piece of it—a prototype of the tanker refueling application? Raj promised, "We'll put a million bucks of DIUx money into it, if you just go do this. Start tomorrow."

By framing this effort as an experiment, under the cover of the new Defense Innovation Unit, Raj and Enrique were able to avoid many of the bureaucratic hoops normally required. It takes years to get new software certified for operational use in the Department of Defense. It helped that this was wartime, and the need was out in the field—it meant that the local commander, Lieutenant General Harrigian, saw risk differently. "I had to accept the fact that we were going to try something a bit different while we were fighting a war. I had to be willing to buy some risk."

Enrique quickly recruited airmen who could code and took them out to Qatar to talk with the airmen that ran the tanker refueling whiteboard. Four months later, Enrique's team built and deployed a tanker refueling application, called JIGSAW, that was deployed to the AOC. The improved planning capabilities it provided meant that the Air Force sent fewer tanker planes into the air, saving $500,000 per week.

The success of this initial experiment—from idea to operational software in four months, record speed in the Air Force—led to Kessel Run getting more resources and people to work on larger projects. Subsequently scaling Kessel Run took a lot more bureaucracy hacking by people across the Air Force, including then-CIO Lt. General Bender, who back-channeled with Congress that the legacy AOC program should end, against the "official" Air Force position (approved by the secretary of the Air Force) that it should continue. Lt. General Bender could not, in good conscience, recommend that the Air Force continue the program in its current state, which would have required another $500 million and would have taken six more years to complete. Moreover, it would not have delivered updated software until 2022—based on requirements gathered in 2006! Lt. General Bender knew there was a better way, as Enrique and team had started to prove.

By the time Enrique retired in the spring of 2020, Kessel Run employed over 1,200 people. In just a few years, Kessel Run had become the flagship software unit of the Defense Department. Like any accomplishment at this scale, the credit goes to many, including those who were critically important behind the scenes. The reform of the AOC and the rapid growth of Kessel Run required significant support and coordination across the Air Force, the Pentagon, and Congress. Bureaucracy hacking at scale is a team sport, and the founding story of Kessel Run is a great exemplar of that.

Start Without the Bureaucracy Noticing

Just as large enterprises have a hard time scuttling innovations in-between their silos, they also have a hard time stopping one person or one small team from local experiments. Use this to your advantage. How can you get a minimum viable product off the ground and into the hands of real customers or employees quickly?

Executing nimbly can be an innovator's biggest advantage. Large organizations don't move quickly. If you can get a real pilot launched in the time most organizations are still studying the problem, you'll be well positioned to have your approach seen and taken seriously by senior leadership. And the more you've already completed, the less risky your innovation will seem next to alternatives that exist solely as PowerPoint presentations or memos.

You could spend the next six months finding data to answer an endless stream of questions and putting your project through formal approval processes—or you could get started. Addressing concerns head-on and using an organization's standard decision-making processes are important to building allies and showing respect for the culture of the organization, as we discuss throughout this book. But the key to successful bureaucracy hacking is also generating momentum, and one of the best ways to get momentum is to show success in the field.

You don't want to announce your new initiative too loudly. Instead, communicate strategically and slowly to avoid setting off too many defense mechanisms too quickly. The longer you can work quietly and prove success, the harder it will be for the bureaucracy to find you and stop you.

Diagnose Your Organization's Experimentation Maturity

Some organizational cultures are pro-experimentation, focused on improving customer experiences, testing new business models, and developing new products, services, or donor bases. If your organization has an experimentation culture, there is likely an established process for how to get permission to start and carry out an experiment. Even if your organization has a more modest experimentation culture, without much structure or organizational commitment, take advantage of using it as a safe shelter to begin work.

Conversely, if you work in an organization that doesn't have a culture of experimentation, you'll benefit even *more* from calling your proposed project an experiment. Describing something as a pilot lowers the threshold of scrutiny, and thus increases the chance you can actually get started. It helps if your pilot is small enough that it doesn't trigger the bureaucracy's antibodies, but real enough that it can show others the art of the possible.

How do you know if your organization has an experimentation culture? It's not just a question of whether people *say* they are experimenting, or a matter of counting the number of experiments in your firm. An experimentation culture exists when your organization understands how to run these kinds of exercises, and make decisions with the results. Harvard Business School professor Stefan Thomke, author of *Experimentation Works: the Surprising Power of Business Experiments*, argues that firms that are aware of experimentation, or only believe that they should adopt more experiments, are much earlier in their maturity. In contrast, firms that commit resources to experimentation (and abide by their results) are further along. The most organizationally mature are those firms where experimentation is widely available to most employees.

Thomke suggests asking questions like:

1. Do our experiments have testable hypotheses?

2. Have stakeholders made a commitment to abide by the results of our experiments?

3. Are our experiments doable?

4. How can we ensure reliable results?

5. Do we understand cause and effect?

6. Have we gotten the most value out of the experiment?

7. Are experiments *really* driving our decisions?

The answers to these questions—across your entire bureaucracy—can give you insights into how your firm values and approaches experiments. Armed with that knowledge, you'll be better equipped in your pitch.

HOW CAN I USE THIS?

» **Call your project an experiment or a pilot.** It's harder to argue with an experiment. Be explicit that while you are excited about the potential, you are unsure if it is going to work as advertised—so you are "just" starting small and informally. Describe your hypothesis (what you believe will happen) and what data you are going to collect to prove or disprove it.

» **Pilot a small but *real* version of your idea.** Start small, because you'll be able to test it sooner. But make it real enough that the feedback on its utility is meaningful.

» **Start in stealth mode.** Avoid the temptation to announce your pilot in the company newsletter or to brag about it at an all-hands meeting. The longer you can work quietly and prove success, the harder it will be to stop you.

» **Avoid duct tape.** It's cheating to solve problems in a pilot that you can't realistically do in the real world, and others will see right through your flimsy solutions. It will be hard, and messy, but you need to develop real solutions, not shortcuts, if you want to create lasting change.

» **Don't get too invested in a particular detail of your plan.** The point of a pilot is to learn as you go and adapt accordingly. You may come across a much better way or outcome than the one you originally had. Or you may come to realize that your first approach isn't meeting the mark. If you're resistant to change, ask yourself: Am I being stubborn? Will this change help me get to my goal?

DEFINE METRICS UP FRONT

Get skeptics to agree to indicators of success ahead of time for your experiments, pilots, and proofs of concept. Also agree up front to failure criteria to make others comfortable with giving you a chance to try. Whenever possible, transparently show how you are performing against those metrics.

When you pitch a new initiative, you want to control the definition of what success and failure look like. When you prime your audience with mutually agreed-upon criteria, you set yourself up to be seen as meeting or exceeding expectations later—and you can potentially raise the bar for your entire organization on how it views and measures success.

The goal of a project is not for people to like it. It's to demonstrate success against clear metrics. Carefully construct these metrics up front and agree on (or at least socialize) them with your ultimate decision makers. It's very easy for something the boss thinks is "a good idea" to never get a follow-up; it's harder if you meet or exceed goals you set together.

This also helps you to convince others that your idea is objectively successful—because, after all, you can point to the mutually agreed-upon criteria for success, and show your project meeting it!

Ideas for Success Criteria

Measures to consider include:

- Number of users

- User satisfaction scores

- Customer service scores

- Cost savings

- Time savings

- Reduced wait times

- Reduced number of steps

- Reduced error rates

- Success or failure rates

- Amount produced (e.g., pages written, comments posted, widgets manufactured)

- Presence/absence of a feature (e.g., no bugs or defects)

- Improvements in scores or amounts

- Qualitative descriptors

- Yes/no criteria related to project requirements (e.g., loads on a mobile phone, includes a privacy notice)

As you pick criteria, make sure you have a clear plan for how to measure each one, and set up these baseline measurements as early as possible. The whole point is to set success criteria out of the gate, defining it before others have the chance to come up with countermeasures; this tactic falls apart if you have to return to the drawing board because you can't actually track your progress.

Agree When to Give Up

Put yourself in your skeptic's shoes: they are thinking about how your new idea or project will impact them. Will your pilot go on forever? Will it take over budget and personnel time they need? Will they have a chance to weigh in on your progress, and if so, when and how?

Frustratingly, while a lot of people will have these concerns—and those concerns will stand in the way of them lending support—very few people voice them. Therefore, we suggest you be proactive: set and share criteria up front that explain exactly when you will pack up shop.

Failure criteria are *not* the same as your project goals. You might believe in your heart of hearts that your new PTA membership drive can get 10 percent higher participation rates from parents, but that ambitious goal shouldn't be the *floor* metric determining whether it can continue into next month. Conflating failure criteria and success criteria makes it all too easy for your detractors to call for the end of your initiative before you've ever had a chance to prove it out.

Set failure measures where you would objectively agree that your idea is not working. When this is agreed to up front, it's a lot harder to argue about later.

Example Checkpoints

Checkpoints for continuing or ending your project (or for unlocking key milestones) might look like:

- **Time:** You agree to end your pilot after a certain period of time, or if you don't start by a certain date. (You probably want to couple this with other metrics.)

- **Usage:** A minimum threshold of people who use the website, buy the book, read the paper, sign up for a newsletter, et cetera. We especially like more detailed usage stats, like how many people stayed on your website for at least one minute or who clicked at least one link.

- **Feedback:** How well does your target audience react? Make sure to set an *objective* measure for this, like average star rating (out of five stars) or Net Promoter Score.

A Rising Tide Lifts All Boats

Clear failure criteria can help make other people more comfortable with your proposal, giving you space for a running start. But it can also lead to something greater: it starts to set an expectation that everyone *else* in your organization should include similar criteria in their pitches, too.

If you believe your idea is a great one, it's easy to think that a hundred other bad ideas in your organization won't hold you back. And they may not. But when there's a lot of competition for resources—time, money, people—it's that much harder to get the resources you need. Forcing yourself *and* others to think through gating milestones for proposals can proactively and objectively weed out resource-sucking bad ideas, leaving more room for yours.

HOW CAN I USE THIS?

» **Define custom criteria for success for your initiative.** Lay out the measures up front. This will make it harder for your opposition to later argue that your pilot wasn't successful enough to continue.

» **Provide transparent progress data when possible.** Let others—especially detractors—follow along! This could be a weekly email update, a spreadsheet at a dedicated link, or a real-time dashboard.

» **Design success criteria that complement your failure criteria.** Your custom success criteria should be ambitious but achievable; your failure criteria should be the *floor* that determines if your project even gets to continue. Ideally, the two will be different but complementary.

» **Give yourself room to pivot and fail.** Taken too far, this advice can trip you up, taking away your flexibility. Pilots are important learning opportunities, and you don't want to take away the opportunity to change course by setting pilot goals that are too aggressive.

» **Understand why you failed.** If you didn't meet your own criteria, why not? Did you learn that a different approach might be more successful, or do you need to start over from scratch? If you uncover a root cause that will keep all your future pilots from succeeding, like a gatekeeping executive who refused to engage, it's worth your time to solve *that* issue before trying again.

SWEAT THE SMALL STUFF

A stitch in time saves nine.

Detractors will get you in the details. Get as much feedback as you can, as early as you can, about what specifics you need to consider. Even seemingly insignificant things, like having the corporate legal notice in a page footer of a website or white paper, can help stakeholders feel seen and heard, and therefore more willing to show their support.

As you pitch your vision, beware of death by a thousand paper cuts. Skeptics may try to poke holes by pointing out missing details, and even well-meaning potential advocates may feel left out or lose trust if your details don't reflect their needs. Confidently addressing the details (or at least being able to explain coherently why you *didn't* address a particular issue) can win support *and* increase your odds of successfully achieving the goals you're setting out to achieve.

Paying attention to details doesn't mean you need to plan for years before you can get started. This tendency to consider every last edge case and requirement is why most bureaucratic plans take forever. Our advice is about *balance*: you will learn a lot more, a lot faster, if you immerse yourself with pilots that *truly* address real-world problems.

Killer Details

Saving lives can take years of training, millions of dollars, or innovative new drugs or procedures. Or: it can take a checklist.

Fresh out of medical school, Dr. Peter Pronovost was bothered by a recurring problem he saw in his hospital's ICU: line infections. Patients were dying not from the condition that put them in the hospital in the first place, but rather from infections they were getting *in* the hospital.

Dr. Pronovost had been taught five steps in medical school to prevent line infections:

1. Wash your hands;

2. Wear a mask, gown, and clean gloves;

3. Put a sterile drape over the patient;

4. Disinfect the patient's skin before inserting the catheter; and

5. Put a sterile dressing over the site after inserting the catheter.

These steps were commonly known and not controversial. So why were so many patients getting infected?

Dr. Pronovost tried a small experiment: he wrote down the five steps and asked ICU nurses to record whether doctors did all the steps for each insertion. About a third of the time, the nurses recorded that a doctor skipped at least one step.

Armed with this insight, he changed the incentive structure: now *nurses* were responsible for the doctors completing this checklist. If a doctor was about to insert a catheter without washing their hands or wearing a mask, the nurses were incentivized to intervene and make sure they completed all five steps.

Dr. Pronovost tracked ICU infections for another year. The infection rate went from 10 percent to essentially *zero percent*. For the fifteen months he tracked the use of the checklist under the nurses, a mere two patients got infections.

Today, Dr. Pronovost is a famous doctor well known for transforming medical systems. But he developed his life-saving, infection-sparing checklist as an observant, brand-new doctor. It was the social capital he was able to earn from that early innovation that later allowed him to design and lead life-saving transformations across healthcare.

In an opposite example, a checkbox in Denver, Colorado, killed David Henderson. Without testing first with real users, Arapahoe County rolled out an electronic form to court officials to facilitate distributing court documents. The form had the box to send all court documents to all parties checked by default. When a clerk errantly failed to uncheck it, all the details of Henderson's cooperation with police in a murder investigation were mailed *to the accused murderers*. Two months later, they murdered David Henderson, too. (They have since been convicted.)

Astonishingly, this same error happened 1,500 *more* times that same year. Nobody paid attention to the details—until someone paid with his life.

Where might a checklist transform your organization?

Places to Pay Particular Attention

We hope this list can serve as a starting point for brainstorming the details that you'll want to address:

- Stakeholders:

    * What are the interests of the specific stakeholders who will openly comment on your idea first? The last thing you want in your first team-wide demo is for legal to complain that you never talked to them and that you are missing key verbiage.
    * Have you looped in people early enough to feel like they can put their stamp on your proposal? Sometimes if you know a stakeholder is keen to give feedback, it can be helpful to intentionally leave in a detail that needs work (or even an actual error) so they focus on *that* and not your core ideas.

- Timing:

  * How far in advance do you need to start, or reach particular milestones, in order to be ready for larger deadlines, like budget request deadlines or project progress reporting timeframes?
  * Send reminders to others to ensure your overall calendar stays on track.

- Prototypes:

  * Fonts, colors, and logos should be consistent with approved branding.
  * Include legal and privacy notices, even if your prototype doesn't have "real" users.
  * Word choice: avoid "lorem ipsum" filler text.
  * Images: Do you have permission to use a photo? Do you know who is in the photo? Marina once used a stock photo of a veteran in a big pitch, only to meet that very woman in the meeting!
  * Technology: Will you be showing a demo on your own laptop, or will attendees use their own phones? Does your snazzy font load on other people's computers?

- Mark proposals as "DRAFT" or "pre-decisional" as is customary in your organization.

HOW CAN I USE THIS?

» **Dot your *i*'s and cross your *t*'s.** If your company has a privacy policy on every page of its website, put that same text at the bottom of your proposed beta site. If someone in marketing cares about using the exact shade of blue in your logo, use that exact shade of blue.

» **Get early feedback on what specifics you need to keep in mind.** Rather than showing legal your new project and asking them to poke holes in it, ask the legal team up front what recommendations they have for you.

» **Admit when you don't know an answer.** It disarms others, in a good way, when they hear you admit that you don't have an answer. This in turn makes it safe for them to share with you when they have questions or knowledge gaps, which builds trust and creates more possibilities for discovering practical solutions.

MAKE THE BUREAUCRACY
WORK FOR YOU

Institutions are rigid. The people who
run them are not.

—ROHAN PAVULURI

---

*Most organizations have more existing resources and
flexibility than you might think—learn how to take
advantage of them.*

Hacking Harvard

"Professor Sinai, can you please convince Rohan not to drop out of
school?"

Nick's mind was racing. Had he been encouraging his student,
Rohan Pavuluri, even implicitly, to drop out of Harvard? Rohan had
been working intensely on his nonprofit start-up idea to help low-income
Americans with bankruptcy, but Nick hadn't realized that he was contemplating dropping out. It seemed Rohan believed that he couldn't be a
world-changing entrepreneur at a place like Harvard, and that his only
way to innovate would be to leave.

As a new professor at Harvard, the last thing you want is to be accused of encouraging students to drop out. Especially by a student's mother.

Most of the students in Nick's field class were graduate students at the Harvard Kennedy School of Government, but he made a few exceptions to include some talented undergraduates. Rohan was eager, bright, and intensely curious, with far more emotional intelligence than most college sophomores.

Like many professors, Nick liked to meet each student for office hours. Especially in a field class where students work in teams, it can be hard to get to know each one individually, like Nick wanted. But it was more than Rohan who showed up at Nick's office one spring Friday.

"Professor Sinai, it's parents' weekend, so is it okay if my parents wait outside?"

Bemused and also slightly appalled at the prospect, Nick responded: "Of course not—they should join us!" and invited them in.

In the middle of a friendly chat about the Harvard campus, Rohan's mother interrupted the conversation with her urgent plea. In the back of his mind, Nick couldn't resist thinking about famous Harvard dropouts Bill Gates and Mark Zuckerberg. But crossing Rohan's mother didn't seem like a smart strategy. Nick reassured her that of course Rohan should finish his studies.

Rohan's idea for his nonprofit, Upsolve, came out of his role as a researcher at Harvard Law School's Access to Justice Lab, where he helped draft self-help packets to help low-income Americans file for bankruptcy. According to Rohan, that law school research position was "where I got the idea that we could scale the impact of these self-help paper packets with a software tool."

Rohan then used Nick's class to learn about product management. "Your class gave me the toolkit to go from problem to solution," Rohan told Nick some years later. "It taught me how to deeply understand the real problem a group of people have through observation and then quickly and cheaply develop tests to explore possible solutions. It taught me to be an entrepreneur."

Instead of dropping out, as his mother feared, Nick encouraged Rohan to take classes that he thought were most relevant to his idea. He rearranged his Harvard academic experience accordingly, taking ten independent study classes—including another one Nick taught—where he chose topics that intersected with his mission. Every couple of weeks, Rohan took the Megabus to New York City—sometimes even the 3 a.m. to 8 a.m. bus—to work with his NYC-based cofounders.

Rohan also used the Harvard Innovation Lab—the "I-Lab"—to incubate Upsolve. The I-Lab was located across the Charles River, near the business school and had plenty of open space, snacks, and white-boards. More than just physical collaboration space, it provided Rohan with a great peer group of other students to learn from and get support, as well as access to entrepreneurs in the Boston community who had already scaled start-ups and were willing to give advice.

"Technically I was a statistics concentrator, but really, I majored in Upsolve!" Rohan liked to joke.

Rohan won the Harvard President's Innovation Challenge for the most promising social sector start-up, which included $75,000 in funding. Including other grants and awards, he ended up with about $250,000 in total support from Harvard by the time he graduated.

Rohan's start-up, Upsolve, is now a thriving nonprofit in New York City, empowering low-income Americans to file for bankruptcy more easily—and to access other civil legal rights, too. It turns out that it's so hard and so expensive to file for bankruptcy that many Americans can't even afford the legal fees to get a clean start. In 2020, *TIME* mag-azine named Upsolve to its 100 Best Inventions of 2020. By November 2020, Upsolve announced it had become the largest nonprofit focused on bankruptcy, reaching an impressive milestone: the company had relieved $250 million in debt for low-income Americans.

But Rohan wasn't done yet. He recognized that low-income Ameri-cans don't just lack access to lawyers to file for bankruptcy—they lack access to lawyers to access many other civil legal rights. He's gone on to give a TED talk with over a million views, coauthor an op-ed with former congressman Joe Kennedy about broadening access to civil legal rights, and file suit against the State of New York to make it possible for trained non-lawyers to counsel debtors about bankruptcy. Upsolve now aspires to be the leading nonprofit brand for financial literacy, and Rohan has become an activist at the national level.

Rohan didn't just stay at Harvard and get his degree. He performed a world-class bureaucracy hack: he used all the Harvard resources at his disposal to make an outsized impact on the world. Rohan hacked Harvard to make his own collegiate experience—he gained practical experience from Nick's class, leveraged the broader Harvard curriculum and faculty to become an expert in simplifying the law with technology, and applied that experience to earn more funding from Harvard than he spent on tuition. He also used the flexibility of the curriculum to focus on his start-up.

It wasn't simple or easy; Rohan had to invest real time to learn the rules to make Harvard work for him. He built authentic relationships with faculty and staff, recognizing that people are inherently more flexible than the rules of their institutions—*especially for people they trust*.

Your company or organization might not seem as accommodating as Harvard was for Rohan, but it's possible you haven't really looked, or asked. Sometimes those accommodations aren't advertised or well-known. Have you investigated how to make your bureaucracy work for you? What resources, programs, or funding can you use—even if they seem outside your immediate scope? Can you find a way to temporarily work outside your firm: Is there a sabbatical, externship, or civic leave policy you can use? If you've built strong relationships, and you make an explicit ask, you may find more opportunities and flexibilities exist than you've been led to believe.

HOW CAN I USE THIS?

» **Don't assume you know all the resources and flexibilities your institution offers.** Even if you have been with your organization for years, you might not know about them. Do your homework, ask around, and research where they might be written down.

» **Leverage your institution.** Take advantage of the full breadth of resources and flexibility that your organization has to offer. Don't be afraid to suggest something new, like an externship program.

» **Get to know the people behind the institution.** Bureaucracies seem impersonal but are ultimately run by people. If you build authentic relationships and trust with the people in charge, they can sign officially sanctioned exceptions and approvals—helping you bend some of the rules, some of the time.

STRANGLE THE MAINFRAME

HARRY POTTER: "So if all of his Horcruxes are destroyed, Voldemort could be killed?"

ALBUS DUMBLEDORE: "Yes, I think so. Without his Horcruxes, Voldemort will be a mortal man with a maimed and diminished soul."

Attack an overwhelmingly large problem with smaller wins that let you tackle it in bite-sized, manageable pieces—often without the bureaucracy even realizing it should mount a defense.

Big organizations have big problems. And they try to solve them in the same way: attempting to eat the entire elephant in a single bite. They create multiyear modernization or transformation plans and put everything else on hold in favor of these all-encompassing initiatives. These plans seek to account for every minute detail and edge case, with genuine intentions to develop a perfect solution, and consume the time and attention of the organization's top talent. Your organization probably has more than one of these plans underway right now.

And yet, these plans fail.

Pointing out that this approach is probably going to fail never persuades anyone to stop doing it. (We've tried. A lot.) Nor does throwing yourself in front of the moving train to try to stop or change the plan. *Multiyear planning is the natural state of a bureaucracy.* Every antibody and defense mechanism will be activated if you try to attack a signature initiative directly.

Instead, you can sidestep this process entirely by using the Strangler Pattern: scope out a small, well-defined chunk of the problem space, then quickly and quietly design, test, and implement a replacement. Each chunk gets you one step closer to realizing your North Star vision, but unlike a ten-year plan, the Strangler Pattern actually works.

What's the Strangler Pattern?

Formally, the Strangler Pattern is a theory of mainframe computer modernization where you chip away one piece of legacy functionality at a time, replacing it with a new, modern one. As you repeat this play, the behemoth mainframe becomes smaller and smaller—eventually small enough that you can replace what's left in one final swoop. This works whether your problem is *literally* a legacy mainframe, or another giant headache within your organization.

The best way we've found to describe the Strangler Pattern is through a Harry Potter analogy. (Spoiler alert!) If you aren't familiar with the books, the Wizarding World has a serious problem: the evil tyrant Voldemort. Initially, the main characters—Harry Potter, Dumbledore, and the Ministry of Magic—try to solve this problem like any normal bureaucracy would: by making grand plans to fight Voldemort and all his minions head-on. As the books go on, this approach causes the deaths of virtually every person Harry holds dear, not to mention billions of pounds of Muggle property damage. Despite the best-laid plans of top wizarding talent, by the end Voldemort is more powerful than ever.

Then Harry learns about Horcruxes, and he unwittingly adopts the Strangler Pattern. Instead of fighting Voldemort directly, he sneaks around the world quietly destroying Voldemort's sources of power one by one: a locket here, a diadem there. Each individual Horcrux may not be exactly *easy* to destroy, but one or two people are able to knock each one out. By the time Voldemort catches wind of what Harry's up to, his once impenetrable power is so weakened that a single timid teenager (Neville) destroys him for good.

Strangling an Unemployment Claim Backlog

In the summer of 2020, at the peak of the COVID-19 pandemic, hundreds of thousands of Californians were panicked. A few lost all hope and even took their own lives. Californians were applying for unemployment benefits in droves—only to go weeks, and then months, with no money and no answers. When they tried to call for help, nobody answered their calls; the unemployment department struggled to even open the mail, let alone process it.

How did this happen? The state unemployment department had put off even tiny changes to its processes or its mainframe computer for many years while it waited for the results of a meticulously planned, decades-long benefits system modernization effort. In theory, the new system would use modern technology that would make it *easier* to make changes and improve the claimant experience. In practice, the modernization effort took almost a decade to plan and was still years away from delivering anything useful. Worse, all of the top claim processing and technical talent were assigned to this project, leaving even fewer people behind to handle the tsunami of incoming claims.

In response, Governor Newsom announced a "strike team" that would help turn things around. In a gambit to find a short-term solution, he told the team (which included Layer Aleph, Marina's crisis consulting firm) that they had just forty-five days to find ways to process over a million backlogged claims. She and her colleagues were in a fast-paced race—with a decades-old mainframe and a workforce that had quadrupled in size overnight—to deliver unemployment benefits to Californians. Every minute counted.

The strike team adopted the Strangler Pattern, breaking off and redesigning small, critical pieces of the puzzle in rapid succession. These included:

- **A claim status tracker.** An analysis of phone calls showed that over 98 percent of people were calling to check on the status of their claim—information that the call center agents couldn't actually provide. A detailed claim status service was part of the planned modernization effort, but had not yet begun. Instead, Marina and her team talked to both real claimants and claims specialists to translate the existing system status alerts (which were mostly three-digit codes) into plain-language, easy-to-understand sentences. They then exported an existing report of these status codes once a night to an external website hosted in a secure cloud environment, which could scale up to meet high-traffic demands that the mainframe could not. In under two weeks, millions of Californians went from waiting on hold all day to using a self-service website where they could instantly learn the status of their claim and what to do next. Over ten million Californians have used this tool.

- **Identification of backlogged claims.** The unemployment department needed a simple way of differentiating between claims that required employee action from those that did not. Without this, claims specialists who were already stretched far too thin were spending time working on *millions* of claims that did not actually require intervention, instead of focusing on those issues that were preventing claimants from getting paid. To build a simple dashboard, the team developed a list of every possible system alert and worked with claims processors to figure out which alerts truly mattered. This dashboard was first built with Microsoft Excel, and then replaced with Tableau, a common visualization software.

- **A workload management tool.** This sounds fancy, but Marina and her team built this entirely in Microsoft Excel, too. Purchasing a sophisticated system for scheduling and workload management was yet another part of the future modernization project. To solve this problem in the immediate term, Marina talked to each business line to gather estimates of how long each step took, how many employees were assigned to each step, and how many claims were waiting at each step. This quickly revealed big opportunities for improvement. One example: the goal was to process every claim in under twenty-one days, yet many claims were waiting at the very first processing step for longer than that. By moving more employees to the front of the process, the unemployment department ensured that no claim spent more than a single day at the initial processing step, which increased the total number of claims that could be processed in under twenty-one days.

These Strangler Pattern solutions in the State of California took minimal time and money, and could have been implemented even *more* easily years earlier. While it helps bring urgency, you don't need a crisis in your organization to make these kinds of improvements.

What Makes a Good Candidate for the Strangler Pattern?

If I look at the mass, I will never act. If I look at the one, I will.

—MOTHER TERESA

How do you solve climate change? World peace? Mental health? Next year's sales goals? When our brains are faced with huge problems, they seem to shut down, overwhelmed and unsure where to even begin. This makes it hard to make progress.

You can effect great change in your bureaucracy—indeed, in the world—if you can show others how to eat their elephant: one bite at a time.

The examples from California worked well as Strangler Pattern candidates because they:

- did not exist as programs or systems already;

- were able to use existing data exports;

- were tightly scoped (e.g., just claim statuses);

- did not require new IT systems or new hires to work;

- could quickly demonstrate utility; and

- could be launched in the context of existing rules and regulations (e.g., the workload management tool was just a spreadsheet that did not require IT approvals, HR training, or changes to business processes).

How do you find places in your organization to apply the Strangler Pattern? Areas in your bureaucracy that may work for this approach include:

- Replacing a process that is done entirely on paper with digital versions. You can improve the effectiveness of the forms by getting out of the office to talk to real users and looking between the silos.

- Tracking metrics that are not currently being measured, to make a change you want to see. A daily or weekly spreadsheet could be all that's needed here. For example, if you ultimately want to move to a multichannel system to improve customer service, but no one is tracking the effectiveness of customer service today, finding ways to deploy satisfaction surveys or measure first-contact resolution rates *first* can set the stage for your pitch.

- Processes that are done differently by area (e.g., where you can pilot and measure changes in your own area of responsibility first).

- Known pain points or requirements that the organization must eventually address, but that are under the radar or boring enough to not attract much attention, such as routine legislative updates.

You don't have to have any idea how to eat the *entire* elephant or even *most* of the elephant when you start—you just need some concrete first steps that will roll up into bigger momentum. These steps need to be specific enough that they feel tractable and achievable to your audience. Marina has what she calls "Marina's Manipulative Math" when giving presentations on how to identify and scope Strangler Pattern efforts. She asks:

- Do you have everything you need to start now?

- Can you talk about it publicly as a win?

- Will it improve employee morale?

- What will it gain you (political capital, financial savings)?

- Who's against it?

- Is it a prerequisite for other changes you want to make later?

- How long will it take?

- What resources (time, personnel) will it take?

Find Your Trojan Horse

In Virgil's *Aeneid*, the Greeks ultimately win a long war against the Trojans using a clever trick. Before departing the battle in "defeat," Greek soldiers construct a large wooden horse, claiming it was a gift for the victors. However, they actually hid their best fighters inside the horse. After giving the "gift," the Greek army starts to sail away. The Trojans, letting their guard down, wheel the horse in past their barricaded walls—only to be attacked and defeated by the hidden enemy. This story has led to the colloquial use of the term "Trojan Horse" to refer to a strategy that gets you past your enemy's defenses.

A Trojan Horse is a great complement to the Strangler Pattern. Much of Marina's early strategy in foster care was explicitly a Trojan Horse. Chronologically, the first step in foster care is the child abuse hotline: someone calls in a report, and it must be evaluated and potentially investigated. She noticed that whenever a state started a foster care transformation project, they would start at the chronological beginning—because why shouldn't you start at the start?

The problem is that the hotline is the most contentious point in the whole system, where employees are most risk-averse—because lives are literally at stake if a call is so much as accidentally categorized incorrectly. Time after time, states that tried to start transforming their foster care systems at the hotline have failed, taken down by infighting.

Wanting to stay far away from all that, Marina found a different entry point: foster parent licensing. Due to an obscure 1993 regulation, states were not eligible for federal funding to digitize foster family licensing, so this process was entirely on paper across the country. Working to improve licensing was a win-win way to build relationships with states and prove her mettle. Over the course of a few years, Marina was able to change state codes and laws, connect to the main foster care IT systems, and deeply understand system change management processes, all the while making it faster and easier for families—particularly relatives—to become licensed foster parents. She used a Web-based crowdsourcing tool called Medallia's Crowdicity to get feedback on what was working (and what wasn't) in licensing from thousands of social workers, private agency partners, and foster parents. With all this knowledge and experience under her belt, she could *then* help states transform other parts of the foster care system, like the hotline, safely and easily.

As you break down your biggest problems, consider what your Trojan Horse may be. Is there an entry point where stakeholders are particularly ready for change? Is there a process that's changing *anyway* that you can attach yourself to? Is there an "undefended" area like licensing where risks are low and potential upside is high?

HOW CAN I USE THIS?

» **Start with existing technology.** If you ever find yourself working with an older, legacy database, something that they are *very* good at is spitting out a spreadsheet of data at regular intervals (e.g., nightly). Rather than wait years (or decades) for it to be replaced, use this to your advantage. If you can get your hands on an existing nightly data report, you can use it to power an extraordinary number of tools outside the mainframe itself, such as status trackers or progress dashboards. Something legacy databases are *not* great at is scaling to enable many simultaneous connections (e.g., a million people directly connecting to the database to check their claim status, and compulsively refreshing). This is a commonly cited reason for why things like self-service tools don't exist more often: the business usually wants this functionality very much, and is just waiting to completely replace the mainframe with a modern database that can handle the load first. Strangle this attitude with an approach that only needs to connect to the database once or twice a day, combining the mainframe's spreadsheet export with a modern tool scalable enough to handle your audience.

» **Don't obsess about having real-time information.** Daily data is perfectly adequate for most business interactions. Sure, some statuses will change a minute after your report is exported—but the majority will not. You can always use the success of whatever you develop with daily data to justify investing in the capability for real-time data later.

» **Find your Trojan Horse.** Consider all your entry points to attack a problem—not just the first one chronologically, or the one nearest to your role. If you feel stuck waiting for a huge project to finish (or start), look around for an opportunity that's not yet covered—perhaps one that's not in the scope, or currently entirely on paper, or under the purview of a different office.

» **Look beyond technology.** The Strangler Pattern may have originated in IT, but you can apply it to nontechnical problems, too. Any years-long plan or initiative has opportunities for shorter-term strangulation (i.e., working on adjacent, smaller problems).

BUILD YOUR TEAM

CULTIVATE THE KARASS

We Bokonists believe that humanity is organized into teams, teams that do God's Will without ever discovering what they are doing. Such a team is called a *karass*.

—KURT VONNEGUT, *CAT'S CRADLE*

You can't go it alone. Find and grow your karass— your informal group of people who want to get stuff done together. Armed with an understanding of which "guild" you belong to, build bridges with those who share your vision—especially those who have attempted your idea before and failed.

Find Your Guild

"So you see," Nick told David Gergen in front of his Harvard Kennedy School class of over one hundred students, "I'm a wonk. And you're a hack."

As soon as the word left Nick's mouth, he feared he had made a mistake.

The CNN commentator, four-time White House advisor, and

popular Harvard professor is much taller and more intimidating in person. Gergen frowned and leaned in toward Nick. They were seated fireside-chat style, and were now uncomfortably close. As the prolonged pause became awkward, Nick remembered that Gergen served in the navy and could probably kick his ass, despite being several decades older and impeccably dressed. The silence was becoming unbearable.

It had all started a few weeks prior, when David Gergen asked Nick if he would guest lecture. As a new adjunct lecturer at the Harvard Kennedy School, Nick was flattered that Gergen would ask *him*, a lowly, young adjunct lecturer, to speak to his students. In addition to being a TV personality who seems to always be on CNN in Nick's house when he visited his parents, Gergen also led an entire research center at the Kennedy School. He was a big deal. But at the time, Nick traveled a lot for work, and was probably too flip in his response, replying that he was only on campus on Fridays.

David Gergen didn't miss a beat and called Nick's bluff: "No problem—I'll move my class to Friday." Nick sheepishly agreed and Gergen left his research assistant to coordinate the details. Nick was horrified that Gergen was making one hundred students change their schedules to accommodate him.

The class started well, and Gergen put Nick at ease asking questions about how the White House works and what Nick did there. Nick showed the whiteboard that our friend and White House colleague Kumar Garg had in his office, explaining the sayings on the board and giving practical examples of each from his and Marina's White House experience. When he got to the saying of "Wonks vs. Hacks," Nick explained to Gergen's class that the White House is a bureaucracy of several thousand people.

One way to categorize the people in a bureaucracy is by the physical buildings they worked in: the Executive Residence (the main part of the White House), West Wing, East Wing, Old Executive Office Building, New Executive Office Building, Jackson Place, and several others that were a half block away.

But a more interesting way to think about the White House bureaucracy is in terms of guilds. There were all kinds of guilds that came to work in the White House. The retired volunteers reading letters addressed to the president had a different perspective than the Secret Service professionals, who generally came from military and law enforcement backgrounds and seemed to have photographic memories.

If you could understand each guild of people—their life experiences, their general orientation, their motivations, their values—you'd have a much better chance of being successful when you ask for their help.

Kumar's board focused on two groups:

- **Wonks:** This was shorthand for scientists, technologists, lawyers, and other subject matter experts. The major policy councils (NEC, DPC, NSC, OMB, CEA, OSTP, CEQ) were mostly wonks. They often came from agencies (e.g., Russia policy experts from the State Department loaned to the National Security Council) or from academia (e.g., economists on loan from Duke to the Council of Economic Advisors).

- **Hacks:** This was shorthand for communications and media, political strategists, and aspiring politicians. These were people who understood how to make ideas accessible to the American people, and who were more attuned to media coverage and public opinion.

One of the hazards of working in a policy council like the Office of Science and Technology Policy—where Marina and Nick both served—is that it's dominated by so-called wonks (scientists and technologists, in this case). If you weren't careful, you could be lulled into thinking that wonks were the top of the food chain, especially when your colleagues had advanced degrees from fancy schools and were experts in things like climate science or physics. But Kumar knew, and liked to remind both of us, that there were more hacks (like David Axelrod, the ex-journalist turned political consultant) than wonks (like Austan Goolsbee, the University of Chicago economist) in the West Wing.

As someone "bilingual" in hack and wonk, Kumar understood instinctively that wonks were likely to be focused on the nuances of policy and programs. Hacks, on the other hand, were much more focused on how to frame policy ideas and make them appeal to the American public. Many of us came to Kumar to figure out how to sell our idea inside the White House, as hacks occupied a number of gatekeeping roles to get something launched as a presidential initiative.

David Gergen was definitely what we would call a hack. But as soon as Nick called him one to his face, in front of one hundred students, he feared it had come out all wrong. There are many meanings of the word *hack*, and just after he said it, Nick worried that Gergen and his class would interpret his comment as an insult.

Just before Nick was about to blurt out an apology, Gergen suddenly smiled broadly and declared in a booming voice: "You are EXACTLY right! You've explained it better than anyone. Having worked for four Presidents, you've captured it perfectly!" He turned to the class, gave them a look like he was letting them in on a secret, and admitted, "I really wish I knew this before I started working in the White House."

Nick was massively relieved. Taking a deep breath, with his mind rushing, he just smiled weakly. They continued chatting, and then Nick took questions from the students.

The point on Kumar's board is much broader than the palace intricacies we saw in the White House—these kinds of divisions exist in every bureaucracy. Think about your organization. How do you group people? Is it by tenure? Seniority? Job function?

In the context of a bureaucracy, a guild can be related to a functional group (e.g., marketing, sales, legal, human resources), but it can also be informed by a set of experiences and backgrounds. Maybe you worked on a particular high-profile product launch or opened a new office overseas. That experience, in addition to your functional skills, can become a core part of your work identity.

Bureaucracies are filled with different guilds that may not spend much time with one another. The factory workers don't spend much time with the top executives, and engineers don't spend much time with salespeople. There are exceptions, of course, but guilds tend to spend time with each other.

It should be obvious, but if for some reason it isn't, figure out which guild you belong to. Other people will see and categorize you that way. Your coworkers—and people outside your organization—start with a bunch of assumptions about your skills, experiences, and interests based on the guild they see you in.

Being part of the finance guild, for example, doesn't mean that you don't have something to offer people in marketing; but you have to recognize that marketing people will see you as someone from finance *first*. If you can understand how people in other guilds think and behave, you'll have a better shot at engaging them productively. Kumar, for example, knew that White House speechwriters were on the lookout for stories involving so-called real people (referred to as "RPs"). He also understood that advance and communications staff cared intensely about visuals. When pitching an idea to them, Kumar would encourage us to include a picture of the prospective event location, or, if on the White House grounds, a picture of the RPs we were proposing to invite.

Uncover Your Karass

Our White House colleague Jake Brewer had a Post-It note on his office desk that read "Cultivate the Karass," a quote from *Cat's Cradle* by Kurt Vonnegut. Jake was killed suddenly in a bicycle accident, and his dedication to this mantra keeps it top of mind for us always in our work.

In the context of hacking the bureaucracy, cultivating the karass means finding (and adding to) your informal squad of people who want to get stuff done together. That means building authentic allyship not just with self-appointed change agents, but also with people who might seem like part of the problem but are actually the key to making true progress.

Cultivating the karass also means building common cause with people who have been working on your ideas for change long before you showed up. Whatever your new idea is for your organization, odds are someone—more likely *many people*—had it first. Instead of falling into the same traps they did, or incorrectly believing that you are special enough to succeed where they previously failed, join forces with them. Befriend them, learn from them, and enlist them to your cause.

It's not enough to find common cause with people who perform similar roles across your organization—of course, accountants in one business unit can befriend accountants in another. Building authentic relationships—built on common understandings and personal connections—across job functions is what makes a karass especially strong.

Bethany McKenzie found her karass two times over. When her son River was diagnosed with type 1 diabetes at age five, she and her husband—an orthopedic surgeon—followed the doctors' advice to the letter. River needed a substantial amount of carbohydrates at every meal, they told her—and she just had to dose enough insulin to cover them. When he ate the carbs, his blood sugar soared past the 200s and he felt awful. When the doses of insulin kicked in later, his blood sugar came crashing down and he couldn't play with his friends. This roller-coaster continued for three years, as the family thought it was just the way diabetes had to be.

Then Bethany found the book *Dr. Berstein's Diabetes Solution* by Dr. Richard Bernstein, one of the oldest living individuals with type 1 diabetes. (Diagnosed at age nine, he is now eighty-seven and in near-perfect health.) Dr. Bernstein advocated that type 1 diabetes is a condition where bodies can't process carbohydrates well, so the best diet was one that instead focused on protein and healthy fats. Bethany also found a community of other parents—her karass—on Facebook, all of whom were achieving normal, non-diabetic blood sugars in their children, and leading normal lives, by reducing carbohydrates and therefore using small, easy-to-manage doses of insulin. Group members also include those with adult type 1 diabetes who found that consistently normal blood sugars reversed complications like retinopathy and neuropathy—complications they had been told were permanent and unavoidable. Bethany was inspired to share this hopeful new solution with others, and founded the nonprofit Let Me Be 83 (advocating for the normal, non-diabetic blood sugar of 83 in all type 1 diabetes patients). Her karass, which refers to itself as the "Type One Grit" community, works together to distribute low-carb dessert recipes, share resources for parents of newly diagnosed kids, run a low-carb diabetes summer camp, and even produce a documentary.

Bethany found her second, related karass at River's school. Like most schools these days, it seemed like unhealthy, sugary treats were part of the daily routine: birthday parties, holiday celebrations, and class rewards, not to mention the standard cafeteria lunch offerings. Bethany wanted to change this, not just for her son but because she believed no child is well served by high volumes of processed sugar every day.

Looking around, Bethany found allies in other parents who had children with food allergies. They also struggled with the frequency of snacks that their children may or may not be able to eat and wanted a change.

Working together, Bethany and the other parents picked up the pen to draft a school policy that replaced food-based treats with other rewards, such as movies, reading time, and more recess. The karass had enough collective power to get the measure passed and improve school fun for *all* students.

Bring the Karass Together

It's not enough to find your karass. You also must regularly bring it together and ensure healthy collisions. Marina started a "Grilled Cheese" club at the VA. Every few months, she would invite all their supporters from all corners of the agency together to see demonstrations of her team's latest work and to eat grilled cheese sandwiches. This club probably broke fire codes, but it built personal connections with executives who subsequently went to bat for Marina.

A karass doesn't revolve around just you, your team, and your goals. That's why you should invest the time to get to know other groups in your organization, on their turf. Our colleague Beth Cobert calls this "playing away games" (as opposed to home games).

One piece of advice Marina received from her predecessor was to buy lunch for the Technology Acquisitions Center team in New Jersey. She wasn't sure who they were or how to find them, and she admittedly dwelled a bit too long on what exactly she'd buy for lunch. But an opportunity came to visit and speak at an event hosted in their office, and Marina sat down next to them. This was the start of a beautiful working relationship with some of the most powerful people in government—procurement officers. Over time, it became a badge of honor on Marina's team to have a "Rook" coffee cup on your desk. (The Rook mug was from the only coffee shop in Eatontown, where the procurement team was located.) If you had the Rook mug, it meant you had driven to Eatontown, New Jersey, from DC to an "away game" with the procurement team.

HOW CAN I USE THIS?

» **Consider where you might find others who are also trying to accomplish your same goal.** Is there a committee? An all-staff event? A mailing list?

» **Sit together.** Find ways for your karass to share or rotate office space, even if part-time, to strengthen team relationships.

» **Remember Joy's Law.** Bill Joy, cofounder of Sun Microsystems, famously said: "No matter who you are, the smartest people always work for someone else." You can get a lot more done by reaching into other teams than trying to concentrate all the talent you need under you.

» **Play "away games."** Regardless of seniority or distance, make an effort to go visit others in their home office or natural environment, rather than expecting your karass to always come to you.

» **Bring your karass together.** You could host formal meetings, informal happy hours, or quarterly gatherings. Also consider asynchronous networking opportunities like a mailing list, group text, or a collaborative messaging tool.

GIVE CREDIT LIBERALLY

It is amazing what you can accomplish if
you do not care who gets the credit.
—HARRY S. TRUMAN

---

*Give credit to others—authentically, generously,
and publicly. You'll generate goodwill and trust
by recognizing their contributions. Welcome when
others take credit for your initiative, because it
means you'll have more champions and allies in the
long term.*

Credit is not a finite resource like matter, energy, or money. If you give credit to others, you and your team can still get credit for the success of a project, too. In fact, the more you give credit and thank others for their contributions, both publicly and privately, the more they are likely to reciprocate. The net result is that all of you will be able to brag about the same project, and more people in your organization will hear about the project's success.

Another benefit of giving away credit: others will see you as a team player and want to work with you. You'll be seen as someone who understands the worth of other people's contributions. This is a good reputation to build. By giving away praise liberally, you build goodwill with people and build authentic allies. Giving other people credit—when they genuinely deserve it—shows high emotional intelligence (also known as emotional quotient, or EQ). It shows that you aren't threatened by their good work, and that you are a team player.

The opposite is true, too. If you are perceived as someone who brags a little too much about their own work, it can be harder for people to trust you or want to work with you. Since trust and a willingness to partner are critical elements of succeeding in any organization, you don't want to get a reputation for hogging the credit.

People can waste too much time worrying about who is getting sufficient credit, and not enough time on making something successful. As Bob Metcalfe, a cofounder of 3Com, a cofounder of Ethernet, and a major contributor to the early internet, aptly put it when talking to us: "There is plenty of credit to go around."

Giving Credit Proactively

Brian Basloe, CEO of corporate ticket management company Concierge Live, shares how liberally giving credit helped him establish rapport with existing clientele as he assumed the helm of the company. "I sought out our current and prospective customers' content on panels, social media, and the news, and then complimented them on it genuinely. I considered this making a 'good credit deposit' on our future relationship. From there, they were much more receptive to a conversation with me than they ever would have been with a cold, generic approach."

Brian's story is a good reminder that you don't have to wait to observe an opportunity to give credit—you can also seek out reasons to (genuinely) recognize people and make them feel good.

Credit in the Obama White House

When we worked in the White House, we subscribed to the saying that "You can get more done if you don't care who gets credit," a variation of Harry Truman's quotation that opens this chapter. Our thinking was partially rooted in the understanding that, as staffers, we weren't likely to get credit for much—we were there to serve the president and his agenda, not our own egos. Even amongst a collection of high achievers and strivers, the "no-drama Obama" White House was known for being quiet workhorses.

But our Truman-inspired philosophy probably also came from being low on the pecking order—at least in the White House. In the Office of Science and Technology Policy, our bosses, the president's science advisor and the US chief technology officer, aren't exactly household names, even inside the Beltway. They didn't have offices in the West Wing. On the other hand, the National Security Council, the Domestic Policy Council, and the National Economic Council, which *did* have offices in the West Wing, were typically headed by people with close working relationships with the president. The Office of Management and Budget, while mostly career civil servants except the top positions, had a ton of legal authority vested in it from Congress. Other than maybe the Council on Environmental Quality, located in a crammed townhouse on Jackson Square, it was harder to be associated with a policymaking council further outside the orbit of action.

Paradoxically, our lack of proximity to power was a tremendous benefit to how we thought about getting things done. It was unlikely our boss was going to outrank their boss, so we lacked "escalation dominance." Instead, it became clear that one of the quickest ways to ensure the long-term success of an initiative was to make sure it would make other principals look good.

Learning to not care about credit was a must for us, but it turned out to be a superpower.

Sharing Credit

Making someone else's boss look good might sound contrarian. Shouldn't you be making your *own* boss look good? Or yourself? Yes— and one way to do that is by giving credit to other people. Okay, but what happens when someone else publicly takes credit for the project you've been working on for months, or even years? Why should they get the glory when you've been sweating the details since the days when glory was far from assured?

We'd say that another person or group taking credit for your project is actually a great sign, if you can put your ego aside. Even—or especially—if they take more credit than their contribution. Here's why: it means they are more likely to champion it, advocate for resources, and generally advance your cause. They now have a vested interest—their reputation—in the success of *your* initiative. Others taking credit builds sustainability and momentum. Ask yourself: Do I care more about being the only person to get credit, or do I care more about my initiative being successful and having an impact? (We're guessing it's the latter.)

Try this thought experiment: What if your idea for change is massively successful—far beyond your wildest dreams—and you get zero credit for it? Would you still be excited about that future? Sure, most people like being recognized for an idea, hard work, and especially for success. There also may be a kernel of truth in someone else taking credit for your initiative—they might have done something to help you, or at least did nothing to block you, that you can't or don't appreciate from your vantage point.

There are some caveats to this bureaucracy-hacking tactic, of course. Giving credit has to be done authentically. If you offer insincere praise, people will see through it immediately. You'll come off as naive at best, and more likely as manipulative.

What does it mean to give authentic credit? The person has to have actually helped you, unblocked you, or advocated for you. They must have done *something*—taken an action beyond their normal course of duties—to advance your project.

There is also a risk when giving credit to people on projects that aren't yet successful. We all like to be associated with the winning team. As the saying goes, success has ten thousand fathers, and failure is an orphan. So lavishing credit to colleagues on a project with unclear prospects isn't doing anyone any favors—save it for later on.

Finally, we're not saying that you should forgo credit on everything, or that credit doesn't matter. Promotions, bonuses, and career opportunities are determined, in part, by who is getting credited with success. Salespeople, for example, get paid on the completed deals they work on—i.e., deals that they get credit for. They wouldn't get paid if they told their manager that other sales reps were responsible. We're just saying that for many projects and initiatives, and in more scenarios than you think, a smart move is to focus on recognizing the contributions of others.

Credit has an equity dimension. Women and people of color in particular regularly have their contributions minimized or disregarded, with others unfairly assuming credit for their work. It's not the sole responsibility of marginalized individuals to highlight their own work. Be an ally by going out of your way to recognize and credit colleagues who are underrepresented or who are being taken advantage of by more self-serving peers.

In the end, bureaucracies are about people working together to achieve outcomes. If you want to build authentic allies, you'll want people to see you as part of a successful team—and not as a lone wolf. Give credit liberally.

HOW CAN I USE THIS?

» **Send a thank you note to your colleague's boss.** If your colleague in another department helps you, send a sincere thank you email to their boss and CC your colleague. The boss will appreciate you calling out their team's good work, and your colleague will appreciate the recognition.

» **Model a culture of giving credit.** In team meetings, find ways to celebrate the contributions of other teams that helped yours. It models what author Adam Grant calls a "giving culture."

» **Use your organization's recognition system.** Find out what awards your organization gives to employees, such as performance bonuses, raises, promotions, and recognition awards, and nominate helpful colleagues on a regular basis.

» **Give credit where it matters: performance reviews.** Find ways to include credit and positive feedback in others' performance reviews. Some organizations have formal mechanisms for coworkers to give feedback on one another; others let supervisors decide. Either way, investigate how performance reviews work in your organization, and how to add input. It might take a little bit of work to write up a positive vignette, but the receiver will appreciate it for potentially years to come.

FIND THE DOERS

The most effective way to do it, is to do it.

—AMELIA EARHART

Find the people who can actually do the work, and pair up with them.

Making change in an organization is a team sport—and you'll need other people to help you do the work. We call them the "doers." Find the doers, recruit them, deputize them, and support them. Bring them into your ecosystem and empower them to do their best work on your team.

What's a Doer?

"Doers are energetic and entrepreneurial people who take responsibility for the execution of an idea," writes our mentor and longtime White House staffer Tom Kalil in an *MIT Press Journals* article titled "Policy Entrepreneurship at the White House: Getting Things Done in Large Organizations." Tom notes:

> Many of the things the White House wants to accomplish are ultimately done by someone else. The White House does not conduct

scientific research, provide grants or contracts, deliver services to citizens, enforce the law, pass legislation, issue regulations, or provide appropriations to the federal government. Even when the president issues an executive order, his decisions are rarely self-executing and require implementation by one or more federal agencies.

Tom had seen too many promising ideas and policies die because they were not fully implemented by the responsible agency—and would therefore encourage his team to focus on finding the doers to make sure *their* projects didn't suffer that same fate.

What does "finding the doers" mean in your organization?

Sometimes finding doers means hiring more people to work directly for you. Hiring a team, whether from external or internal sources, is a great opportunity to pick people who have skills, experiences, and relationships relevant to your project. If you are interviewing internally, you have a chance to build more relationships and tell more people about what you are working on.

But more often, it means finding others who are willing to work on your project from within their existing department or business unit, in their existing role. Most doers won't formally work for you, and that's okay.

Why do people volunteer to work on things that aren't their job? Maybe they are junior, looking for something beyond their immediate, assigned duties. Perhaps they are in administrative or clerical work, and ambitious to grow their skills. Or they want to transfer into your group or department because you throw the best office parties. Or they feel a sense of responsibility to the mission of the organization and are inclined to say yes when asked to help. Or maybe, just maybe, they are passionate about your project. Regardless of their motivation (though you should make sure you understand it), there is human slack in any large organization. You need to tap into it.

When we worked in the White House, finding doers made all the difference. Our boss might take a cabinet secretary to lunch at the White House Mess—the intimate private dining room on the bottom floor of the West Wing, served by active-duty navy personnel—to get her agreement to do something. Subsequently, that commitment might get announced in a White House press release, a powerful public marker. But if we didn't first identify the doers that worked in the department, and work closely with them to actually achieve the intended outcome, our chances of success went way down.

One challenge with bureaucracies is that there are plenty of people who *talk* about the work, but surprisingly few people who *do* the work. Sometimes you'll identify people who are eager to network but who aren't good at rolling up their sleeves. That's okay—they can still be important allies, tell your story, provide important information, provide air cover, and help in many other ways. But don't rely on them for results.

What does it mean to do the work? It depends on your organization, industry, and project, but here are some examples:

- They can draft a report or presentation.

- They can research a topic, product, or person.

- They can write policies, proposals, grants, or contracts.

- They can analyze data or build a website.

- They can help with administrative or logistics needs.

- They can get the right people to attend a key meeting.

Doer 101

Where are the doers? How do you find them? One obvious place is newer and more junior employees, who are often eager to prove themselves. Others may appear as you socialize your idea across your organization.

What does it mean to recruit doers? It means that you've had at least one, but ideally multiple, conversations about your project, and that they explicitly said they're willing to help on a specific piece of it. This is different from simply liking it, supporting it, or unblocking it. We're talking about people who have affirmatively said they want to work on your project. They can volunteer this on their own, or you can ask them proactively, but either way, you've had a clear conversation about the actual work.

How can you deputize doers? Start small. Give a potential doer a discrete task to see how they perform. Our friend Kumar Garg used to give prospective doers a small amount of homework—such as asking them to write a one-pager on a policy idea they just discussed—and would invest more time with the 20 percent of people who actually completed the task. You want to build trust and confidence, especially if you haven't worked together before.

How can you support your doers? In addition to recognition and gratitude, think about other discrete opportunities you can offer. Can you get them into a meeting that they couldn't normally get into? Can you provide positive feedback in their annual review and help them get promoted? Can you get them transferred to the office or role they want? Are there other perks of your organization that you can help them access? Be sensitive that this is a completely voluntary relationship, if a doer doesn't work directly for you.

A final note: doing the work is noble. This isn't about Tom Sawyering others into painting the fence; it's about maximizing the total amount of work you and you team can get done.

The flip side to our advice to find the doers is valid, too. If you are just starting your career, or feel stuck mid-career, consider volunteering to work on projects that you think are important, or with people who you want to work with. *Be* a doer.

HOW CAN I USE THIS?

» **Find doers.** Keep your eyes and ears open for doers in other parts of the organization who might be open to helping.

» **Hire doers.** If you can hire people directly or accept internal transfers, you can build a team of doers that works directly for you. When you reference-check candidates, make sure they have a reputation for *doing* the work, not just talking about it.

» **Vet potential doers.** Before making significant commitments to work together, test out someone's capabilities with a small project, like a draft one-pager. If they never do it at all—and most won't—you've saved yourself the hassle and narrowed down to the true workhorses.

» **Cultivate doers.** When you've recruited people to help on your project, you are making an implicit commitment to help them in return. Make time for them, and make sure they are getting something out of the trade.

» **Support your doers.** Especially if they don't formally work for you, find ways to recognize your new teammates with the kinds of rewards they value most, such as recognition, positive performance reviews, access, or experience.

» **Be a doer.** Earn political capital and trusted relationships by rolling up your sleeves for others.

MAKE IT EASY FOR THE OTHER PERSON

Help other people help you by making it as easy as possible for them to do what you need.

Think about a time someone has asked for your help, like a friend asking for an introduction to a prospect or possible employer. When it came time to sit down to make the introduction, how long had it been since they first asked? If you're like most people, it probably took longer than you meant. Perhaps the original email slipped too far down in your inbox; perhaps you kept finding it hard to phrase the introduction the right way, putting it off until later; or perhaps you simply didn't have the time. Many of these kinds of requests never get fulfilled at all.

We've seen this time and time again in the bureaucracies where we've worked and advised. Coworkers have the best of intentions—until their list of things to do inevitably piles up. How can you break this cycle of good intentions but little follow-through?

Start by assuming that people never follow up—not because they don't like you, or secretly don't want to help you, but because they're just too busy. Instead, recognize that the best way to get your favors fulfilled is to make it as easy as possible for the other person to fulfill it.

Beyond being busy, friction is another culprit. "It is human nature to follow the law of least effort, which states that when deciding between two similar options, people naturally gravitate toward the option that requires the least amount of work," writes author James Clear in *Atomic Habits*. His third law of behavior change, "make it easy," focuses on reducing friction to build everyday good habits like exercising or eating right—and we'd argue that the same principle holds for reducing friction in working with others.

Your colleague may genuinely want to make that phone call or email on your behalf, but if they need to ask you for clarification, look up phone numbers, compose a fresh email, or do other tasks that take time or mental energy, then it's that much easier for them to delay. They might even forget altogether, and by the time you remind them, it might be too late.

Now think about a time when someone made it easy for you to help them—they sent you an email you could forward in two seconds, ghostwrote the reference letter they needed, or even formatted a calendar invite to automatically dial the conference code and PIN for you to drop in to a meeting. Be more like that person.

Make It Easy to Learn

If your project will require others in your organization to learn something—how to use a new software application, how a new pharmaceutical works, why a new chemical will improve your factory outputs, etc.—then you need to make it *easy* for them to learn. If you don't, you run the risk of friction or dissent derailing your project simply because someone feels out of their depth, and perhaps worries for their job security. Nobody wants to be seen asking "dumb" questions in front of their colleagues or direct reports.

Our colleague Erie Meyer had a brilliant approach to making it easy for government IT executives to learn about APIs (Application Programming Interfaces), a way for software applications to talk to one another and exchange data. This can sound scary at first to a group of professionals who are concerned with security, because it meant outsiders would be able to exchange data with sensitive government systems. In the 2010s, the federal government was not using APIs much, and Erie wanted to change that. Getting ahead of potential objections, she hosted a series of formal presentations called "APIs for Executives." They had professional invitations, were held in a fancy room in the White House, and included expert industry speakers. It was designed to look and feel like the trainings with which these executives were already familiar. But the content was actually more along the lines of "Introduction to APIs," starting with the basics and not assuming any prior knowledge. (Please note that she was never patronizing—our advice is to make it *easy* to learn, not to make senior executives look or feel foolish.)

You could take this a step further and make it easy for colleagues who *no one* expects to know your material—say, because they are in a different department—to become familiar with the basics, too.

Copy and Paste

When foster youth reach adulthood without being adopted or reunited with their family, they abruptly "age out" of the foster care system and lose the associated support overnight. Every day during the COVID-19 pandemic, children were aging out of foster care into a scary world: limited jobs, limited housing, and limited ways to build or maintain relationships. But state policies at the time specified the exact day foster care ended (in most states, it's a child's eighteenth or twenty-first birthday), and with those policies in place, social workers were powerless to extend money or other resources to these kids.

Nobody actively wanted this to happen, but welfare agency leadership teams were overwhelmed with the pandemic on every front. Directors said they wanted to change the rules, but there were so many other competing pandemic-related priorities, and no capacity to explore solutions.

But what if there was?

Sixto Cancel, the CEO of Think of Us, a nonprofit focused on helping older foster youth to heal, develop, and thrive, saw an opening to make fixing this problem easy for states. Sixto formed a coalition to help solve emerging child welfare issues related to the pandemic. Unlike states, this coalition had the capacity to quickly explore and crowdsource solutions from across the country. The group learned that Illinois passed an executive order issuing a moratorium on aging out, allowing older youth to stay in care until the pandemic ended. The coalition also found other states that had taken similar, but slightly different, policy actions to achieve the same goal, like issuing internal policy amendments and passing new laws.

Sixto and his team published a playbook that compiled the various, tested pathways to stopping youth from aging out, and they shared the specific policy language that Illinois and other states had successfully used. Other states literally copied and pasted these materials, enacting their own moratoriums within days. By making it as easy as possible for the agencies to do the right thing, Sixto kept tens of thousands of vulnerable youth from being kicked out of foster care during a pandemic.

HOW CAN I USE THIS?

» **Follow up quickly.** Within twenty-four hours of someone agreeing to help you, thank them and provide all the necessary information, such as timelines, contact information, instructions, and/or ghostwritten copy.

» **Ghostwrite emails, letters, blog posts, and speeches.** Whenever possible, when you need someone else to send it on your behalf, write the actual email or letter yourself. They will likely have edits, but if you write simply and factually, you've gotten them a lot closer to the final draft—which gets you a lot closer to a response. At a minimum, share talking points in bullet form that can easily become final prose.

» **Send materials they can forward.** Email is still the dominant form of communication across many organizations; writing a forwardable email is always a good tactic to make it easy for the other person. Your email should be clear, brief, and specific—one they can forward with only a single sentence of their own endorsing you and your message.

» **Give context.** Why does helping you matter? In the case of a mutual introduction, does the person helping you know why? Do they understand what you are trying to do?

» **Make it easy to learn.** If your idea involves a technology or concept that is new to the other person, go out of your way to make a safe space for them to learn the basics without having to ask in front of their peers or employees.

» **Include a timeline in your asks.** Politely give people deadlines. Without a deadline, it's easy for even the best-intentioned colleague to let a request slip.

DON'T BE A TOURIST

Find a way to help or get out of the way.

President Obama was mere minutes from entering the Green Room in the White House Residence. An official but intimate parlor room on the main floor, with dark green silk walls, the Green Room is used for small meetings and receptions. Next to the much larger East Room, it's the kind of place where the president can have a private conversation with a handful of guests. It's a great place to witness history—if you can get in the room.

Deesha Dyer, the White House social secretary, came in and scanned around for a final check. She was the last line of defense before the president arrived. It was the White House Science Fair, which had become an annual event. It took over two full floors of the residence. President Obama was moving from room to room, touring the exhibits, and generally enjoying the chance to meet with precocious children and teenagers showing off their robots, models, and prototypes. But in this quieter, fancy room, there were only a few grown-ups waiting.

Deesha saw the scientist who had been invited to spend a few minutes with the president, patiently waiting. She saw a familiar staffer, Phil Larson, who worked closely with the communications teams across the White House. Then Deesha saw a face that was out of place. She asked Nick: "Why are you here?"

Nick stammered and attempted an explanation: he was from the Office of Science and Technology Policy, he had been helping set up, etc. But his blue badge—emblazoned with a large T, indicating he had only temporary clearance to be in the building and wasn't a West Wing regular—gave him away. It was clear in her mind that Nick was only

209

there to try to see the president with only a few people around, and she rightly asked him to leave.

Her job as social secretary was to make sure that people were prepared to meet the president: telling them to relax, bend their knees, and not to hand him gifts. But Deesha's job was also to be an effective gatekeeper—and superfluous staff trying to hang with the president was a definite no-no.

Nick was being a tourist in the White House—a near-cardinal sin. There are tens of thousands of tourists who visit the building every year, not to mention all kinds of invited guests, from heads of state and winning sports teams, CEOs, heads of civil rights organizations, advocates, and many others. But staff are there to *work*. Phil, for example, had helped set up that day and was talking with the scientist to keep him occupied. Had Nick genuinely been part of the crew that set up that room, or had some working history with Deesha or her team, he might have stood a chance. But without a good reason to be there, he was a tourist in her eyes.

Think Like a Gatekeeper

Ask yourself: Am I essential to the work, or am I a tourist? It's not just a question for the social secretary of the leader of the free world. Would Deesha kick you out of the meeting? Are you just gawking at the CEO, important guest, or a spectacle that's unfolding—or are you a key piece of the puzzle?

There are two problems with being a tourist. The first is that your time is precious. There is an opportunity cost to watching rather than doing. But the second and more pernicious problem with being a tourist is that others will negatively perceive you as a gawker, rather than a doer. This makes it harder to gain traction and social capital for your own projects later.

If you are in management, you might think that your job is essentially to be in meetings all day: to relay information, coordinate across silos, et cetera. You're not being a tourist if your job is to observe and coordinate, right? While it's true that any management job has a fair amount of this kind of work, managers can also spend too much time as tourists. Are you actively mentoring, coaching, and providing input—or are you slipping into tourist mode?

We are not saying to skip celebrations, promotions, or retirement parties. Every organization has a rhythm to how it celebrates its people and important milestones, and attending them to recognize peers' accomplishments can be a good way to *build* relationships. Participating in these events shows that you belong to the group and that you appreciate the mission and culture. Celebrations are fundamentally about holding people up, and you'll need other people to help you be successful. Plus, who doesn't like cake now and then?

We're also not saying to avoid important meetings. A decision has probably been made before or after the actual meeting, as we talked about in the chapter "Do the Work Outside the Meeting," but many meetings matter culturally. Meetings are an inevitable part of most organizations, and you can't understand how your organization works without attending at least some, however unproductive they might be.

Our recommendation: attend meetings where you plan to contribute. Some meetings are part of your job; others are optional. If it's an informational meeting, consider skipping it, especially if you can learn via asymmetric channels (emails, Slack messages, presentations, meeting notes, etc.). But if you have a perspective or input that is valuable to the meeting, then attend and contribute. If you are just going for the spectacle—skip it.

It's important to cultivate a reputation as a workhorse rather than a show horse. And a workhorse is usually too busy doing things, and helping teammates, to be a tourist.

HOW CAN I USE THIS?

» **Be helpful.** Ask yourself: How can I, specifically, help? What can I unblock?

» **Remove yourself when you aren't helpful.** The more people involved in a meeting, the more friction. Are you really needed in every meeting on your calendar?

» **Consider the optics.** Joining a small ceremony to recognize a colleague's accomplishments is good; joining a small ceremony that's being photographed because you want to be seen in the photo is not.

MAKE YOUR JOB

> Change will not come if we wait for
> some other person or if we wait for some
> other time. We are the ones we've
> been waiting for.
>
> —BARACK OBAMA

Bureaucracies are mostly filled with people hired to satisfy a specific, and sometimes outdated, job description. With some creativity and entrepreneurial spirit, you can create a new role that better leverages your specific skills and passions.

Do the Job You Want

Three months into his post–White House fellowship at the Harvard Kennedy School (HKS), Nick practically told the dean and academic dean they were committing academic malpractice. After a few months of talking with students, other fellows, and faculty, it was clear to Nick that the premier graduate school of government wasn't teaching enough technology—and he wasn't afraid to share this perspective. As a mere fellow on a six-month gig, Nick was able to channel his bureaucracy-hacking experience to help Harvard solve its problem.

Nick certainly wasn't the only one sounding the alarm. Denise Linn and Alison Flint, leaders of the student club Tech4Change, polled their fellow students and found that 82 percent of respondents were interested in technology skills workshops, and 68 percent of students surveyed were interested in more HKS technology courses.

So Nick did what any self-respecting, hard-hitting change agent would do: he wrote a memo. Nick sent his memo to the dean and academic dean, observing that Harvard Kennedy School is supposed to be the best school of government in the world, yet it didn't really teach technology, innovation, or design—three topics that are critically important for the next generation of public sector leaders. But instead of just complaining and pointing out the lack of courses, Nick tailored his pitch to show how his ideas for new tech curriculum fit neatly into their existing goals and ongoing efforts to recruit new faculty in these areas.

How could Nick convince this storied institution to start teaching hands-on tech skills? Harvard, founded in 1636, isn't exactly known for changing quickly. It took until 1946 for classes to be co-ed (with women denied access to most libraries until the 1960s), 1972 until the dorms were co-ed, and all the way until 2007 to reach undergraduate gender parity. Also, adjusting course offerings wasn't exactly what Nick was hired to do as a fellow—he was supposed to be reflecting about his White House experience, writing research papers, and meeting with students.

Bureaucracies are built to withstand criticism. In fact, they often don't respond to it *at all*. At Harvard, he had to make the case that his diagnosis and suggestions weren't criticisms, but rather would simply improve upon the institution's existing worldview.

The reception was better than expected. Instead of firing Nick or being dismissive of his ideas, the dean offered him a new role teaching to help address the issue. Nick created a field class where student teams work with government clients over the course of a semester. Called "Tech and Innovation in Government," students learn design, innovation, and product management skills in a novel way: by actually doing them.

In the first part of the semester, student teams work with their clients to better understand their problems, and more importantly, get out of the classroom to embed and speak with end users (as described in "Talk to Real People"). Just before spring break, the students present their research findings to the rest of the class. In the middle of the semester, students brainstorm ideas to solve the problems they've identified, then rapidly prototype and test their solutions with real people. Their interventions and solutions can be websites and apps, but could also be lower tech process changes. In the last part of the semester, the students focus on the "so-what." They take what they've learned from the research and prototyping phases and their knowledge of the client organization to develop near-term and longer-term recommendations. Everything is fair game—including ideas for policies, product, personnel, procurement, and pronouncements. At the end of the semester, the students present their research, prototypes, and recommendations at a Demo Day, attended by other faculty, students, and the government clients. (You can see Nick's class on our website.)

The class proved to be a hit among the students. After teaching it for five years, Nick was asked to help design and teach a new class about implementing policy—a core class required for all new master's in public policy students at the school. Making his own job meant he now has the opportunity to make sure that every master's in public policy student at Harvard has practical exposure to technology, design, and innovation.

Nick didn't set out to teach at Harvard or plan to change the curriculum. But he ended up creating a new role—teaching a field lab that gives students experiences solving real government problems—that leveraged his passion, experiences, and skills. His core skillset was curating an experience for the students, and that was the class he designed and taught for five years—with Marina as his favorite guest lecturer, of course! Now he is teaching technology, innovation, and design across the school.

Ask yourself: Am I most passionate about the job I was hired to do? Given what you know now, is there a more compelling opportunity in your organization? With some hustle and creativity, can you make the pivot inside your bureaucracy by framing a proposal that fits (or looks like it fits) squarely into the existing goals and framework?

Go Where You Are Rare

Maximize your potential impact by seeking out projects, problem areas, and teams where your skillset is rare. You can have an outsized influence if you take your skills and experiences to a project or team where your abilities are in short supply. For example:

- A technologist can make an outsized impact on a project that has little or no technical capacity.

- A data scientist embedded in the marketing team can create new, data-driven insights to complement existing campaigns.

- An ex-consultant can help a team that wants to advocate for change but isn't sure how.

- A designer can bring significant value to a team of engineers building a functional but ugly product.

This advice doesn't mean quitting your job to switch to another company, or even necessarily switching departments. It just means thinking about your competitive advantage, and, when given the opportunity, creating a role where your comparatively rare talent can deliver outsized results.

HOW CAN I USE THIS?

» **Create a role that works for you.** Organizations have defined needs, with detailed job descriptions. But sometimes there is flexibility to define a new role based on a specific candidate and their strengths and interests.

» **Do the job you want.** If you are already inside a large bureaucracy, take advantage of the resources and expertise across the organization to grow your own experience, whether by assisting colleagues in other units with their projects, volunteering on cross-functional committees, or filling in talent gaps on your own team.

» **Volunteer for teams where your skillset is rare.** See if you can take an assignment where your skillset is not dominant. You'll wow them with your talents, even if the task isn't that hard for you.

» **If you are building a team, recruit people with uncommon skills.** Be intentional about adding skills to your team that are outside your team norms.

CREATE PEOPLE FLOW

It can sometimes seem as if one person
will not be very effective. However, change
in the world always begins with an individual
who shares what he or she has learned
and passes it on to others.

—DALAI LAMA

---

*Add people to your project through fellowships,
internships, in-residence programs, and other
temporary, nontraditional, and part-time
mechanisms. New talent, paired with experienced
teams and mentors, can create breakthrough
momentum for your project—and just might make
an even larger impact over time.*

On Inauguration Day, January 20, 2017, with less than an hour left of President Obama's tenure, White House staffers were scrambling to get one last bill in front of the president for his signature. They were running out of time.

Although the bill was bipartisan and uncontroversial, once Trump was in office, there was no guarantee he'd sign it. Plus, it was an accomplishment of the Obama administration, and President Obama deserved to sign it himself. Coordinating with the House of Representatives clerk responsible for physically shepherding legislation for signature, and the aides who physically accompany the president, staffers managed to get the bill in front of the president just before time ran out. In the halls of Congress, at 11:07 a.m.—mere minutes before handing power over to Trump—President Obama signed legislation to make the Presidential Innovation Fellows (PIF) program a permanent part of the federal government.

The PIF program is how we met: Nick helped start and run it, and Marina was a fellow in the initial cohort. The PIF program is a great example of a "people flow" bureaucracy hack to create systemic change over time. The concept is simple: add to your organization by using nontraditional or interim pathways. Bringing people on board via temporary mechanisms can seem less risky to your company, because the positions are short-lived. If someone doesn't work out, it's not as big of a deal.

There are many different flavors to this play, including using it to add only a single person to an existing team, but we're fans of a cohort model, where a set of fellows joins the organization for a set period of time. The advantage to a cohort model for fellowships (or internships) is that there is both a peer group for the incoming talent, as well as a peer network for the hosts.

The Presidential Innovation Fellows

The story of how PIF started in 2012 begins with Nick's boss at the time, US Chief Technology Officer Todd Park. Todd was a wildly successful private sector entrepreneur before entering government—he cofounded and built two multibillion-dollar market cap companies, Athena Health and Castlight, before he was forty. (He has since built another one, Devoted Health, after his government service.) Todd would alternate between a thoughtful, intense listening mode and an unrivaled, authentic passion for whatever he was pitching.

Todd was a natural at bureaucracy hacking: he solicited and incorporated feedback with gusto, expressed genuine enthusiasm and gratitude, and gave credit liberally. Todd's energy was infectious, and he had a legendary work ethic even by White House standards, where long hours and weekends were a given. But his true superpower was recruiting and motivating people, whether they worked for him directly or as part of the larger federal government.

Todd was inspired by nonprofit Code for America's fellowship program in local government, and wanted to try something roughly similar at the federal level, building on existing White House staff conversations about bringing in diverse, interdisciplinary mid-career talent from the private sector. Todd recruited John Paul Farmer, a former minor league baseball player who had moved into Wall Street finance before joining government, who in turn recruited Arianne Gallagher, a bright young staffer from the Office of Personnel Management.

Todd, John, and Arianne—along with Nick and other White House officials—established the Presidential Innovation Fellows (PIF) program to bring both technologists and entrepreneurs into government. Similar to the way DARPA program managers have a planned expiration date, PIFs had an explicit duration for their fellowship, under the theory that it would create a useful sense of urgency. The PIF program was also designed to recruit and staff fellows around a well-scoped problem; it wasn't just bringing in talent for its own sake.

There were some bumps in the road. Initially, the fellowship was just six months, but that proved too short of time to gain traction, as PIFs were just figuring out how to maneuver in the bureaucracy by that time. Subsequent cohorts were one year, with some PIFs staying even longer.

Federal hiring processes were also too slow to competitively attract top technology and entrepreneurial talent. As a result, John had to figure out a way to cut down the time-to-hire. Using a somewhat obscure hiring authority that exempted fellowships and other short-term hires from the civil service hiring processes (which usually took a year or longer), John was able to compress the hiring timeline down to a handful of weeks from application to offer.

Part of the PIF model, and other cohort models we have observed or helped create, is that it paired fellows with the right people internally—in this case, talented career civil servant innovators inside each agency who knew how the levers of the bureaucracy really worked. In addition to being Nick's mentee, Marina was paired with master bureaucracy hacker Richard Culatta at the US Department of Education. When done well, it meant PIFs weren't positioned as complete outsider change agents. As Todd once described it, "These talented tech minds come into government and they team up with the best people already on the ground in government agencies, and *together*, they make amazing things happen."

The focus on internal teammates was important to the success of the PIF program, because it showed civil servants that this program was really about helping *them*. By being as authentically passionate about internal government talent as he was about the PIFs, Todd was able to generate enthusiasm and support across many federal agencies.

The PIF program has brought exciting new talent into government since 2012: some for only a short period of time, others for a few years. A few fellows, like Marina, moved into leadership roles in an agency or in the White House. Over time, the PIF program has become the flagship fellowship for mid-career technical and entrepreneurial talent in the federal government. PIFs have founded other digital units in government, helped rescue HealthCare.gov, contributed to executive orders on artificial intelligence and customer experience, and built COVID-19 tools for veterans and the federal workforce.

The Fellowship Model

We've seen the fellowship model work in many places. The French government modeled their Entrepreneurs d'intérêt général (Entrepreneurs of General Interest) after the PIF program. The UK government launched the No. 10 Innovation Fellowships to recruit fellows to work on digital education, COVID-19 response, and humanitarian assistance projects. TechCongress has recruited over fifty fellows to bring technical savvy to Congress. And PIF cofounder John Paul Farmer, who went on to become the chief technology officer of New York City under Mayor Bill de Blasio, used the model at the city level to create the NYC[x] Innovation Fellows, embedding technologists into city departments to help with pandemic response.

The fellowship model doesn't need a fancy chief executive though; Marina continues to use the fellows model at the nonprofit Foster America, recruiting mid-career executives to work inside state foster care agencies, with her mentorship. Fellowship is also well known in the academic context—Marina and Nick have both served as nonresident fellows (a fancy way of saying part-time) at various research centers at Harvard. Many organizations, public and private, are familiar with a fellows model.

If your organization has experiences with fellows, interns, or other temporary talent, see if you can tap into that talent pool to bring new energy and skills to your project. Or propose creating or revitalizing a fellow program, ideally with allies who also want new short-term talent of their own. By actively shaping the program, you'll have influence over what projects they work on and who they work with. You may also be able to get your organization to experiment with people from less traditional or overlooked talent pools, and to overcome barriers for them, like ensuring adequate salary and benefits for a diverse set of applicants.

Flow People Out

Our advice on people flow goes the other direction too: find ways to let people leave your organization in temporary and nontraditional ways. Think externships, exchange programs, sabbatical programs, cross-organizational details, and civic leave programs. Instead of employees outright leaving your organization, can they use mechanisms to only leave temporarily, and come back better than ever?

Admittedly, letting people leave your company more easily doesn't seem like it would help you make change on a specific project. It might sound counterintuitive to make it easier for people to leave—but look closely at businesses that are hypercompetitive for talent. Many elite management consulting firms offer employees the ability to work temporarily at social impact and philanthropic organizations; top law firms talk about their pro-bono efforts; big tech firms have sabbatical programs; and so on.

In the fall of 2021, Insight Partners, the venture capital and private equity firm Nick works with, started hosting Defense Ventures fellows, a six-week immersion program for active duty military servicemembers. Bringing on a Naval aviator, an Army Special Forces operator, and Air Force innovation and intel personnel brought a varied set of servicemembers and their experiences to Insight. As Insight evaluated investment opportunities in software companies with defense and national security focuses, having these individuals work at the firm—even for a short period of time—helped Insight gain familiarity with the national security mission, and improved the diligence process for specific companies that Insight was considering. But the true value of the Defense Ventures program will be what the fellows learn about the innovation economy and bring back to the US military. The Defense Department recognizes that it needs to modernize and innovate—and is therefore wisely flowing servicemembers *out* into the innovation economy (for short periods of time) to bring new ideas and practices back into one of the largest bureaucracies in the world. Recall Colonel Enrique Oti, from our "Pilot Is the Password" chapter: as an active duty Air Force officer, his fellowship at Stanford gave him a new, important perspective about software innovation, which contributed to him cofounding Kessel Run.

Is the Defense Ventures fellowship working for the Defense Department? The participants definitely think so. As one Air Force weapon systems officer said after the fellowship: "I learned more in two months than in sixteen years of Professional Military Education."

HOW CAN I USE THIS?

» **Create a mechanism for new talent.** Are there new or underused ways to bring new people into your organization? Whether they are interns, fellows, adjuncts, entrepreneurs-in-residence, executives-in-residence, special advisors, or some other influx of talent, a small cohort can make an outsized impact. Create a new program, sponsor an existing one, or repurpose an underutilized program with new talent pools.

» **Champion externships, sabbaticals, pro-bono leave programs, and other ways for existing employees to get external experience.** Your celebration of these programs signals confidence in your organization, and that you value the professional development of others. While the temporarily departing employee might not be able to help your immediate project, your ability to recruit other people across the organization as informal helpers and advocates, or as actual team members, should increase as a result. And when people return to the organization (some will!), they will be more inclined to work with you.

GIVE PEOPLE A CHOICE,
AND A CHANCE

"Come to the edge," he said.
"We can't, we're afraid!" they responded.
"Come to the edge," he said.
"We can't, We will fall!" they responded.
"Come to the edge," he said.
And so they came.
And he pushed them.
And they flew.

—GUILLAUME APOLLINAIRE

You won't win everyone over to your way of thinking, but you may win over some by giving them an honest chance to join you. For example, if you are trying to convert to a new technology system, the current team needs a genuine opportunity to learn the new application and be part of the roll-out.

If you want people to adopt your changes, you need to give them a reasonable chance to change. This often means time, training, additional resources, or all of the above. But it's more than just accommodations—people want to have a *choice* in the matter. If someone's first introduction to your new idea is that it will be forced upon them, upon penalty of termination, they may come out of the gate kicking, screaming, and sabotaging you—even if your idea is ultimately in their best interest.

Ask yourself: Who will bear the brunt of my changes if I'm successful? How can you help them gain the skills or resources to make your successful change a success for them, too?

One scenario where we've seen people reacting poorly to proposed changes is in the adoption of new technology tools. The new application you want people to adopt may save millions of dollars and employee hours, all while making customers twice as happy. But what happens to the team who were experts in supporting the *old* application? They need a choice, and a chance.

Choices could include:

- Being looped into decision making early enough that they feel part of designing or proposing the change;

- Clear and accurate information about what they should expect if they choose the status quo; and

- Fair alternatives, including early retirement, lateral transfers, and job separation, with help finding another role and a positive reference.

Examples of chances include:

- A trial period with a new team or way of working;

- Training (including the time, money, and other supports to complete the training);

- Clear criteria for what you expect from them and what success looks like;

- An opportunity to apply to join a new team; and

- Advance warning about adverse consequences (e.g., you will give them seven days before you talk to their supervisor).

Much in the same way as you'd have a structured onboarding process for a brand-new employee, design a way to onboard colleagues and stakeholders to your idea, or your new way of thinking or working. For example, let's say you want to demonstrate a new way for IT and business to work together to solve customer problems, and part of that includes a team meeting on Friday afternoons where everybody shares one thing that went well and one thing that could be improved from the prior week. This type of meeting is known as a "retro" (short for retrospective). It would be unfairly disorienting for an interested outsider to come to visit on Friday and find themselves hearing criticism (something that could be improved), without advance notice that this is your team's norm.

Your team doesn't have to have its own human resources department to make this work. You can help give others a chance by:

- Maintaining a glossary of the vocabulary you use;

- Making it very easy to get training on your new concept, technology, or process—ideally on their own, without having to ask for it; and

- Writing down the way you work, including the tools you use to communicate, norms for meetings, and expectations for team members.

Not everybody is cut out for every change. Unfortunately, some people will really want a chance, yet will not be able to make it in the new environment. That's why it's important to have clear expectations about performance in addition to providing a fair chance: because good intentions do not always lead to good results.

HOW CAN I USE THIS?

» **Consider who will be negatively impacted by your proposal, and make a plan to give them a choice and a chance.**

This plan might include looping them in early, making training available, or even enticing a naysayer with an early retirement package.

» **Have clear success criteria for people who sign up for a chance.** This helps them decide if they think they can achieve it and makes it more objective for everyone to measure whether it's working out.

STAB PEOPLE IN THE CHEST

Hell hath no fury like a bureaucrat scorned.

—MILTON FRIEDMAN

Be open and honest with your detractors about where and how you disagree. This builds a unique sort of trust, where, despite your difference of opinion, your colleagues will gain confidence that you won't blindside them down the line.

If everyone in your organization agreed with the changes you want to make, you wouldn't be reading this book. You're not going to win everyone over with your new idea. So how do you interact with colleagues who want something different—or who want to maintain the status quo?

You stab them in the chest.

In other words—*ensure they see you coming.* If you know you don't see eye to eye with a peer, avoid the temptation to talk about them behind their back, spring news on them at the last minute (even good news), or wait to show your cards until you're both in a decision meeting. (Remember: nothing ever happens in meetings.)

How do you do this? You:

- Send your memos, slides, and proposals ahead of time directly to the individual who will disagree with them. A mass email still counts as stabbing someone in the *back*.

- Offer to sit one-on-one and review what you plan to say in response to *their* memos and slides.

- Take them out to lunch! Just because you disagree on a particular issue doesn't mean you can't form a friendly relationship.

- Make sure that if you're planning to say something that you expect someone to disagree with in a meeting, that you say it to them ahead of time (or: do not say that thing at all).

This advice might make you feel uncomfortable. You have to sit, one-on-one, with your biggest critics, walk through your slides one by one, and show them how you intend to take their idea apart?

Absolutely. It may not feel great in the moment, but this technique establishes a deep, if unusual, type of trust. Your opponents may not agree with your pitch or your outcomes (or, at least, they may not agree with your approach), but they *will* start to trust that you won't surprise them. This also affords you a chance to refine your argument: in these conversations, you might learn new information, including a deeper appreciation for your opponent's position.

Will this strategy lead to you skipping off into the sunset holding hands with your biggest detractor? Probably not. But the goal here is not to become everyone's best friend or to make everyone happy: it's to *get things done.* And a high-trust working relationship with your colleagues is a mission-critical piece of that puzzle. Being up front about your disagreements and not blindsiding colleagues builds an authentic trust that can help you get more done, at scale.

HOW CAN I USE THIS?

» **Stab people in the chest.** If you fundamentally disagree with someone, the time to bring it up is *not* in a meeting in front of other people. Schedule time to meet with them one-on-one and share your concerns. Be clear about what you might bring up later. Never surprise someone with criticism in a meeting. This can develop a real, if unconventional, form of trust with colleagues.

» **Don't surprise people.** Develop a reputation as a reliable narrator: send agendas out ahead of time, share success criteria ahead of time, and let people know you disagree with them (and why) *before* you're both in front of your boss. This doesn't only apply to disagreements; you shouldn't spring good news on a principal in public, either, because it exposes them as being out of the loop. On the other hand, surprise birthday parties are still okay!

MAKE IT STICK

USE THE BUREAUCRACY
AGAINST ITSELF

Use the routine practices of your organization—like committees, approvals, and reviews—to formalize your changes within the bureaucracy's current ways of doing business.

This is one of our favorite hacks: getting the bureaucracy to change *itself* in the ways you want, by using its own practices against it. Think judo (using your opponent's motions), instead of karate (striking directly).

As tempting as it is to take shortcuts, rewiring a bureaucratic process *itself* is what leads to bigger and lasting change. As we've discussed, you need to follow existing processes to learn where they are failing. Then, you need to change the unfavorable rules and processes themselves, so that a future opponent will have to work that much harder to derail you. Results may be slower than you like at first, when you have to change *how* your organization operates, but the people coming behind you will thank you, and you'll ultimately make a bigger, more permanent impact.

How the Berlin Wall Fell

The Berlin Wall fell in a matter of minutes. While this was not an intentional bureaucracy hack, we think it's a great illustration of how, if you leverage the way an organization *truly* works, monumental change is possible very quickly.

On November 9, 1989, East Germany's government released a memo intended to clarify minor procedures for East Germans to travel. At the time, memos were considered the authoritative source of truth, and there was no social media, texting, or email to rapidly validate or discredit information. The memo was promptly and confidently read aloud at a press conference: "Private travel outside the country can now be applied for without prerequisites."

The sentence was missing key context—that the policy only applied to *East* Germans. (The East Germans should have considered usability testing their communications.) But the spokesman was in no position to question the memo. Immediately, throngs of people approached the wall, trying to cross. Interviews with border guards later revealed their thought process: they had just heard their superiors announce the opening of the border at a press conference, and they cross-referenced the announcement with their authoritative memo. From the perspective of the bureaucracy at large, the wall was *down*—and once the border was open, it proved impossible to close again.

How It Works

We consider this an advanced tactic because it has a number of prerequisites. You can't show up on day one and change a rule, because you don't yet know where the rule came from, who will resist the rule changing, how to go about changing such a rule, or what perverse incentives your new rule will introduce—not to mention, you probably don't quite know if it's *really* a rule at all. That is why we want you to learn your organization first!

Using the bureaucracy against itself builds on the other tactics we've discussed in this book. You'll need to:

- identify a problem you want to solve or a goal you want to achieve;

- immerse yourself with real people and follow the real process, looking across silos as necessary, to truly understand it end to end;

- try the normal way first to suss out the obstacles to success;

- understand the *why* behind these obstacles, getting down to the letter of the law or policy;

- map out and socialize a new future process that would remove enough obstacles for you to complete your mission; and then

- use the rules, practices, policies, and people of your bureaucracy to make what you need the easiest, least-risky path for others to follow.

If you're feeling stuck by your bureaucracy, identify the specific tension point that's holding you back—and then look for how, at a higher level, you can change *that*. People are wandering all over your organization today bemoaning their inability to get things done; but almost *nobody* is doing something about, or even thinking about, the root causes.

For you, this might mean:

- changing a form;

- changing a rule;

- changing a process;

- changing a goal or measured metric;

- changing the makeup of a team or committee; or

- changing expectations.

In other cases, you might not need to change a rule or process at all, but rather, change how you interact with it.

How to Put a Cloud in an Evidence Bag

When Marina was at the VA, one of her early goals was to be able to move software applications into a cloud computing environment. Up until her arrival, all applications were installed on on-premise servers, generally in a single room. These servers were slow, often down, and required a lot of human time and work to upgrade. Worse, some were located in broom closets or directly under fire sprinklers, running the risk of losing veteran data altogether.

Similar to electricity, cloud computing scales up and down based on need and charges by usage. A good cloud has almost no downtime, and is relatively easy to upgrade or patch; in fact, automatic upgrades are often included. This kind of flexibility and reliability requires many servers across many locations. By Marina's estimates, the cloud would save more than 80 percent of costs per year, while providing faster, more reliable service to employees and veterans. Why wouldn't the bureaucracy love it?

Marina's first obstacle was the rule that before a new computer system could go live, she had to sign off that she physically jiggled the doorknob of the server room to confirm that it was locked. This sounds logical—when you're using on-premise servers. But when Marina tried to get approval to use the cloud, this requirement halted her progress— because there's no longer a server room, and definitely no doorknob. For security reasons, cloud providers like Google and Amazon won't even tell you their exact location—and they most certainly will not let you jiggle their doorknobs.

Marina tried to fill out "N/A" in the box on the paperwork asking if she had jiggled the doorknob. It got denied.

She tried explaining to the nice woman checking the paperwork why the box didn't apply. It got denied.

She tried writing a description of how she *conceptually* jiggled the doorknobs by checking other, relevant security controls. It got denied.

Fed up, Marina researched where this form came from in the first place. A small committee of three people oversaw the form's revisions. Marina explained to *them* why the box didn't apply, proposing they create a new form without the doorknob question that would apply to cloud computing projects.

This worked. Marina was able to submit the new form with no missing fields. It was approved.

Over time, she and her team drove more changes to this form that flipped the doorknob challenge around, adding questions that made it difficult for new systems that *didn't* use the cloud to be able to complete it.

Her second challenge remains one of her proudest professional achievements. The VA's investigative body, the Inspector General, originally issued a memo banning cloud computing because they could not put the cloud in an evidence bag. When they had to investigate alleged malfeasance, investigators would go into an office or server farm, pick up the computer(s) in question, and put them in an evidence bag to begin a forensic analysis. The lawyers didn't see any way to do their work without physical servers in physical bags.

In a cheeky move, for the winter holidays Marina made sugar cookies in the shapes of clouds and distributed them around the office in evidence bags.

More productively, Marina's team built a relationship with the Inspector General team, showing them how they could use cloud-based tools to conduct their investigations instead. Once they learned how, the lawyers *loved* this new process—they could conduct investigations faster and more easily, without having to lug heavy computers around. Two years later, they issued a new formal memo: the Inspector General now *preferred* logical access through cloud computing over physical servers. This legal memo was the final piece of her puzzle to unlock buying cloud services across the agency.

It's All in How You Look at It

Sometimes your bureaucracy will present you with a way to use its current rules and practices to get a completely different outcome.

For example, when Marina was advocating for her team to be able to deploy code more frequently to the VA's website, she made a case for a concept called "automated deployment." Instead of using a manual process to push software changes to the production servers, her team would write scripts that would do this automatically. This dramatically reduces the chance of human error, and makes code launches repeatable and dependable. This practice is quite common in modern software development environments.

But the existing team that oversaw manual deployments was, unsurprisingly, not in favor of this plan. They were used to a committee process called go/no-go in which each committee member could vote on whether each change was allowed to go forward. From this team's perspective, the new automated process was all risk and no reward; if something bad happened, they'd be responsible, without having gotten a say in the first place. They voted "no" on Marina's proposal.

But here's the funny thing: Marina didn't need them to vote "yes"—she had enough votes from other teams. But she did need them to *vote*. And it typically took them two weeks to submit every "no" vote, because they had to meet, draft a decision memo, and then submit it, each time.

Seeing an opportunity, Marina offered to include their "no" vote in her automation. Whenever a vote was needed, a script would automatically generate the memo with the correct format and timestamp, documenting that the release team voted "no" on the current release. Paradoxically, the release team *loved* this—they would save time, and never have to assume any risk for any release. And Marina loved it because she no longer had to wait two weeks for their predictable dissent. Win-win.

Another process at the VA was found to be similarly fungible. The agency's budget process required submitting a roadmap for exactly what each team would be delivering, three years in the future—right down to the month! But modern software development uses much shorter design and build cadences, so this level of detail is virtually impossible to know so far out. This meant talented employees often found themselves trapped, doing work that a predecessor had promised years prior, regardless of whether it was the right thing to be doing any longer.

Kelly O'Connor was familiar with the hazards of a multiyear budgeting process from other organizations, and she knew just how to manipulate it. When she had to write down what her team would be doing three years, or even three months, from now, she wrote broad descriptions like "healthcare" or "help veterans access their benefits." These statements were generic enough that almost any project would count—and that was the idea. Nowhere in this budget process were people required to list *detailed* plans—they just had to list *a plan*.

This trick gave Kelly's team tremendous flexibility to let data and veteran feedback drive what they worked on next, instead of being beholden to an outdated mandate.

Using the bureaucracy against itself like this is not limited to the federal government. Over in Connecticut, elementary school mom Kathy Rice was frustrated that on days with unannounced early dismissals, generally because of snow, some kids would be stuck behind for hours because staff couldn't reach their parents. Out of concern for privacy, only two secretaries were allowed to call parents—at a school with over six hundred students. This took hours, with no time for them to try back or call multiple numbers (like both home and work).

Recognizing the primary risk from the school administration's point of view—privacy—and balancing that against the primary problem—that two humans couldn't call six hundred parents fast enough—Kathy got together with other parents to propose a volunteer phone tree. First, parents would sign a permission slip, giving permission to reveal their contact numbers to the volunteers. The volunteers also underwent privacy training and signed a confidentiality statement. This used the bureaucracy's favorite thing—forms—to address privacy concerns. The phone tree, built in a spreadsheet, was given the green light for a trial run. On the next snow day, volunteers reached all parents in under thirty minutes, and no kids were stuck sitting in the empty gym for hours waiting to be picked up. The Board of Education made the volunteer phone tree permanent.

Yet another example comes from a grant writer we know, Lucy. Nonprofits live and die by their grant criteria; if they don't meet them, they don't get the grant money (not to mention, they miss out on future grants). Lucy and her colleagues wanted their organization to work on diversity, equity, and inclusion (DEI) goals, but their executive director was always prioritizing other things. So the grant writing team used the grant proposals *themselves* to circumvent their boss, inserting detailed statements of work and goals whenever a grant application asked about equity. When the organization subsequently won the grant, they had to follow through on those promises. Understanding the intense incentives to win grants but also the minimal attention paid to the specific details included in initial grant submissions gave Lucy and her team a powerful opportunity to shift the way her organization impacted their community.

When Bureaucracies Invite Your Changes

Sometimes bureaucracies go so far as to *announce* they want change. This might take the form of a suggestion box, an innovation lab or idea fund, or an employee ideas contest. At HP, then-CEO Meg Whitman encouraged employees to send in ideas for cutting red tape; at Novartis, a pharmaceutical company, employees are invited to compete to take part in Project Genesis to receive funding and laboratory resources for their research. The CIO of the US Air Force, Lauren Knausenberger, launched an initiative called Project Flamethrower to ruthlessly attack manual processes, outdated policies, and redundant IT. The State of Utah has created a regulatory sandbox where new innovations can apply to legally work with the state, piloting their new ideas to *inform* subsequent legislation and policy, instead of this process happening in reverse.

Sometimes a bureaucracy doesn't solicit *your* ideas but pays a consultant a pretty penny for them. If your organization has an outside consulting firm show up to make recommendations, try to get time with them, and share your thoughts. Consultants are often quite game to include your ideas and materials (even if they're inclined to take all the credit for them). As much as it doesn't make logical sense, we've seen a lot of organizations that ignore internal pitches for years snap to attention when a high-priced consultant says the same thing.

HOW CAN I USE THIS?

» **Organize yourself in the image of your bureaucracy.** If every team has a project manager, your team should have a project manager. If teams normally have all-hands on Tuesdays, you should have all-hands on Tuesdays. This can help your initiative to otherwise blend in and makes it easier for others to understand how you work and how to work with you.

» **Change your obstacles.** Change a rule, change a process, change a committee member—change the *underlying* cause of your challenge, instead of trying to fight it head-on or reason it away.

» **Look for innovation invitations.** These don't exist everywhere, but if your organization does have a sandbox, innovation center, or employee idea fund, use it to your advantage.

PICK UP THE PEN

I wrote my way out of hell
I wrote my way to revolution
I was louder than the crack in the bell
I wrote Eliza love letters until she fell
I wrote about The Constitution and
defended it well
And in the face of ignorance and
resistance
I wrote financial systems into existence
And when my prayers to God were met
with indifference
I picked up a pen, I wrote my own
deliverance

—LIN-MANUEL MIRANDA
(AS ALEXANDER HAMILTON)

Large organizations depend on written rules, processes, and plans. Find opportunities to help those who are writing down the rules. Where possible, volunteer to write the rules yourself for long-term influence.

An often overlooked strategy for making change in a bureaucracy is *literally* offering to take the pen. Bureaucracies love paper—strategic plans, slide decks, memos, and missives. But behind each piece of paper is an author, and in most organizations, few people are fighting for that role.

When you write (or ghostwrite) a policy or proposal, you can control the precise language and the proposed parameters, which can, down the line, define success. While this won't necessarily be effective for moving the ball on a hotly contested issue, it can be a *very* effective means of getting visibility and accountability for your projects.

Picking Up the Pen, HOA Style

All Melanie wanted to do was take a quick dip in the pool. It was sweltering outside in the record Connecticut heat, and she could see the pool right outside her window—a pool she was paying for with her monthly homeowners association (HOA) dues.

But a pesky little sign stood in her way: CLOSED DUE TO COVID-19. Inquiring with her HOA about the expected timeline for reopening the pool, the president of the HOA replied that they couldn't reopen until a formal COVID-19 pool policy was approved.

The letters HOA tend to strike fear, or at least frustration, in many hearts. Once the HOA has decided the pool's closed, it's closed . . . right?

But Melanie knew the power of picking up the pen. The board needed *a* policy. But it didn't have one yet. If she wrote the first draft of a version that would open the pool right away, she would have an advantage: anyone who felt strongly about keeping it closed would have a bigger hill to climb, because they'd be forced to write a competing policy from scratch *and* have to respond to hers. To up the ante, Melanie's proposed policy suggested that if the pool were to remain closed, then condo owners' monthly dues should be reduced until it reopened—a budget reduction she knew her HOA wanted to avoid.

The strategy worked. The following week, Melanie's version was accepted by the HOA, with no opposing policies proposed. While the heat wave may have passed, she still got to enjoy reading by the pool on her lunch hour every day for the rest of the summer.

Protect Yourself with the Pen

Carla Geisser was an engineer at Google responsible for preparing the release of a long-neglected but important piece of infrastructure. She *was* the entire team, and while the software didn't change too often, occasionally someone would come to her with an emergency change that needed to be made right away. If she said no, people would argue or try to go above her head. This became stressful and distracting.

Eventually, Carla realized that she could write and enforce her *own* policy for emergency changes. She authored a brief document entitled "Release Policy" and published it on the company intranet. The policy listed the schedule for making changes and the name of a higher-level manager to whom people could escalate emergency changes, if they needed it.

The next time someone came to ask for an exception, Carla merely pointed them to the official release policy (which she had written only days before). Suddenly: no argument, no escalation. The words in the release policy weren't any different than what she'd said to people directly in the past, but because it was now "official documentation," other people's behavior changed accordingly.

Which Pens to Pick Up

All pens (and papers) in a bureaucracy are not created equal. When we were at the White House, *everybody* wanted pen on the State of the Union. Getting your policy idea, even as a mere sentence, into the president's speech was very difficult, and there was a complex and established process for suggesting contributions. David Litt, one of President Obama's speechwriters, was not going to consider it a personal favor if you sent him a first draft. There are hundreds of policy staffers in a White House and only a handful of speechwriters, so it was an unwritten rule that we wouldn't bother them with unsolicited material. But if they asked you for an example or a clarification, that was a golden opportunity to engage. The same is true if you want to get your idea placed in a shareholder meeting or CEO keynote.

One area where your help and expertise might be accepted: strategy and long-range planning groups, including committees that ultimately feed up into the organization's mission. One of Marina's most success-ful uses of this tactic was to write a goal into the President's Manage-ment Agenda (PMA) that the VA would host the first-ever agency digital services team. As the management blueprint for the executive branch, the PMA isn't exactly talked about on CNN. But the Office of Manage-ment and Budget measured agencies on their performance against the PMA goals on a regular basis and reprimanded those that were out of compliance.

Marina found herself on the PMA committee at first not because she was particularly passionate about it, but because she was the only one at the VA on the access list for the White House compound, and therefore did not have to stand in the long security line to attend PMA meetings. (Her colleagues were happy to avoid the swampy DC humidity.) Once there, she noticed no one raised a hand to take a first pass at the technol-ogy goals section—so she volunteered.

Having already spent a year trying to create a digital services team at the VA without success, she worked this goal into the draft slides, figur-ing it would probably be cut out later. But as week after week went on, her bullet remained. When the final PMA was announced, it was still there—and now the VA, not to mention the Office of Personnel Man-agement, was formally on the hook *to the President of the United States* to make Marina's hiring goal happen.

This advice is not to join every subcommittee or to write everyone else's reports for them. But if there's a change you want to see, looking for ways to write it into the very fabric of the bureaucracy itself is one easily overlooked way to generate alignment.

HOW CAN I USE THIS?

» **Sign up for key opportunities.** Take advantage of chances to literally write your vision into your organization's new and exist-ing strategic plans, partnerships, quarterly agendas, newslet-ters, and other venues, or to tweak language so it will make your project particularly shine.

» **Write the draft yourself.** The next time you hear about a proposal or decision you don't like—or the next time you notice yourself fearful of the decision someone else will make (as with Melanie's pool policy)—consider drafting the policy yourself.

» **Help others write.** Volunteer to draft for other people, or even to ghostwrite proposals for them (while giving them all the credit). When you write the draft, you can determine the format, the criteria, and the initial ideas.

» **Join boards and committees that impact you.** Do decisions from your local school board, homeowners association, or historical preservation society drive you nuts? Join them. Volunteer to run committees. Pick up the pen and shape their decisions.

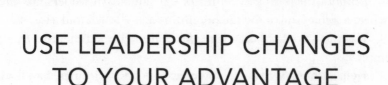

USE LEADERSHIP CHANGES
TO YOUR ADVANTAGE

*Changes in leadership bring new opportunities to
gain a champion. Shape an incoming leader's agenda
by talking with them directly and influencing what
they learn early in their tenure. Even if they have a
long history with your organization, once in a new
role, a leader is less likely to see constraints as truly
fixed and more likely to be open to bold ideas.*

When we worked in government, we would hear the oft-told joke about the civil servant and the new boss. The civil servant would tell the boss: "You're the A-Team, and we're the B-Team. We 'B' here before you got here, and we'll 'B' here long after you're gone."

It's a stupid joke, but it held a kernel of truth: we all knew that leadership changes frequently in the federal government. While the president was guaranteed four years and could win four more, the average political appointee had a shelf life of a couple years and was eager to make his or her mark in that time. The average civil servant, on the other hand, was likely to be around far longer than that, with some serving their entire career in government. The result: there was strong incentive for political appointees to try to accomplish goals relatively quickly. The inverse was true, too: civil servants who didn't agree with their senior management had an incentive to stretch things out, to try to run out the clock.

While your CEO or organization head might not have term limits, they will eventually turn over. At your business unit or division level, there is probably already healthy turnover. In his book *Inside Bureaucracy*, Anthony Downs refers to "lumps" in leadership, which is when a group starts at an organization together and rises up the ranks together—only to then leave around the same time, too, in a big "lump."

Every leader will have their own preferences, priorities, and leadership style. A proposal that doesn't make the top ten list for one leader might be a top three mission for the next one.

Leadership changes are important because they are opportunities for the organization to try to do something different. New leaders want to make their mark. They want an agenda. And they don't yet have all the answers. Many new leaders spend their first thirty, sixty, or even ninety days doing a listening tour, talking with customers, employees, and stakeholders. Get in on that tour agenda early.

New leaders want quick wins in their first year—it's human nature. If you have a compelling plan of action detailing the specific steps needed to make your idea into a reality, and you can get it in front of the new leader, you've just performed a perfect bureaucracy hack—using leadership changes to your advantage.

Finally, leadership changes aren't just about a single new person. New leaders often bring new staff, new executives to the management team, and new priorities from their board or governing body. Look at the full slate of new people coming in with a leadership change, not just the top person.

HOW CAN I USE THIS?

» **Brief the new leader.** Volunteer to brief the new leader on a topic you think they will be interested in learning about, even if it has nothing to do with your pet project.

» **Get to know a new leader's staff.** Their assistants, security detail, and direct reports could be even more helpful than the new leader herself.

» **Write to the suggestion box.** If the new leader says they have an open door policy, use it to pitch your ideas.

» **Prepare your boss.** Prepare your own boss to meet with the new leader. Making your boss shine in front of new management is a double win.

» **Align to the new agenda.** Learn the new leader's agenda. What are their new priorities? What are they focusing on getting done and what are they refocusing the organization on? Tailor your pitch as being part of those new priorities.

ALWAYS BE READY FOR FIVE MINUTES WITH THE HEAD HONCHO

You never know when you are going to run into your big boss, or another important stakeholder outside your chain of command. Having a few talking points prepared will serve you well in a chance encounter.

"You'll either get fired or promoted," Nick told his younger brother, Jim, when he heard what Jim had done.

Jim was twenty-three years old and had just started his career at Bloomberg—first as a customer service rep answering phones, and then on the analytics help desk supporting traders with advanced Bloomberg Terminal functionality. Bloomberg's hiring model at the time was to recruit young people right out of school, teach them how the company works by having them operate the switchboards, and then teach them how the software works by having them support end users. The unspoken trade was this: "Do these roles well, and you will be in the pipeline to join our prestigious sales organization." But two years in, Jim was watching some of his most talented peers leave Bloomberg, because no one was moving up into sales.

One thing Jim didn't lack was boldness. When he started, Jim sat a few desks away from the CEO. (The CEO sat in the call center to make a point!) Jim emailed the CEO and asked if he could get a quick coffee with him. When they sat down for fifteen minutes a few weeks later, Jim, who had just a handful of years of professional work experience in his life, proceeded to tell the CEO about the morale issues on his team and the fact that great folks were leaving because they weren't moving up. The CEO thanked Jim for his suggestions, and it seemed like that was the end of it. As an older brother with a few more years of experience, Nick was impressed with his younger brother's audacity *and* naivete.

But a week later, the CEO walked onto the floor to personally announce the promotion of five people into sales. Shortly thereafter, Jim transferred into sales, too. He went on to become a very successful salesman at Bloomberg, and later became a marketing executive at Salesforce, and more recently at Procore, which he took through IPO. Jim's start in sales was because he knew how to leverage those few minutes with his boss.

What Would You Say?

One of the common sayings we had in the White House was, "If you have five minutes with the President, what would you say? And are you working on that right now?" Part of this thought exercise was to make sure people were working on important things. But it also helped prepare people for an unscripted moment. You never know when you might have a few minutes with your boss—or your boss's boss's boss—in an elevator, a nearby restaurant, or an airport gate. While it was pretty unlikely that you'd randomly have a few unscripted moments with the president—Obama came by Nick's desk exactly once in four years, on one of the few days he went home early—it was a great thought exercise for new and experienced staffers alike.

As a thought experiment: What would you say, beyond small talk, if you had time with the big boss? What is the thing you are most passionate about changing in your organization? And if you aren't working on it, why not?

Less-Than-Coincidental Encounters

We are *explicitly* not advising you to stalk your executives, or to creepily stand around their elevator doors or favorite restaurants. But to some extent, you can make your own luck when it comes to opportunities for an audience outside your chain of command.

When Marina first worked at the VA, it was customary for her boss, Secretary Eric Shinseki, to walk the floor to say goodnight before he went home. This was often 9:30 p.m. or later. While this was not good for marriages or for work/life balance, it did offer a reliable window to share a quick story, highlight someone's good work, or plant a gentle reminder. If she knew she'd be there late anyway, she tried to make sure that she had something more interesting to say than just "Good night!" when he popped in.

Look for natural ways to get more face time, like:

- a leader who normally walks the floor once a week or at particular times of day;

- social gatherings like awards ceremonies or holiday parties; or

- early or late office hours when fewer people are around.

HOW CAN I USE THIS?

» **Have your talking points ready.** Have a rehearsed update— and even an ask—for your boss, CEO, or a key stakeholder if you encounter them in an elevator, the cafeteria, or out in public. These talking points will also benefit you any other time you're seeking support for your ideas.

» **Have a point of view on how to improve your group, unit, or department.** Instead of just complaining about something that doesn't work, pitch how to fix it.

» **Practice for your five minutes.** Caught unprepared, you're likely to stammer nervously through introductions and talk about the weather. While you don't want to seem like a scripted robot, you *do* want to have an introduction and a segue to your talking points that feel natural to you.

DON'T WASTE A CRISIS

There are some things you learn best in
calm, and some in storm.

—WILLA CATHER

*Bureaucracies are more receptive to change during
times of crisis, especially if your idea is related to
fixing or recovering from the problem at hand. Being
prepared with a one-pager—or even a full plan
that's ready to go—will best position you to take
advantage of an unexpected opening.*

Everything's going along swimmingly—until you're at the airport waiting for a connecting flight and spot your boss on CNN announcing his resignation. Congress initiates an investigation into your project and calls your biggest detractors as witnesses. A disgruntled employee, whose safe worldview is challenged by your new idea, takes his case to the press and drags your name through the mud.

In other words, it's Friday in the federal government. But corporations, nonprofits, and universities have their share of scandals, too. Accounting irregularities, a leadership scandal, or maybe just a particularly unflattering media story during layoffs—every industry and organization has the potential to go through a public embarrassment.

Whether you prefer Winston Churchill or Rahm Emanuel, we've all heard the saying "Don't let a crisis go to waste." Perhaps you think like Jim McNerney, the CEO of Boeing, who calls it "planful opportunism." But what does that mean exactly? What are some concrete tactics for leveraging a crisis to gain momentum for your own goals? How can you identify openings that may not have existed before—and that won't last very long?

Sometimes you'll face a crisis like COVID-19 that affects the whole world. Other times, you'll face a crisis that specifically threatens your market share or the viability of your team or organization. Regardless of the severity and type of the crisis, you can hunker down and hope that the scrutiny and change blow over, or you can use the crisis as a unique opportunity to get more done.

COVID-19 Innovations That Stuck

- The COVID-19 pandemic forced child welfare systems across the country to change the way they worked. Previously, group homes had been the easiest option for placing children, though they are the absolute worst when it comes to children's well-being. Overworked case workers in foster care agencies tended to pursue the path of least resistance (placing children in group homes) in the face of common foster home shortages. However, in the pandemic, group homes became ground zero for infection, and many group home employees quit or refused to come to work. Suddenly, at least temporarily, putting children in group homes *was not* an option. Case workers at foster agency placement desks were forced to reconsider their work. Marina worked with multiple states to introduce simple ways to find more family members instead. (One tactic that seems obvious in retrospect but that wasn't being done: asking youth directly if they have a place to go.) Incredibly, New Mexico's new focus on finding relatives increased its relative placement rate from 3 percent to over 60 percent in just a few months! As the pandemic subsides, these new foster care placement practices have stuck, and fewer kids will ever see the inside of an institution as a result.

- Bob Schaeffer, the executive director of the National Center for Fair and Open Testing, had been working for years to make more colleges and universities "test-optional"—which means they won't require SAT or ACT tests from applicants and won't prioritize applicants who did take those tests. These tests are increasingly seen as biased against children of color and children from lower socioeconomic households. In 2020, he had successfully persuaded 175 schools to sign his test-optional pledge. But once the pandemic hit, and many students literally couldn't access ACT or SAT testing sites, Bob's idea started to get real traction. The next year, in 2021, nearly 1,500 schools signed his pledge, including highly selective institutions like Brown, Columbia, and Harvard. While some schools will likely return to standardized testing, his forward momentum is likely to have staying power with many others.

- Newer technologies that bureaucracies resisted adopting for years, like digital signatures replacing wet signatures, or telemedicine replacing in-office medical visits, took off during the pandemic, as medical and legal bureaucracies needed to continue to operate in a remote environment. The government lifted HIPAA restrictions on using remote technology like Zoom for confidential medical purposes, and repealed barriers like the federal Ryan Haight Act, which had forbidden doctors from prescribing controlled substances online. In the legal world, suddenly criminal hearings and adoptions were happening over Facetime. Even insurance companies, the epitome of old-school bureaucracy, began accepting digital signatures. At the time of publication, many of these measures are temporary—but we predict that many of them will become permanent, as it will be hard to argue going forward that all those remotely signed adoptions, contracts, and prescriptions should go away.

Examples from Other Crises

- The 2013 failure and rescue of HealthCare.gov, the website for the uninsured to buy discounted private insurance, catalyzed a new generation of technology talent in government, known as the United States Digital Service. A version of this story was even featured on the cover of *Time* magazine. But the untold history is that plans for a digital SWAT team inside the government—originally called GovX—had already been underway for years. The near failure of President Obama's signature healthcare initiative helped wake up the West Wing to the importance of technologists in government. A small team—led by our friend and Code for America founder Jen Pahlka—had been developing this idea inside the White House for a while. Jen and her team had done the hard thinking and planning about what a digital rescue team might look like. Jen took advantage of the crisis and had a proposed budget, memo, and approvals all ready to go. Since then, US Digital Service has brought hundreds of top-notch technologists into government, who have made improvements to nearly every top citizen-facing service, from veterans benefits to immigration to Medicare.

- The creation of Amazon Web Services, a cloud hosting environment that today dominates more than one third of the market, was one engineer's response to a crisis. In 2000, Amazon—which primarily sold books at the time—wanted to launch Merchant.com to let other vendors like Target use its online shopping technology. But under the burst in traffic, the website kept going down, creating a huge internal nightmare. To solve the immediate problem, a small team began breaking the servers into discrete components to better distribute the load—an idea that Andy Jassy had been interested in for a while. This not only saved the day, but went on to become the building blocks of cloud computing. Andy went on to become the CEO of Amazon Web Services two years later, and became the CEO of *all* of Amazon in 2021.

- A thirtysomething engineer used a crisis to demonstrate his idea that high-pressure water could be used to extract gas from deep underground (a process known as fracking). Nick Steinsberger worked for George Mitchell, a Texas oil tycoon who was dying of cancer and on the brink of bankruptcy. Competitors (and creditors) were hovering around the company, which had been experimenting with using sticky gums and other materials to frack, to no avail. Steinsberger learned about using water for fracking sandstone from a fellow engineer at a competitive company (Ray Walker at Union Pacific Resources), and approached his boss about giving it a try. Everyone thought Steinsberger was both nuts and wrong—but George was desperate enough to give him the go-ahead to experiment.

  It worked. Steinsberger is now an internationally sought-after expert, and George went from bankruptcy to selling his company for $3 billion. While fracking is controversial due to its environmental impacts, it has also played a key role in low-cost natural gas and America's energy independence. One engineer capitalized on a moment to create an entire industry that's worth over $40 billion a year today.

Set Up a Central Command Center

Another opportunity to not let a crisis go to waste is to earn political capital by helping solve it, even if the solution is not exactly the project you've had waiting in the wings. If you see a leadership vacuum, and you have the capacity, you can stand up a central command center to address the crisis. Bureaucracies, in both public and private sectors, *love* command centers.

The central command center model was critical for the rescue of HealthCare.gov—and you can replicate this strategy in your own organization. Here are the components of success, as told by Mikey Dickerson, Matthew Weaver, and Carla Geisser, who each led the HealthCare.gov rescue team at various points (and who are all Marina's business partners today at Layer Aleph).

A successfully integrated operations body will have these features:

- A single, shared, always-on communications line monitored by a designated single point of contact, an operations lead or incident commander. This position should be staffed in rotating shifts if possible. The single point of contact also owns reliability and accessibility of the communications line.

- Low-complexity, easily distributed information for accessing that communications line. Phone conference bridges with stable dial-in and join information have proven very effective in the past.

- Direct (zero degrees of separation) access to the top of the chain of command (president/secretary/governor/CEO) or their delegate. This person must be able to make decisions requiring any magnitude short of an act of legislation.

- Convening power for the leads of each line of effort.

- A daily working rhythm of morning and evening check-ins from the single leads of each area of effort, and experts who know ground truth on issues firsthand. These check-ins happen at the same time every day and are mandatory.

- The ability to track the top three issues and top three needs on a daily basis for each line of effort.

- A daily read-out of the operational terrain (issues, needs, and personnel status) directly to the top of the chain of command (president/secretary/governor/CEO) or their delegate.

HOW CAN I USE THIS?

» **Be prepared with written materials and plans.** In bureaucracies, more than anywhere else, a crisis can temporarily reconfigure the rules of the game. With the right preparation and approach, you can use this opportunity to turbocharge your plans and even potentially cement new rules. Starting your master plan *after* the crisis might work, but being ready to go the moment one hits is much better.

» **Create a command center.** If there's a problem to solve and no clear person to solve it, can you take charge? Running an effective command center isn't rocket science; it's about getting ground truth information from the people on the front lines, on a regular basis, and applying resources to the highest-priority problems.

» **Be self-aware about whether you can really help.** It's possible to get carried away and try to insert yourself, and your idea, as the savior to every crisis. Ask yourself: Do I really have the skills to help? Does my idea credibly help the organization recover, respond, and rebuild? Sometimes the best thing you can do is help others with *their* newly pressing project, or stand down and stay out of the way.

» **Step up locally.** See a current crisis on the news or in your community? Step up to help; find ways for your existing projects, teams, or ideas to align with addressing the crisis.

LEVERAGE THE BIG BOSSES

Large organizations are hierarchical, with a lot of focus on what the big boss thinks, says, and does. Use this to your advantage and find ways to gain attention and air cover from your higher-ups.

Invite the Principal

The White House is arguably a singular institution—a small bureaucracy focused around the leader of the free world. But even in the White House, there are a number of important people—called "principals" in White House lingo—that you could leverage for a meeting. Sometimes it would just be for a few minutes ("a drop"), or a brief standup meeting before a larger event ("a clutch"). Through experience and plenty of experimentation, we understood when inviting a principal to a meeting or event would be catalytic. If the mere presence of the principal was enough to energize the attendees, a clutch or drop would usually be sufficient. But if there was substance for the principal to hear, or if part of the reason of the meeting was to make the group feel heard, a full meeting is what we would shoot for.

Your institution has its own big bosses—a university or nonprofit president, C-suite executives, major donors, board members, and so on. No matter how they communicate internally—speeches, videos, emails, or town halls—what they say and where they go matters. Finding ways to strategically include them in your meetings or events, whether for a "drop" or a keynote speech, can garner a lot more respect and attention when done well.

It's worth thinking about how the boss or a principal attending an internal or external event might add legitimacy to your project, then learning exactly how to get them there. Do you know how the schedule and calendar are decided for these leaders? Can you find a way to invite them to participate in your event? Can you do the background work to make it more likely their staff will say yes? Their attendance can boost your credibility, highlight the project you are focused on, and help you build more allies across your organization.

We're not saying this is easy. When we wanted a principal in the White House or at the VA to say a few words, either to our team or external stakeholders, it required writing an event memo, submitting sample talking points, and sometimes having staff meetings to discuss. We were competing against many other groups and priorities—not to mention various national and global crises. You likely are competing for attention, as well.

Our advice: make the ask *both* the formal and informal way. If there is a process for asking for the CEO or other senior executive to participate, like submitting a memo, then take the time to do it well and on time. Submit your request far enough in advance for the office to give it full consideration. But if you have a personal or informal connection, or your boss is willing to make the call on your behalf, it's perfectly fine to leverage those avenues, too. However, if you have your boss ask the CEO directly, and you haven't done the staff work ahead of time, you risk the CEO's support team undercutting your efforts. As Marina found out when she was trading paperclips, those who control calendars wield significant power.

There's No Such Thing as a Blank Check or a Blanket Waiver

One way *not* to leverage your big bosses is to try to get special exemptions or permissions from them. There's no such thing as a blank check or blanket waiver. We've looked everywhere. If the president of the United States can't issue a blanket waiver to Marina to connect one measly computer to another, you're not going to get one for your project, either.

Bureaucracies are literally designed to withstand rapid change. Going around the rules or even getting formal permission to break the rules might seem like the fastest path to success, and you are correct in a way: you will probably move faster, at first, than following the normal path and making fundamental changes. But it's only a matter of time before this catches up with you: lawyers, accountants, new senior leaders, or simply a grumpy executive assistant *will* find and report your transgressions. Then all your progress will halt; you'll lose a ton of political capital; and you may not be able to salvage your project, no matter how good your intentions or the results. Even if you can declare success on a project before the bureaucracy catches up with you, rest assured the next person won't be able to follow in your footsteps.

We don't mean for this to be discouraging—there are *plenty* of ways to drive real change in a bureaucracy, which is why we wrote this book. If you're tempted to ask for a waiver, we encourage you to particularly consider the tactics "use the bureaucracy against itself," "understand incentives and risks," "consult a thesaurus," and "try the normal way first."

Follow the established approval processes or change them—but if you want your project to succeed long term, don't seek special exceptions.

Seek Air Cover

While you might not be able to get a blanket exemption that lets you do whatever you want, there is a powerful corollary you can get from senior leaders: air cover.

Air cover is a signal from the higher-ups that they support your project. It won't get you out of filling out required paperwork or having to follow the rules, but it will send a strong signal to your detractors that you have the big bosses' attention. If someone tries to block your progress or stand in your way, they won't just have to face *you*, they'll also well have to explain themselves to a senior leader—an embarrassment they may very well want to avoid.

Matt Cutts, widely regarded as creating the spam-fighting function at Google, shares how he leveraged air cover from VP of Engineering Urs Hölzle to help establish his team. When he needed reinforcement in a meeting, he'd ask Urs to attend and confirm that Matt's project was approved and supported. Matt referred to this tactic as "the hand of Urs." Today, Google (especially Gmail) is practically synonymous with fighting spam.

Air cover can sometimes mean special permissions, but only in the context of what's already allowed in your bureaucracy. You might get to go first or early in an established line or agenda; you might get included in meetings or initiatives that you wouldn't otherwise have been in; or you might get more favorable interpretation of a fuzzy rule or policy. The more trust you earn with your executives, and the more successful your projects are, the more air cover you can earn.

Treat air cover as the precious resource that it is. As an informal privilege, it can be taken away in an instant, whether because your senior leader loses trust, becomes busy with other priorities, or departs. Relying on air cover alone to get your project to the finish line is unwise.

HOW CAN I USE THIS?

» **Invite the big boss to your existing event.** Perhaps they could say a few words expressing enthusiasm without staying for the entire event. Maybe they could participate in the visual of the event, without having to stay for the rubber chicken dinner.

» **Create an event for the big boss.** A new event from scratch is much more work but ensures that you can craft a narrative that best highlights your senior executive while also advancing your objectives.

» **Plug into planned events.** Package up your project. Help write a speech, or offer talking points to help the communications or public relations team meet their deadlines.

» **Seek air cover.** When a higher-up has a vested interest in your success, they might not be able to break the rules for you, but they can prioritize getting the resources, attention, or decision-making you need to make brisk progress. Air cover can be informal, or it could be a documented email or memo from an executive affirming their commitment.

» **Don't look for a blanket waiver or a blank check.** This is wasted time and energy you could instead devote to real bureaucracy-hacking efforts.

» **Find formal, approved ways to move faster.** Instead of skirting rules, look for ways to work with them: call your project a "pilot" to escape early reporting requirements; participate in an "innovation" program that has its own, smaller set of rules; or, instead of simply assuming the status quo will never work, try the normal way first—then document and fix issues with that process directly, for the benefit of everyone (including your future self).

WORK FROM THE OUTSIDE IN

Leverage external stakeholders who can provide
outside support for your initiative, or even own part
of the solution.

Every sizable organization has outside stakeholder groups. The question is: How can you appropriately leverage them? Can you steer them in the right direction? Can you help them be more effective? And perhaps most importantly: How can they help you?

Effectively working with outside groups is not entry-level bureaucracy hacking. A lot can go wrong. You might be aligned with an outside group and have similar objectives, but you never want to be seen as captive or beholden to them. As an example, regulators, even if they are sympathetic to the industry they regulate, are wary of being seen as "captured" by industry. But if you can find a way to work with outside stakeholders in a strategic fashion, you will have another arrow in your bureaucracy-hacking quiver.

Your CEO or leader will have various external constituencies, but they don't all have equal importance. The average alumnus isn't going to get the same attention as a billionaire classmate contemplating a hundred-million-dollar donation. A small shareholder isn't going to get the same attention as a major one. The union head is more likely to get a meeting than an individual worker, and so on.

In large organizations, managing external constituencies is too much work for a single person. Your organization probably has several people, across several functions, to manage these relationships. For example, investor relations might handle investors, government affairs engages with government officials, and human resources handles employee alumni. A warning: if you go around these internal teams to engage with a group they are in charge of managing, don't expect them to do you any favors later.

Nick learned this the hard way. His first job in government was at the Federal Communications Commission (FCC), on a blue-ribbon task force called the National Broadband Plan. He led a small team focused on how broadband and advanced communication could improve energy and environmental issues. One of his team's flagship recommendations was that electric utilities should make it easier for consumers to access their own energy consumption data. Congressman Ed Markey (now Senator Markey) ultimately authored legislation, the Electric Consumer Right to Know Act, calling for utilities to make this information available to consumers.

Nick was hugely proud that his first policy job in Washington, DC, resulted in actual legislation and was doubly proud that Markey invited him to testify about the topic. But having been too headstrong in talking with staffers on the Hill without first consulting the Office of Legislative Affairs inside the FCC, Nick didn't have their support or trust. Unsurprisingly, they didn't allow Nick to testify.

Ways to Leverage Outsiders

Ways you can build momentum for your internal initiative with outside forces include:

- Building partnerships with other organizations to achieve shared goals.

- Generating positive news coverage in articles, news shows, or blogs.

- Finding new voices to highlight problems that your bureaucracy isn't taking seriously (especially the voices of the people directly impacted by the problem).

- Recruiting new talent from other industries to bring a new perspective to your project (or perhaps even a bidirectional staffing rotation, to expose your internal employees to other organizations).

- Facilitating data collection through surveys or independent research.

- Enlisting volunteer talent when you don't have enough budget to do the necessary work to achieve your shared goal.

- Bringing fresh solutions to standing problems from other industries or even the public.

- Creating rallying cries for specific changes, like a write-in campaign led by an advocacy organization.

Again, we recommend following your bureaucracy's normal procedures for engaging with outside constituents, whether that be reporters, customers, or peer organizations.

HOW CAN I USE THIS?

» **Understand the major stakeholders.** Draw a map of the stakeholders inside and outside your organization. Who are they, and what are they focused on? Who inside your organization is charged with managing them? Who are the people that lead those outside groups, and what relationships and experiences do they have with your organization?

» **Help outsiders be on message.** If an outside group can help your cause but isn't quite landing its message, suggest a tweak in how they communicate with your company or organization.

» **Invite outside stakeholders to own part of the solution.** An outside group might be willing to perform a function that your organization is struggling with. For example, you might partner with a group that can disseminate information or collect data that your organization cannot. If you have an extremely complicated process that people are struggling to navigate, a short-term fix could be an outside group publishing a plain-language guide or a navigation wizard, or setting up a helpline to give advice.

GET PUBLIC COMMITMENTS

> You get in life what you have the courage
> to ask for.
>
> —OPRAH WINFREY

Get your organization to publicly commit to specific actions—and find ways to leverage that commitment to generate momentum for your initiative. If your organization also has the power to convene and celebrate other groups, ask others to make public commitments on shared goals that you can unveil and collaborate on together.

The Schedule Is Your Friend

At the White House, unveiling new Executive Branch commitments to action was extremely challenging—*by design*. No one wants the federal government to commit itself to action lightly. The typical process for determining what the federal government should sign up to do, beyond the status quo, was something that layers of interagency committees and meetings worked on.

And to get to the top of their agendas, it helped to have a deadline.

One of our frequent sayings—from Kumar Garg's whiteboard—was "The schedule is your friend." Whether it was the State of the Union in January, the United Nations General Assembly in September, or a scheduled presidential trip to Colorado in a few weeks, we quickly learned that any presidential event, which usually included speeches and appearances, could be a very helpful forcing function.

We thought about using upcoming events as a way to get work done, especially items that were important but not urgent, or that were completely new and not yet part of anyone's plan. When we were engaging with an agency about their policy initiatives, we would ask if they had something the president might be able to announce.

We were banking on the idea that the president *wanted* to say something substantive during a speech. Uplifting stories and demands that Congress pass legislation are par for any presidential speech, but there was an inherent desire to have something new and newsworthy, too. The hope was that the media would cover it, instead of (or more likely, in addition to) the routine political coverage of polls and elections.

Any actual policy announcement would have to be vetted, both by us and many others at the White House, to make sure it was (1) genuinely new, (2) sufficiently ready ("baked," as we liked to say), and (3) interesting enough to catch the fancy of the communications and speechwriting teams. While we would never promise anyone that we'd get their points into a presidential speech, the potential alone was enough to create an artificial deadline for them to make more progress, faster.

As an example, Nick coordinated an initiative called the Open Government Partnership. At international summits, with world leaders present, countries would unveil their latest plans to promote transparency, participation, and inclusion. Civil society groups would celebrate progress and put pressure on governments to do even better. The process of getting governments to agree to reforms—like improving freedom of information or declassification efforts—was not a particularly beloved portfolio in the White House. But President Obama, who had co-launched the Open Government Partnership, needed to show progress nonetheless.

Using the upcoming deadline of the September UN General Assembly in New York City, which President Obama was going to attend, Nick and his team (led by tenacious ex-journalist and public interest lawyer Cori Zarek) wrangled Executive Branch commitments to increase transparency in spending, develop privacy protections in healthcare, and create an open-source software policy. Sitting in the cavernous hall with translator earpieces available at every seat as part of the US delegation and watching Obama and other world leaders make speeches in the UN was certainly awe-inspiring for Nick and Cori. But the real work—getting internal agreement to make new stretch commitments that would push the federal government for years to come—was done in the months leading up to the event.

Getting Your Organization to Make a Public Commitment

A public declaration that your organization is going to do something can be a useful stake in the ground—especially if your CEO or senior executive personally makes that commitment. Once she has committed publicly, your organization will likely invest significant resources to try to achieve that action or meet that goal, even if there is no explicit penalty or consequence for failure.

A public commitment means a new, or incrementally new, course of action. It's not the same as restating what the organization is already doing, or has published as its status quo plan. A public commitment also needs to be specific enough to be measured, like a company pledging for the first time to get to net-zero carbon by 2030. Simply highlighting a strategy, reemphasizing an existing goal, or issuing a fluffy press release with feel-good sentiments doesn't count.

There are various ways for your organization to publicly commit to action, including:

- Your CEO making a speech or media appearance

- Your company issuing a press release or fact sheet

- A member of your management team testifying in front of Congress, your regulator, or even a city council meeting

- Your CEO or company signing a pledge by a third-party group

Once your organization has made a new commitment, there will be both internal and external pressure to show progress. Internally,

champions will remind the company about its commitment and organize resources and action in support. You can position yourself to take
advantage of these additional assets and attention.

Externally, the accountability mechanism is public scrutiny. A company can be proactively transparent about its progress (at least on a peri-
odic basis), or only provide updates when asked. No one wants to put
their CEO in the position of having to answer a difficult question in a
public forum—from a journalist, Wall Street analyst, or shareholder—
about why your organization isn't delivering. Once a commitment
has been made, the fear of being called to account can be a real motivator, too.

You can use your organization's desire for attention, as well as its
desire to make announcements, to advance your actual work. Ask yourself: What motivates my organization to make announcements? How
does it use public forums to share news? What forums does my CEO
or leader participate in already? Armed with this knowledge, consider
how you might insert your project into the planning process for a public
commitment, or even use the process to get approval to announce one
yourself.

We recognize this is a challenging bureaucracy-hacking tactic. Public companies, for example, tend to be very careful about public pronouncements because they can move the company's stock price. Any
proposed pronouncement will likely have rounds of vetting, including
investor relations professionals. At the same time, public companies
may also be more familiar with the idea of a CEO making public decla-
rations, and might even have an established process for considering new
commitments.

Multiparty Coordination: Outside Commitments

The federal bureaucracy obviously does not have all of the answers or
resources to address complex societal problems. To make up for this, the
Obama White House also used a commitments model where we encouraged outside third parties (corporations, universities, foundations, local
government, etc.) to make public commitments that the president could
unveil and celebrate.

Our mentor and friend Tom Kalil learned how to use this approach working for President Clinton, who in 1999 urged CEOs to invest in underserved communities like East Palo Alto and the Pine Ridge Indian Reservation. He continued to catalyze public commitments while working at the Clinton Global Initiative (CGI), the nonprofit that Bill and Hillary Clinton spearheaded post-presidency. CGI was explicitly designed as a "do tank," rather than a think tank, with public commitments at its core. At its annual convening, participating companies and organizations were required to make public pledges of action. The accountability mechanism was simple: CEOs and nonprofit leaders wouldn't be invited back if they didn't fulfill their prior promises. Leaders who made a public commitment, sometimes directly on stage with Bill Clinton, *wanted* to come back the following year to bask in the glory and report on their progress. In contrast to other annual gatherings, CGI was designed to highlight and encourage new work.

Tom frames the outside public commitment model in the Obama White House as one of voluntary inspiration:

> President Obama often highlighted the importance of an "all hands on deck" approach to solving problems. When actions by the federal government could not solve a particular issue, the president would often issue a "call to action" to inspire stakeholders to make specific commitments that advanced the administration's priorities.

The fuller story is that, however inspiring a presidential call to action can be, an outside public commitment model requires dedicated staff work. Public commitments by third parties are completely voluntary— CGI and the White House weren't telling anyone what to do, and there was never a stick beyond not being included in an event. But the prospect of being celebrated and generating positive press was sufficiently motivating for many organizations. If we worked with them in the months—sometimes even years—leading up to an event, we could help them develop meaningful commitments that built on what they were already doing.

For example, Tom Kalil and colleagues launched President Obama's BRAIN Initiative, which was designed to increase our understanding of how the brain encodes and processes information. The initiative included not only increased funding for agencies like the National Institutes of Health and DARPA, but commitments from the private sector to leverage its expertise in technologies such as miniature, implantable microscopes. By encouraging the private sector to make specific commitments, he made the initiative an all-hands-on-deck effort to transform our understanding of the brain and, ultimately, to treat diseases of the brain.

Data Jams and Datapaloozas

Todd Park jumped onto the table, in his suit and dress shoes, with so much enthusiasm he was practically quivering. It was a Tom Cruise on Oprah's couch moment. He called out to ask who was willing to continue to work on the ideas they had been workshopping and brainstorming over the last few hours. His unbridled passion and childlike excitement were hard to take your eyes away from, and even the most cynical in the group found themselves volunteering to work on their ideas post-workshop.

Todd nicknamed this and other brainstorming workshops a "data jam." With several dozen entrepreneurs, software developers, and education subject matter experts all in one room, Todd, Nick, and teammates had been helping small groups think up new ways to use government education data to support students, teachers, and school districts.

This idea of open data—think temperature and wind speed data from the government that feeds your local weather report—had been around for decades. President Obama even signed an executive order in 2013, which Nick helped draft, making "open data the new default." But executive orders aren't self-executing, as we liked to say. So here was Todd, in 2013, literally on the table, calling for commitments.

Todd's enthusiasm, cross-fertilization of bias-for-action people, and call for service worked. Several of the entrepreneurs and software developers at the data jam spent the coming weeks turning their brainstormed ideas into real demonstrations. At this data jam, and many others, Todd, Nick, and team held out the promise of celebrating progress at larger, public events that Todd nicknamed "Datapaloozas." Bringing senior government officials, technology executives, and nonprofits together in data jams and then subsequent Datapaloozas, Todd, Nick, and colleagues found ways to highlight the potential and drive the progress of government data being used in new ways—all to help the American people.

How to Make Outside Commitments Real

All organizations don't have the kind of convening power we had in the White House—but many foundations, government agencies, and even celebrities do. Most at least have annual convenings where they can highlight news and accomplishments. If you work in such a company, consider using the public commitment model during your next big event. You could ask your customers, partners, or suppliers to commit to actions against a certain shared goal (e.g., hiring veterans, getting to net-zero emissions, etc.). If your organization has what we call "stage equity"—i.e., the ability to convene parties and shine a light on the event via media—you can try a model where you ask third parties to make public commitments at the event, too.

To set the framework correctly, you'll need to give public credit to *newly* announced commitments, not just existing players and ongoing activities. People generally share stage equity to make themselves look smarter or more connected. You might invite a famous author to your annual conference, or celebrate a cause by having the executive director of a charity that your corporation funds as an honored guest. But with an outside public commitment model, you use that convening to celebrate those doing new work.

The outside public commitments model is essentially a multiparty coordination mechanism. It's hard to get multiple organizations to work together, and it really helps to have a deadline. An event for public announcements helps focus every participating organization on whether or not they can make a specific commitment, and on exactly what that commitment can look like in the given timeframe.

An advantage of announcing commitments together is that they collectively feel bigger. Most things your company or organization is going to work on might seem small in the context of the overall problem or in the face of daunting societal challenges. Commitment devices help you connect to a larger umbrella and framework, and to situate your work as part of a bigger movement.

HOW CAN I USE THIS?

» **Frame your ideas in the context of a public commitment.** If your initiative is something that your organization can publicly commit to, see if you can tee it up to a chief executive or senior official. Frame it as a win for them, with the knowledge that you can use that public statement to remind your bureaucracy that your idea matters.

» **Use events to encourage and celebrate third-party commitments.** If your organization has star power, see if you might invite outside executives or celebrities to make public commitments that advance your organization's priorities.

PAY THE BOX GUY

Honor the promises you make to people—or they may be the one to take your entire project down.

War Dogs

Efraim Diveroli became a millionaire at just eighteen by selling supplies to the US military. Part of his strategy was to undercut the big government contractors on smaller-dollar contracts, but he also took advantage of the Department of Defense's small business contracting goals, which required awarding at least 20 percent of contracts to small firms like his.

Over time, Efraim got greedy—and unethical. His annual sales to the government soared from just over $1 million in 2004 to over $200 million three years later, and then he hit an even bigger jackpot: a huge contract for ammunition. Except, there wasn't this much ammunition to be had (legally) in the entire world. To fulfill the order, he resorted to illegally reselling Chinese bullets from the 1960s. (It's against US federal law to buy Chinese ammo.) To help him get away with this scheme, he hired a guy named Kosta Trebicka to repackage the Chinese crates into plain cardboard boxes, for a fee of just $50,000—on a *$298 million* contract.

Although Kosta (the "box guy") successfully repackaged all the munitions, Efraim never paid him—he cut him out of the deal, replaced him with a different packaging company, and left Kosta holding the bag for labor and supplies. So Kosta exacted his revenge: he spilled the beans to the *New York Times*. The subsequent front-page headlines tipped off the FBI, and Efraim went on to serve four years in prison.

This true story was memorialized in the 2016 film *War Dogs*.

The Political Capital Ledger

Now, we certainly don't want you to use this book to commit crimes or defraud the US military. But the lesson to pay the box guy stands. As much as we suggest an attitude of giving first, you are going to find yourself owing people who help you on your particular project. In some cases, you'll seek out a favor; in others, people will offer up contributions unprompted. In all cases, you need to pay them back.

Keeping track of what you owe people is never going to be as simple as borrowing and paying back $10 because you forgot your wallet at lunch. Sometimes you'll make an explicit quid pro quo agreement with someone: you help me get the budget for this contract, and I'll make sure my consultants include your problem in their scope of work. But other forms of help you want to recognize and repay include:

- Mentioning your initiative in a high-profile meeting (to gain support)

- *Not* mentioning your initiative in a high-profile meeting (to preserve stealth mode)

- Loaning you a team member

- Sharing back-channel information that helps you

- Warm introductions

- Persuading a third party to listen to or believe in you

- Including your needs in their budget or contract

- Voting for or prioritizing your initiatives

Repayment where you work can take many forms. You owe something to the secretary who gets you in early on the new manager's calendar, but you probably don't repay him by getting him in early on someone else's calendar; instead, you might nominate him for a performance award, submit that report he's worried about a day early, cover for him one day when he is late to the office, or share career advice over coffee.

Just as we counsel you in this book to understand other people's risk and incentive frameworks in service of persuading them to work with you, you should have a framework for thinking about how to pay people back. Most importantly: it depends on the person. The career advice over coffee might be highly coveted by a secretary whose dream job is the one you have; it would be insulting if that same secretary doesn't want any career advice, or if you don't have good advice in the first place.

And when you can, repay with interest! A strong source of political capital comes from exceeding expectations. People expect their resources returned and their favors repaid; that's table stakes. But if you make it big, and you share the riches with those who helped you—that won't be forgotten.

What Happens If You Don't Pay Them?

As we cover throughout this book, bureaucracies are booby-trapped with ways your new project—no matter how cost-effective, how well-designed, or how mission-critical—can get shut down in a snap. And your equivalent of the box guy knows all of them.

The repercussions may not be calling a major newspaper to spill your secrets. It could start with little whispers here and there about how you took advantage of them and never repaid their kindness...slowly calling into question your reputation and trustworthiness, and eroding your social capital. Maybe they ask a pointed question that you can't answer right in front of a key decision maker, or they "forget" to include you on a meeting invite.

Or perhaps they casually—or not so casually—suggest your project is breaking a rule and that someone should investigate what you're up to. Just because you *aren't* breaking a rule doesn't mean you can't be subjected to weeks, months, or even years of inquiries and investigations from legal, human resources, and elsewhere. Once, an anonymous person sent in a whistleblower complaint on a project of Marina's at the VA, asserting her new pilot program violated a required data standard. And it actually did: the data standard, written before women could serve in the military, required "left testicle" and "right testicle" values for every physical exam—a data field she had removed for women's gynecological exams. The subsequent investigation, as ridiculous as it was, caused her to miss a key deadline, presumably to the great pleasure of the so-called whistleblower.

Taken out of context, perfectly innocuous things can be made to look bad. That exciting afternoon you and some colleagues brainstormed together is now recounted as a "secret meeting" that left others out. Your strategic decision not to share a draft with Melissa until it was more polished, because she is a stickler for details, becomes you hiding your plans from Melissa. A back-of-the-napkin estimate can be mischaracterized as a lack of understanding about what it takes to get something done in your organization.

Just pay the box guy.

HOW CAN I USE THIS?

» **Keep track of your commitments.** Write down your commitments to people, however small, and keep track of them. As you build resources (money, political capital, team members), work in ways to honor those commitments.

» **Communicate early.** If circumstances change and you truly cannot honor a previous commitment, communicate as early and often as you can with the people you will let down. Go out of your way to find other ways to help them get what they need.

» **Pay others back with interest.** It never hurts to go out of your way to show others' contributions are appreciated.

PICK YOUR BATTLES

Not every problem needs to be overcome,
just the ones stopping you from getting
where you want to be.

—ANN HILL

You need a clear understanding of what you can compromise on, and what you can't, to achieve your objectives. Consider the extent of the disagreement and the players involved to help figure out whether you should give in or fight back over a particular detail.

You're in the throes of your project, you have real customers or employees testing your prototype, or you've found your moment to shine, perhaps thanks to a new crisis. But then…someone picks a fight, or at least creates a needless distraction. They need you to include their new feature (immediately!), they need their name on the press release (even though they did nothing!), or they need your team to drop everything and work on *their* project instead.

What do you do?

You pick your battles.

As ICUs filled past capacity during the COVID-19 pandemic, many states were scrambling to get more healthcare workers. One immediate barrier that came up: healthcare workers need to be licensed in individual states, which costs money and takes time—time that no one had. To get around this, some states hurriedly implemented systems for out-of-state providers to register, granting them special permissions to work.

In one state, the form to register out-of-state doctors and nurses was literally minutes from being launched when a key stakeholder spoke up: they couldn't launch the form because it did not include "acupuncturists" in the dropdown list of specialties.

Now, we are not against acupuncturists, but they were not exactly at the top of the list of needs in the ICU. And if this request were granted, they would *literally* be at the top of the list, which was alphabetical. The team's first inclination was to fight this request and leave them out.

But what was their goal? To get more nurses into the ICU, *stat*. The longer they waited to launch this form, the longer it would be until the first out-of-state professional made their way there. Including acupuncturists was annoying, but it wasn't going to stand in the way of success. They adjusted the dropdown and launched the form, on schedule.

The Pointless Domain Name Battle

One of the strangest, and dumbest, battles Marina has ever found herself in was over which federal agency should own the domain name "veterans.gov." If you think the answer is the Department of Veterans Affairs, we think you *should* be right—but you're not. Since 2013, this website has been owned and operated by the Department of Labor.

Marina spent years of energy and political capital trying to get this website address back. This even escalated to numerous White House meetings trying to mediate the dispute. Marina had her heart set on launching her new, modern website at veterans.gov; she had written it down in her plans; and by gosh she was *stubborn*. She was going to win.

Except, she didn't. And in retrospect, getting this domain did not matter one bit. At the final hour, her team ended up buying "vets.gov" instead, and launched the site there. It was eventually so successful that it merged into VA's main website, VA.gov, a few years later—with the simplicity and ease-of-use of Marina's vets.gov replacing the clunky functionality of the VA's former website. *That* was what mattered—making it easy for veterans to discover, manage, and access their benefits and healthcare. The exact website address they used to do this did not matter to anyone.

HOW CAN I USE THIS?

» **Keep your goals front and center.** When someone challenges part of your project, or you have to pivot, consult your list and ask: Will this compromise derail what I'm trying to accomplish? Am I being stubborn?

» **Consider the other side.** Maybe a feature request or a copyedit is annoying, but could it help another stakeholder feel part of your project? Could a minor change or tweak get you more support?

DON'T TRY TO MAKE
THE BUREAUCRACY CARE

If you're going to sin, sin against God,
not the bureaucracy. God will forgive
you—the bureaucracy won't.
—HYMAN RICKOVER

Bureaucracies, unlike the people that inhabit them, don't have feelings. You cannot persuade your bureaucracy to change through emotional arguments. Instead, understand exactly the criteria that are going to be used to make a decision—and meet them.

No Thanks for Saving the World

The bureaucracy doesn't care about you. Your organization does not care about your feelings or your noble intentions. We have seen many people try, and fail, to persuade lawyers or security officers to overlook a step or a missing requirement with emotional pleas about human consequences, like homeless veterans or foster youth. But a bureaucracy will never make a decision, or accept a risk, based on emotions. Align accordingly.

You may have heard the story of Stanislav Petrov, who is widely credited with saving the world from nuclear annihilation. A Soviet Air Defense Forces officer in Russia in 1983, he received a satellite report of an incoming missile attack from the United States. It was strict protocol to report this attack, which would have resulted in an immediate counterattack. Russia and the United States attacking one another with nuclear missiles was not going to end well for anyone on Earth.

But Petrov did *not* report the attack. He believed—correctly—that it was a false alarm and waited until it was clear that the "missile" was actually just the sun hitting the clouds.

His bureaucracy did not care. In exchange for literally saving the world, the Soviet government reprimanded him for not using the correct form to file his report and forced him into early retirement.

The CIA Triad

If you have ever filled out IT paperwork or taken a cybersecurity training class, you have probably come across the CIA triad. This is not a reference to the Central Intelligence Agency, but rather to the concepts of confidentiality, integrity, and availability. Whether you are building, buying, or simply trying to use new software in your organization, your IT or security shop will probably require you to explain how the system will adhere to these three requirements.

The CIA triad cares about:

- How you will keep data confidential

- How you will maintain data integrity (e.g., not allowing unauthorized tampering or editing)

- How you will make the system available to users most of the time (e.g., minimal downtime, bugs, or crashes)

The CIA triad does not care about:

- How many foster kids will be homeless during the pandemic because you have no other way to keep a list of their names and phone numbers if you do not get IT to approve your shared spreadsheet

- How many veterans will be homeless if the VA and HUD cannot share a list of homeless veterans in a given community

- How you can place 20 percent more foster kids with relatives than with strangers if you could just access Facebook on your work computer to find them

- How many veterans can have their dishonorable discharge reversed if you could proactively send them the correct, prefilled form.

How do you make the bureaucracy care? *You don't*. It doesn't matter how noble your mission is. If you want homeless veterans in houses, and foster kids safe with their loved ones, and you need permission for a new tool, policy, or practice to make it happen, then you leave your emotional arguments aside and you fill out the CIA triad form. You throw all your energy into showing how something as simple as a shared spreadsheet will be confidential, with high integrity and high availability. You get permission to use your spreadsheet, and then use it to achieve your real goals.

In a similar vein, you can't rely on good intentions to protect you if you break a rule or deviate from the approved process in your bureaucracy. If that worked, we'd rename this book *Have Good Intentions* and leave it at that. Elsewhere in this book, we encourage you to build authentic relationships and allies. Sometimes these individuals *can* come to your aid—and they can definitely care about you. But the bureaucracy itself won't, and can't, care.

HOW CAN I USE THIS?

» **Follow the required steps to get to your goal and leave emotional arguments at the door.** With your endgame in sight, fill out the form. Follow the rule. Meet the criteria for the committee to vote yes. You might not enjoy the process, but it's the results that count.

PLAY THE LONG GAME

The ascent of Everest was not the work of
one day, nor even of those few unforgettable
weeks in which we climbed....It is, in fact,
a tale of sustained and tenacious endeavor
by many, over a long period of time.

—SIR JOHN HUNT

---

*Your bureaucracy isn't going anywhere, and no
change is going to happen overnight. Expecting
that your entire project or initiative will be adopted
quickly and at scale is unrealistic. If you have your
endgame in mind, you can make strategic chess
moves that get you closer and closer to that goal, one
bureaucracy hack at a time.*

What was Samantha Bee's worst nightmare? Agreeing with President Trump. And in her 2019 Halloween episode, her nightmare came true—the result of years of behind-the-scenes, cross-administration machinations from Jennifer Erickson and dedicated, data-driven reformers. They played a long game of bureaucracy hacking across administrations, states, and public and private sector actors to achieve their North Star goal of ending America's kidney donor shortage.

Large organizations are complex. Fixing a problem systematically often requires fixing multiple issues—which necessitates using many of the tactics in this book. Bureaucracy hacking, paradoxically, is most powerful when you pair a fierce urgency for action with a patient perseverance. We had a saying in the White House about dogged persistence: "Like water on stone." Over time, water eventually cuts through rock and reshapes the earth. Your efforts to reshape your organization might take some time—but even the largest and most stubborn bureaucracies can change.

Jennifer and her colleagues at the White House—including Robbie Barbero, Megan Brewster, and Alefiyah Mesiwala—built a process to solicit the best new ideas and commitments to increase organ donations. They teamed up with Greg Segal, cofounder of Organize, a patient advocacy group that held an Innovator in Residence position at the US Department of Health and Human Services, and set to work to follow the data, find the best research, and follow users in every part of the process: organ donor families, the doctors who perform transplants, the committees who decide what organs are viable and who will receive them, and the delivery services that transport them. In fact, Jennifer is so dedicated to user research that in her will, she has a clause directing an investigative journalist to follow her organs after she dies to make sure they make it to donors. After all, research suggests that the biggest predictor of donation rates in any region is how positively a deceased donor's next-of-kin rates their interaction when being talked to about donation (was the person pushy or compassionate?).

Shockingly, as she looked between the silos at handoff points, she learned that there are enough potential donors available in America for there to be no waiting lists at *all* for some organs, and 28,000 organs go unrecovered each year by the organizations charged with picking them up. As a result, 33 people die waiting for a transplant every day, with more than 100,000 Americans wait-listed for an organ transplant.

The organizations responsible for picking up donatable organs—many of which are utterly failing at their jobs—are all federal contractors. Not a single one has lost their contract based on their performance, because their contracts don't require performance. They are incentivized to meet the other terms of their government contracts, such as reporting deadlines, but without an incentive to reach performance metrics, they aren't performing at what should be their core mission: picking up organs. What one might *think* were guaranteed behavior changers didn't budge their actions a bit: not negative investigative reports and federal probes dating back to the 1990s, and not the completely preventable deaths of thousands of Americans every year at their hands.

The bureaucracy doesn't—*can't*, even—care about you, or about people dying for lack of organs. So a small group of like-minded Democratic and Republican health policy experts set out to create the incentive and risk frameworks to *make* the bureaucracy pay attention.

Working on this issue across multiple administrations, Jennifer is a master bureaucracy hacker. Her team focused on influencing the levers that really changed behaviors: regulations and government contracting. By changing the contract requirements as these organizations come up for renewal, they pulled the one lever that will actually make organ procurement organizations (OPOs) change their behavior and pick up more organs: the fear of losing their government contract (and therefore losing their entire business, because the federal government is their only customer).

To shed light on this issue and foster more support, Jennifer cultivated a karass of unlikely allies over the years. In 2016, she brought together these allies through President Obama's White House Organ Summit. Three years later, she and Greg—then working outside of government with a group of often surprising bedfellows—picked up the pen and worked with both Republicans and Democrats to support an executive order to enact sweeping reforms to the national organ donation system, which President Trump gladly signed and made official in 2019. This received national acclaim from other karass members—like Samantha Bee.

The 2019 Executive Order on Advancing American Kidney Health is a master class in "Show, don't tell." It lays out multiple pilot programs for iteratively testing and improving initiatives to improve kidney health overall, as well as save thousands of lives each year with transplants. The order directed the secretary of HHS to start a handful of new, outcomes-focused efforts to rapidly arrive at new solutions, including bioengineering implantable artificial kidneys.

To continue to carry out this work, Jennifer made her own job by pitching the creation of an Innovation Fellow role to Schmidt Futures, where she was able to continue her work post-government.

In advance of the 2020 election, Jennifer, Greg, and Abe picked up the pen once again and published one of the very first Day One Papers for the incoming administration, with leaders from the American Society of Nephrology and the Global Liver Institute. Knowing that transition teams are always overwhelmed and don't have time to come up with lots of detailed project plans from scratch, they laid out a plain-language, thirteen-page action plan for ending America's kidney donor shortage. This plan is serving as a North Star vision for a world where no American dies from lack of an available organ.

The following year, Jen and her team's efforts to get the US Department of Health and Human Services to show the hard numbers worked, too. For the first time, data about kidney donation outcomes, including data broken down by race and ethnicity, was publicly available. The data showed what Jen had long suspected but now everybody saw in black and white: the majority of organ procurement organizations are still failing performance standards, resulting in thousands of unnecessary deaths each year. Her work to use the incentives of the bureaucracy to drive it to change *itself*, by inserting the first-ever performance standards, will be live in 2026—yet another 60,000 Americans will have died waiting for an organ until then.

The data showed not only 28,000 unrecovered organs every year, but also staggering racial disparities: there was a 10X delta in recovering organs from Black donors, leading to massive, unnecessary Black deaths. Jen used this data to drive additional media coverage and calls for action, highlighting an urgent health equity issue that we can (and must) fix through greater transparency and accountability.

This incremental approach of strangling the "mainframe" of America's core organ donation operations capitalized on both crises and windows of opportunity to slowly but steadily change one component of the system at a time. Completely rewriting the rules of organ donation in one fell swoop sounds appealing but was not possible or feasible. But creating new payment model pilots for improving quality outcomes for kidney patients through an executive order; changing the contract rules so organ procurement organizations have no choice but to increase collection rates if they want to survive; and other bureaucratic judo moves are setting the stage for her North Star to become a reality.

Bring Your Lived Experience

Jennifer Erickson clearly has grit and persistence. She used many of the tactics in this book and is a master bureaucracy hacker. Her colleagues, inside and outside of government, know she is passionate about organ transplants. What many of them might not know is why.

Jennifer's drive to fix organ donation in America was inspired by her personal experiences. Her father was a fighter pilot who was shot down and suffered from long-term kidney damage as a result. While he wasn't eligible for a kidney transplant, she watched her father quietly endure dialysis. That powerful lived experience has informed her current passion for improving organ transplants.

Your lived experiences can also bring detailed knowledge that can be especially useful to guide your agenda, recruit the right people, and drive system-wide change. As an example, consider what happens when those advocating for structural reform are subsequently put in charge.

Larry Krasner was the most unlikely district attorney in Philadelphia. He spent three decades as a defense attorney railing against the abuses of prosecutors and police and being vocal about the failures of mass incarceration. Before becoming the DA, he spent his career as a public defender, filing over seventy-five lawsuits against the Philadelphia Police Department. He surprised everyone when he announced his intent to run in early 2017, and shocked the political establishment by winning later that year.

On a snowy Friday in January 2018, four days into the job, Krasner fired a number of career prosecutors that he believed couldn't carry out his ambitious reforms. He has since hired over a dozen new lawyers (many of whom are former public defenders), data scientists, and long-time criminal justice activists. Determined to address police misconduct, Krasner pursued a homicide case against a police officer who shot a fleeing suspect in the back and expanded the unit focused on reviewing potentially problematic convictions.

A fierce critic of a cash bail system that he views as punitive to the poor, Krasner has declined to prosecute many low-level offenses, like prostitution and drug possession. He has worked to reduce the number of people in jail awaiting trial, taking it from 6,500 down to 4,800 pre-pandemic. (During the pandemic, to avoid prisoners becoming super-spreaders, he reduced it further to just 3,800 people in custody.)

According to Krasner, his office has achieved "the lowest level of incarceration in Philly since 1985."

Krasner used his lived experience as a longtime public defender to convince the general public that the DA's office needed reform, and that mass incarceration wasn't the answer. Once inside the DA's office, he pursued a number of reforms with the zeal of a longtime progressive activist. The Philadelphia voters seem to appreciate his agenda—in May 2021, they rejected his primary opponent—a former prosecutor he had fired—by over 30 percentage points.

HOW CAN I USE THIS?

» **Develop grit and resilience.** Large-scale changes—and sometimes even tiny changes—can take a *long* time to bear fruit in a bureaucracy. But if you find a small way every week to keep the ball moving forward, one day you will be able to look back over the previous months or years and be glad you didn't give up.

» **Be prepared to pivot.** Bureaucracies may not change on a dime, but *you* may need to pivot quickly to accommodate feedback, criticism, or new insights. Don't be overly rigid, and you can arrive at an even better solution.

CREATE A NEW ORG

If opportunity doesn't knock, build a door.

—MILTON BERLE

---

*Consider whether your idea might flourish faster
somewhere beyond your home bureaucracy.*

Sometimes the project you are most passionate about has the best chance of flourishing outside your home bureaucracy. That was certainly true for a trio of Harvard undergraduates who were in a hurry to make an impact. Neel Mehta, Athena Kan, and Chris Kuang, students who took Nick's field class, were interested in using their technology skills for public good—and wanted to get their peers involved, too.

Neel was a traditional computer science student, serving as a teaching fellow to Harvard's popular introductory computer science course. With a skateboard tucked under his arm, speaking a mile a minute, he was a natural, confident leader.

Athena Kan was a year younger than Neel, whip-smart, and totally unflappable. During her time at Harvard, she interned in Uber's engineering department and took some time off to become a micro-VC with Dorm Room Fund, investing in other student start-ups.

Chris Kuang, the youngest of the group, was a first-year student in 2016. Unlike Neel and Athena, who were taking computer science classes, he was focused on applied math and economics, with an eye toward policy. He was a student leader in the Institute of Politics, participating in their weekly pizza and politics study group that brings in politicians to talk with undergraduates. A Boston-area native, he was a big Patriots and Red Sox fan.

Neel, Athena, and Chris were interested in civic tech and social impact broadly, and they came to Nick with the idea of starting an organization called Coding it Forward, which would share information about civic technology opportunities with their fellow students.

But they had bigger ambitions. Inspired by Marina and other guests in Nick's class, and their exposure to public leaders through the Institute of Politics, they all wanted an internship in the federal government. Yet when they looked on USAjobs.gov, the federal employment website, all they could find were internships to install Microsoft Sharepoint, the intranet software that no one likes.

For Neel and Athena, top computer science students at Harvard, whose other summer internships would include engineering and product roles at Khan Academy, Microsoft, and Uber, it was like a budding Picasso only being able to find jobs painting houses. They wanted opportunities where they could put their software development skills to work—and work on something of importance. Managing a clunky intranet on outdated computers didn't cut it.

So the Coding it Forward team did what any entrepreneur would do: they created their own way. Not finding one that worked for them, they decided to create a summer internship for technical students in the federal government themselves.

Among other challenges, they had the practical problem of timing: it was the spring of 2016. By then, talented Harvard students usually have their internship already lined up. But the three were determined to see what they could get off the ground, even as a "beta test" for the summer.

Nick introduced them to Jeff Meisel, the chief marketing officer at the Census Bureau, who was also responsible for new talent programs for Census. Jeff was a former Presidential Innovation Fellow (PIF), and unlike a lot of PIFs with technical training, Jeff instead had a sales and marketing background. Jeff had been trying to start up an internship program at the Census Bureau for a while but hadn't yet succeeded. Jeff's initial attempt the year prior to meeting the Coding it Forward students was a failure, though it wasn't for a lack of trying.

Sensing complementary needs and missions, Nick introduced Jeff to his students who were passionate about building a peer network to share opportunities about civic technology. Coding it Forward started as a way to spread information and opportunities to fellow students—via newsletters and social media—but had quickly spread beyond Harvard to tech students across the country. They were building a network of students that self-selected into a "civic tech" niche and could be a fantastic recruiting pool for Jeff, Census, and government more broadly.

After Neel connected with Jeff for the first time on March 1, 2017, it kicked off a mad dash to accelerate the planning. Nine days later, Jeff traveled to Boston from DC so they could all meet in person and build a preliminary plan.

Neel, Athena, and Chris found an empty classroom in Sever Hall, a brick building in the middle of Harvard Yard. They rallied a handful of students to participate. Nick donated from his (very modest) faculty budget for a couple of cheese pizzas, and they all came together one snowy March day before spring break to brainstorm how this might work.

During the brainstorm, Jeff dusted off his data science fellowship concept that had failed the previous year, asking the students for help on how to improve it. He came prepared with a few constraints around timeline, funding, and existing contract vehicles to ground the discussion in operational reality. The focus of the meeting was: "How might we transform the government talent pipeline, and start this summer?"

Neel's, Athena's, and Chris's perspectives as students proved pivotal to understanding how federal agencies could deliver a compelling experience and out-compete tech companies in Silicon Valley for top talent. Both sides left the meeting fully committed to turning this idea into a reality—smartly framed as a beta test, given the especially short timeline they had. The motto "Let's build a fellowship for students, by students" became their rallying cry.

Inspired by the students and their ambitious vision, Jeff immediately pitched the idea of this new fellowship concept to Census leadership. In the course of a few weeks—incredible speed in any large organization, especially a federal agency—Jeff had the approval to fund a dozen interns that summer, a contract vehicle, and an operational partner (The Washington Center) that had deep expertise in running the behind-the-scenes logistics.

Neel, Athena, and Chris put out a call for students to apply, and news quickly spread among like-minded technology student groups across the Ivy League, and then to other college clubs. Over 220 students from eighty schools applied in less than ten days, which was impressive given it was early April—and *especially* impressive given the program didn't really exist yet! (They were "making stone soup," the tactic in our chapter "Act 'As If'.") Like many private sector entrepreneurs, their marketing was at the very edge of what they could actually deliver.

As Neel put in an inaugural blog post in early April 2017 calling for applications, the problem was clear:

> CS [Computer Science] students want internships where they can work on modern software problems, and there's just no supply of that from the federal government.
>
> The second problem is that the "user experience" of a government internship isn't up to scratch. Silicon Valley interns have cohorts, mentors, speaker series, intern programming, housing, and other perks. And did I mention pay? Federal government internships rarely provide that. Plus, the application process is clunky and unstructured, and many times the only way to get a federal internship is by knowing the right people.

It was important to Neel, Chris, and Athena that the internship, which they dubbed the Civic Digital Fellowship, be funded for reasons of equity and access. The federal government, like many industries, has too many unpaid internship roles, which unfairly sustains privilege. But getting approvals just for hiring—let alone the mechanics of getting federal money to flow—in that timeframe is unheard of. It helped that Jeff had tried the summer before, and that Census Director John Thompson was personally committed to talent initiatives.

When the Census Bureau saw the quality of resumes, it was impressed. As Jeff likes to say, it was a "holy shit moment" that confirmed to them that they were on to something big. And while Jeff was excited about the quality of technical talent applying, he also understood that this was about more than Census getting a few summer interns. Census was in the position to be the founding agency for this new Civic Digital Fellowship and help pave the way for the rest of the government.

The first group of Civic Digital Fellows didn't just show up for a fun summer in DC. They delivered groundbreaking work, including a new learning platform on how to use Census data (called Census Academy), a machine learning approach for the commodity flow survey, disclosure avoidance techniques to protect personally identifiable information for the 2020 Census, and more. But most impressive of all, the Civic Digital Fellows demonstrated that a sea change was underway in how government agencies should think about their talent pipeline.

The Civic Digital Fellows, unlike the technology industry, were diverse from the beginning. The initial group of interns at Census came from private and public universities across the country—and over 50 percent were from minority or underrepresented groups. A majority of the cohort (and of the four that have followed) was female. Much of Coding it Forward's continued diversity and representation came from having such a balanced first group. It became a visible commitment of the program and a reason why many people applied in later rounds.

The Harvard student entrepreneurs behind Coding it Forward— Neel, Athena, and Chris—seemed to understand momentum right out of the gate. They also understood instinctively how to tell the story of their program, and how to spread that message on social media, trade press, and simple one-page summaries—useful for potential funders and busy government executives alike. It didn't hurt that Neel, Athena, and Chris had developed and practiced exactly those skills in Nick's class.

By showing they could recruit, screen, and place technical talent, they immediately had credibility with agencies. They were in effect making their own jobs—and a larger movement.

While they might have started by looking for their own summer jobs, they very quickly realized they could create opportunities for many more people. According to Chris, "We saw an open door thanks to Nick, his class, and the network, and instead of just running through that door ourselves, we wanted to make sure we could hold that door open and bring as many other students along with us."

Choosing to become a nonprofit instead of a Harvard student club, Coding it Forward raised money from Chan Zuckerberg Initiative and Schmidt Futures, and has hired a full-time executive director in cofounder and Wellesley graduate Rachel Dodell. Part of the inaugural class of interns in 2017, Rachel quickly realized that the team could use help with branding, communications, and operations. While she was still in school that following year, she commuted from Wellesley to Harvard nearly every Saturday to work with the team.

Over the years, Nick proudly served as an advisor to the group and continued to introduce them to senior federal executives—sometimes less memorably! Bruce Greenstein, the chief technology officer of the US Department of Health and Human Services (HHS), admitted in a 2017 *FedScoop* interview: "I don't know how they ended up in my office, but I was blown away by the sophistication." He felt that the entire program—the cohort model, the mentorship, and thoughtful selection criteria—was "so well thought through" that it was obvious that HHS should participate, too.

Coding it Forward has increased their intern classes each year, growing to almost a hundred interns across ten federal agencies in 2021. Coding it Forward has also started placing interns in federal government agencies outside of Washington, DC, including Special Operations Command (SOCOM) in Tampa, and the Air Force's Kessel Run in Boston. Recognizing the need for early-career technical talent at all levels of government, Coding it Forward also launched the Civic Innovation Corps, a new program in 2021, placing fifty-five interns in three states and six cities across the country in its inaugural year.

More than four years later, Rachel is now leading Coding it Forward as a full-time employee, along with another former student of Nick's, Ariana Soto. Neel is a product manager at Google, and Athena went on to found a start-up called Dreambound to help low-income Americans get accelerated training and licenses for better-paying vocational jobs—like certified nursing assistants—creating a ladder of opportunity during the pandemic.

Chris also joined Coding it Forward full-time once he graduated from college but couldn't resist an opportunity to continue to hack the bureaucracy by creating yet another new organization to solve the problem at a different scale. With Nick's mentorship and help, and a fair amount of "making stone soup," Chris joined up with Caitlin Gandhi, a Teach for America executive, and the two of them joined the General Services Administration. Together, Chris and Caitlin took aim at the painful technology talent gap at the early career level within the federal government. At the time, only 3 percent of federal government technologists were under the age of thirty and only 26 percent were women. Despite increased visibility of the problem due to such startling metrics and the increasingly loud voices of civic technologists inside and outside government, there was yet to be a whole of government approach to address this challenge.

With the support of the General Services Administration, in the summer of 2021 Chris and Caitlin launched a brand-new two-year fellowship for early-career technologists called the US Digital Corps. Their first cohort of fellows started work in June 2022 at over ten different federal agencies. The US Digital Corps serves as a bridge between mission-oriented early career talent from a diversity of backgrounds and experiences, including those who may have participated in Coding it Forward's internships, and federal agencies in need of such talent but without the means to effectively recruit, matriculate, and develop that talent on their own. The US Digital Corps has plans to scale commensurate with the need, hoping to reach annual cohort sizes in the hundreds or even thousands over time.

Watching these students hack government to find a place—and just as importantly, a voice—for their generation of technical talent in public service has been inspirational. They have used many of the tactics in this book to create impressive momentum and impact, including being thoughtful about founding units that have greater growth potential by being located outside their existing organization.

HOW CAN I USE THIS?

» **Stand up a new unit where it can flourish, even if it's outside your current bureaucracy.** By choosing to create a non-profit outside of Harvard, instead of a student club on campus, Neel, Athena, and Chris had greater freedom and were able to scale beyond Harvard more easily. As you look to create a new group, division, or unit, find the place where it can best grow and succeed—which may be non-obvious or even outside your organization.

» **Leverage mentors.** Nick was excited to introduce Neel, Athena, and Chris—and later, Rachel and Ariana—to federal officials, because he believed in them and saw their passion for doing good. Find people that believe in you, and who will delight in opening doors.

STAY CALM AND CARRY ON

It's not a matter of if something is going to go sideways, it's a matter of when. If you can stay calm when you hear unpleasant news, or when a crisis comes out of nowhere, you'll build credibility and trust among your colleagues. Bureaucracy hacking requires grit and patience.

Don't freak out over problems, and people will come to you with problems. This probably applies to all aspects of life, but it's an important piece of getting things done in a bureaucracy, where backstabbing, gossip mills, and fear-mongering are common obstacles to stop change. If you lose your cool or give up at the first sign of trouble (whether real or perceived), you'll never reach the finish line—and people will remember your reaction and use this ploy to stop you again next time, too.

Making It Safe to Screw Up

David Koh learned the value of having a safe space to fail in his first days as a software engineer at matchmaking website OkCupid. Fresh out of college and in his first job, he sent out a routine marketing email to users letting them know they had a potential match, including a link to their match's profile. But he mistakenly created a link that logged the email recipient in *as their match*—a huge security breach. Worried for his job, he watched helplessly as his more experienced colleagues fixed his error (miraculously, before a single person did anything malicious).

But instead of letting him go, the company kept him on and helped him learn how to not make that same mistake again. He went on to become OkCupid's director of engineering, maintaining this no-blame, let's-fix-it culture.

When David later joined the federal government, working in the US Department of Health and Human Services on the Medicare Quality Payment Program (QPP) for doctors, he was surprised to find that possible security issues usually went unreported. It was routinely up to him and his colleagues (who were temporarily assigned to the project, and not on the permanent core team) to identify and resolve issues, some of which were quite severe. It seemed that staff was so afraid of negative consequences they didn't even try looking for bugs or security flaws.

Wanting to change this behavior, David called an all-hands meeting to share his OkCupid blunder story. He announced that he not only wanted, but expected, everyone on the team to report issues. If someone reported an issue, he promised they wouldn't get in trouble. Each time someone did raise a flag, he visibly praised them and rolled up his sleeves to help solve the issue—no blame, no disciplinary action. By the time David left, one of his coworkers told him at a happy hour that the team now had "an almost unreasonably supportive culture," unlike any team he had ever worked on before.

Someone Will Always Be Unhappy

You probably have specific ways you want to change your bureaucracy: to better serve others, to improve customer service, to create a new service, or to improve an existing product. But your goal should *not* be to make everybody happy. If you've followed our advice in earlier chapters, your stakeholder map and conversations with people across the organization should have given you a good idea of who will be upset, and why, if you're successful with your mission. Tactics like building your karass (your informal network) can provide emotional support for the journey, and strategies like stabbing detractors in the chest (being up front with those you disagree with) can help to soften the impact on those you know will dissent.

Not only will someone else surely be unhappy with your goals, or at least the specific ways you plan to achieve your goals, but you'll also sometimes be faced with unhappy people because you aren't supporting *their* goals in the way they want. Newt Gingrich once tried to get Marina fired, proclaiming in an email to the VA secretary that she had a "not invented here attitude" when she didn't support his plan for helping homeless veterans. Suspecting the idea—which involved using cell phones to track the locations of veterans experiencing homelessness, and only renewing their cell service if they answered a lengthy survey once a day—would not work, but willing to approach it with an open mind, she proposed first starting with an inexpensive pilot using disposable cell phones and a free website form. This was not the multimillion-dollar grant Newt's project was looking for. Marina still sleeps fine at night.

You need to prepare for the reality that not everyone will be pleased with your accomplishments, and not derail your own success in order to try to please these people.

This advice is *not* to be mean or a jerk. And of course, we encourage you to take responsibility for unforeseen negative consequences, and remedy them when you can.

How to Keep Calm and Carry On

Changing a bureaucracy is *hard*. Marina was burned out like crispy toast by the time her tenure at the VA ended. Three things helped her to keep going:

1. Her North Star plan, which she kept on her desk.

2. A front and center reminder of why she was there. In her case, this was a photo of a recently widowed military spouse sitting on her husband's grave at Arlington Cemetery, holding their newborn son. When she wanted to give up and go home, Marina would remind herself that it was *her* job to make sure that baby boy got every last possible benefit that his father earned—the bureaucracy be damned.

3. A quote from the CEO of GoDaddy, Bob Parsons. Bob recounted that when he was founding his first company, he was afraid of failure. His father retorted, "Well, Robert, if it doesn't work, they can't eat you." When Marina was anxious or fearful about taking a next step, she'd ask herself: "Well,

can they eat me?" It may *feel* like Congress or your board of directors can eat you alive, but unless you're hacking a zoo or wildlife preserve, you're probably safe.

There is also a useful concept that applies here called ring theory that we borrow from caring for someone with a serious illness. In the center of the ring is the patient; the first ring around them is their immediate family; the next outer ring is extended family; then close friends; and so on. Your job is to locate yourself in the rings and share your negative feelings *out*, not in. If your sister-in-law has cancer, you **do not** go crying with your fears that she is going to die *to her*, or *to her husband or children*. You only do that to people *outside* your ring, such as to a friend or a work colleague.

Similarly, if you're fearful that your project isn't going to work out, you *don't* talk about that at a team meeting with your direct reports. You *could* get support from a trusted peer in another department, your own manager, or a personal friend.

This advice is designed to help you regulate your emotions to stay calm enough to be a trusted, rational team player. We are *absolutely not* saying that your team shouldn't discuss real risks or how to mitigate them; that you can't share disappointing data; or that you should otherwise hide relevant project information from your team. But sometimes you need a friend or a counselor to share your fears with, and that can't be the same team you are leading.

Don't Read the Comments

You rightly want to get feedback from everyone who may be impacted by your proposed changes: colleagues, current users, potential customers, trusted advisors, etc. But don't confuse this with having to listen to the whole world, or, more specifically, listening to internet trolls. If there's a blog post or news article written about your idea, resist the urge to read the comments. (We know—it's hard.) If you get anonymous feedback via email or Twitter, give yourself permission to ignore or delete the negativity.

HOW CAN I USE THIS?

» **Rehearse staying calm in the face of bad news or harsh criticism.** Imagine some possible bad news related to your project: a key team member leaves, you're going to miss a deadline, your direct report complains about your management style, or there's a bug in production. Now practice calmly responding and fixing it.

» **Make a safe space for people to surface problems.** Demonstrate that you won't fly off the handle or punish people for coming to you with bad news, and more people will come to you with bad news—information you *absolutely* need for your project to be successful. This is unusual enough in a bureaucracy that it can pay dividends.

» **Consider if you are too focused on other people's happiness.** Were you tempted to change your proposal slides just to not upset Susan in the front office? Are you leaving out key information because it could hurt someone's feelings? Weigh these choices carefully against the goals you're trying to achieve.

» **Develop your own motivation arsenal.** This might be a future press release you developed from the chapter "Think of the End at the Beginning," a photo of an end user, or an inspirational quotation (or all three). Make these easy to see, such as on your office wall or on your computer desktop.

» **Reassure in, complain out.** Before you vent to someone, consider: are they inside or outside my rings? If they report to you, or are on a voting committee, then choose another audience.

» **Don't read the comments.** Just don't.

LEAVE YOUR BUREAUCRACY
BETTER OFF

Don't stop when you're tired, stop
when you're done.

—MARILYN MONROE

---

*Consider how your changes will persevere after you
leave the organization, and what you can put in
place now to make lasting change after you're gone.*

They Will Wait You Out

Your changes are not guaranteed to last. The longer someone has been at your organization, the more times they've seen people try, and fail, to make change stick. They've also seen plenty of people fail to make any change in the first place. We too have seen the bureaucracy regress. In fact, we've seen people wait as long as a decade or more, only to swoop in and undo things the moment a change-maker turned their attention elsewhere.

You can complain about this, or you can acknowledge it as reality from the start, and plan accordingly. You do not have to stay at your job forever in order to ensure your changes endure. Rather, you have to make the structural changes to make them permanent, and recruit enough champions and allies to continue the fight after you're gone.

Keeping Your Changes from Falling Apart

Many of the tactics we lay out in this book are designed with resilience in mind: when you use the bureaucracy's own incentives and policies to institute your change, it's that much harder to undo. This is a big part of why we don't endorse quick fixes, duct tape, or temporary waivers: they're too easy to dismantle. Our approach will help you create systems that outlast leadership changes.

As you start to think about leaving, you should carefully consider how others could slow or stop your progress once you're gone. This is not always obvious, which is why we encourage thinking about it from day one. Some things to consider include:

- Who will replace you? Have you groomed a number two? Can you influence the hiring committee or criteria? Does your job description accurately reflect the responsibilities and experience needed to carry out your mission?

- Can your team function without you? A few months before she left the VA, Marina's team added a new target to its goals list: "The team can function without Marina anymore." (As a political appointee, Marina's job was always going to end on the last day of the Obama administration; you may not have this much notice.) Every week, they checked in on progress against this goal. For her last two months, she stopped going to team meetings and stopped responding to project-related emails. This helped identify any remaining spots where she was still a single point of failure, *before* she left. (You can also practice this before you actually leave, by taking time off.)

Knowing When It's Time to Leave

Everyone contemplates leaving from time to time, whether you've achieved outsized successes (but still want more) or you still haven't found traction.

If you have had success, do your future self a favor and, as early as possible, write down your current ambitions. As time goes on, return and review your progress against this list. Marina did this with the "21st Century VA" vision document she published in her first year as a senior executive (which you can see on our website, in case it sparks ideas for you). Years later, on the eve of her departure, she had many new goals—but realizing she had accomplished almost all of her initial ones gave her a lot of peace in leaving for her next adventure.

As for knowing when to "give up," we have a simple question when people call us for advice on whether it's time to leave an organization where they haven't yet accomplished their goals: "Do you see any more doors?" If you still have another operating theory for how you can succeed, and you have the energy: stay and try it. If not: it's okay to move on.

Sometimes leaving can help *further* your goals. In 2018, the CEO of Taco Bell, Brian Niccol, read an article about competitor Chipotle's *E. coli* and salmonella outbreak crises. Niccol had been wanting to expand more into sustainable fast food practices and saw this as an opportunity. He reached out to Chipotle and soon became *their* CEO.

While becoming CEO of a competitor might be an extreme jump, perhaps you're a consultant who sees a gap you could fill at the company you're advising; a nonprofit employee who sees the chance to fill a social impact role at a corporate donor; or an academic who sees a chance to drive change in a commercial company you've been studying. Many solutions require advocates in multiple spots: someone in the organization, in an outside nonprofit, at another school or university, at a standards or legislative body, et cetera. In the course of building your karass and breaking down a monumental problem into bite-sized pieces, you may identify another role that's a missing piece of the puzzle—and one that *you* may be well-situated to take on.

Jim Fruchterman took this approach when he sought to expand his new invention, a machine that would read to people with visual impairments. Proudly, he showed it off to the venture capital board of his for-profit tech company, sharing that it could drive as much as $1 million in revenue per year.

The board scoffed—any new invention had to bring in *at least* $100 million for them to agree to it. So Jim, wanting this machine out in the world, left his cushy job and founded a nonprofit to manufacture the machines. He initially assumed he'd recruit a bunch of engineers like himself to volunteer to distribute the machines, until some of his early users told him that there were a lot of talented people with visual impairments who couldn't get hired at traditional firms. Jim set up an independent dealer network under his nonprofit, hiring mostly blind people as sales agents. Three years later, sales exceeded $5 million per year—still not enough to incentivize his former bosses, but plenty to keep the nonprofit going. After ten years, he sold the reading machine business to a for-profit company, which is still manufacturing them twenty years later.

HOW CAN I USE THIS?

» **Write down your list of goals.** Over time, go back and read your list. Have you made progress against them? Have you since moved on to new goals? This list can help keep your progress in perspective—after all, nobody can fix every last thing.

» **Map out where your project's success relies upon key players.** It might be best if you stay put, or success may call for you to switch to a different department or even an entirely different bureaucracy.

» **Ask yourself: "Do I see another doorway to success?"** Bureaucracy hacking is not synonymous with smashing your head against a steel wall. It's possible there may not be a pathway right now, and if so, it's definitely time to focus elsewhere.

» **Consider ways to bolster the resilience of your changes.** Can you influence who succeeds you? Sign a longer contract with a trusted vendor? Build a strong enough karass that it will continue to support your project long after you're gone?

» **Say thank you.** Colleagues, stakeholders, and other allies had a vested interest in your success. A thank you note as you depart can go a long way in reminding others to keep up the fight.

» **Think about any unique opportunities you have by leaving.** Is there something productive you can now safely say or do that you couldn't before?

» **Take time off.** Even a one-week vacation where you are *truly* disconnected can help reveal areas where you need more coverage. If you are the only one who can do something, your change is not sustainable.

CONCLUSION

President Obama, when asked about a philosophy of getting things done, said it can be boiled down to two things: being kind and working hard. We mostly agree.

Hacking your bureaucracy does require kindness—including respect, appreciation, and candor. You'll build stronger relationships based on mutual understanding, trust, and reciprocity—and be able to get more done at greater scale—if you are a compassionate human.

Working hard is also key to bureaucracy hacking. The tactics in this book aren't rocket science—but they do take work. Whether it's getting out of the office and talking to real people, making it easier for the other person, or picking up the pen, you have to do the work. You have to sweat the small stuff.

But being kind and working hard, while important, isn't going to be enough to make change in organizations that are *designed* to resist change. You need to also have intentionality about making change in a bureaucracy, of any type. That's why we wrote this playbook—spanning problem definition, understanding your org, pitching, experimentation, team building, and scaling. We learned a number of these plays the hard way.

Navy SEALs like to advise trainees to "embrace the suck"—meaning that you should lean into the unpleasant stuff and get comfortable with the uncomfortable. We're confident that your work experience, or the organization you are trying to navigate, is not as hard as Navy SEALs training. But we still think it is a good idea: embrace what lies ahead.

Embrace the bureaucracy as you seek to maneuver through it to get things done. Embrace the people, the mission, the culture—and the rules!—as you seek to improve on them, reform them, and even radically change them. Embrace the continuity while you seek to disrupt it.

We hope the stories and tactics in this book are helpful in your professional or personal life. Let us know how they work for you (at our website: HackYourBureaucracy.com). Good luck!

APPENDIX:
LIST OF TACTICS

Define the Problem

1. **Talk to Real People.** Get out of your office to observe and listen to prospective, current, and former users—ideally in their natural environments. Ground your ideas for change in their real-life experiences.

2. **Be Your Own Customer.** Experience your organization's product or service the way customers or constituents do. You'll uncover customer service gaps, confusing instructions, and opportunities for new products, services, or features.

3. **Look Between the Silos.** The Achilles' heel of an organization is the space between the silos—i.e., between business units, academic departments, or government agencies—where broken handoffs or miscommunications can lead to poor customer experiences or wasteful repetition. Few people are paying attention or defending the status quo in these gray areas, making them ripe for quicker and more well-received changes.

4. **Play the Newbie Card.** Use your newness in an organization or a role to your advantage. Don't be afraid to ask questions about how things work in your institution, which can uncover significant opportunities that your longer-tenured colleagues can't see.

5. **Remember Employee Needs.** Spend time in the field shadowing frontline employees to gather insights about what's really working—and what isn't. Prioritize improving internal processes just as you would end user improvements; use those internal improvements to gain buy-in for other changes you need employees to make that benefit external users.

6. **Beware of Red Teams and Problem Lists.** Avoid the temptation to make and share a laundry list of problems. You might gain some short-term attention for your insights, but you'll alienate too many people in the process. Worse, if you incorrectly characterize a problem, you might find yourself on the hook for having to solve it. Instead, focus your efforts on creating and testing solutions to problems.

Learn Your Org

1. **Figure Out the Real Org Chart.** Relationships, knowledge, and power aren't captured by traditional org charts. Making your own map of who knows what, who controls what resources, and who is in cahoots with whom can help you strategically map out who to include, in what order, on your schemes.

2. **Understand Incentives and Risks.** Everyone in your organization operates within a framework of incentives and risks. If you want a coworker to do something differently, you need to understand what's stopping them from making that change today. Where possible, change their incentives to make doing what you want them to do the lowest-risk, highest-reward path.

3. **Know the Consequences.** Know the consequences for breaking rules or not following existing processes. On one extreme is breaking the law and facing fines or imprisonment; on the other hand, if the worst that can happen is that you don't meet a performance goal next quarter, it might be a risk you're willing and able to take.

4. **Understand Why.** Getting to the root reason behind a particular practice is often the key to changing it. It's possible the original rule, policy, or law gives you much more flexibility than people think—and sometimes that original reason may not even apply anymore! Asking *why* repeatedly and tying current practices back to specific reasons makes it clear what needs to change, and what may not need to change at all.

5. **Try the Normal Way First.** Before declaring that a process is broken and looking for ways around it, try it first. Your first-hand experience will help you gather real data about why and where the process isn't working. Armed with the nuances of what a truly effective new process could look like, you'll have more credibility to convince others that you can design a new way of doing things.

6. **Relax Fixed Constraints.** In a bureaucracy, it's easy to see the status quo as unmovable, akin to laws of physics, rather than just the result of human inaction. Question assumptions about which constraints are really fixed, and see if you can develop a sense of shared agency with others.

7. **Beware the Obvious Answer.** When it comes to long-standing problems in large organizations, solutions can appear obvious, especially to outsiders or newcomers. But it's rarely that simple.

Pitch the Solution

1. **Write a One-Pager.** Talk is cheap. Write down your idea on a single page to clarify your thinking and message.

2. **Think of the End at the Beginning.** Be specific about what the future you envision looks like by doing things like writing the launch press release or mocking up potential media coverage. Use this future state vision to drive your day-to-day planning.

3. **Set Your North Star.** A compelling vision of the future that is both inspiring and broadly accessible makes it easier to get others across your organization to join forces with you. That vision, when written down and widely shared, can inspire and drive change in your bureaucracy.

4. **Use the Power of Visual Design.** Make your ideas stand out with written proposals printed on heavy stock, professional-looking presentations, and visually compelling prototypes. Even the most formal of reports can benefit from professional design elements.

5. **Consult a Thesaurus.** In your organization, specific words have connotations based on years of history. Choose your words carefully to find the ones that maximize what you're trying to accomplish while minimizing baggage.

6. **Show the Hard Numbers.** Showing real numbers that contrast with the way most people in a bureaucracy currently perceive reality—especially data that they have not seen before—can be a powerful catalyst for change.

7. **Tailor Your Pitch.** Align your idea with your organization's strategy, goals, and priorities. Reframe your messages in the context of what your audiences and organization care about most.

8. **Do the Work Outside the Meeting.** Do the hard work before and after a meeting to make sure that nothing unscripted or spontaneous happens. This work includes sharing materials ahead of time, having one-on-one conversations with key participants, and prepping allies with helpful talking points and questions to ask.

9. **Sell, Baby, Sell.** Gaining buy-in and resources for your idea is ultimately a sales job. Recognizing this, and learning the fine art of enterprise sales, can help your bureaucracy hacking gain traction.

Start Small and Build Momentum

1. **Find Your Paperclip.** No matter where you sit in a bureaucracy, it can feel like you don't have enough resources under your control to accomplish your goals. You might be surprised at what you can accomplish when you trade with others for what you need.

2. **Act "As If."** Bring your idea to life by acting as if it's already reality, even if it's not quite there yet.

3. **Delivery Is the Strategy.** Plans and pitches can be effective bureaucracy-hacking tactics—but if you really want to drive progress toward your goals, start delivering on those plans. Even a seemingly small project, like improving a tracking spreadsheet for an internal team, can put you years ahead of where you'd be if you spend all your energy describing what you're going to do one day.

4. **Go Second.** The more established the bureaucracy, the less likely it wants to be the first one to try a new process or adopt a new technique. Going first is often seen as risky and prone to errors or failure. Find or create precedents to make it seem like your organization is going second to create powerful peer pressure while mitigating risk.

5. **Give Real Demos.** Once a decision maker interacts with a real working demo or prototype, you've changed the bar for the game—subsequent presentations with smoke and mirrors won't cut it. When you provide real, interactive demonstrations of your future vision, you make it that much harder for your competitors to win out.

6. **Pilot Is the Password.** Show a prototype of your idea and get feedback from the actual customers or the people impacted, in order to convince your organization to explore it further.

7. **Define Metrics Up Front.** Get skeptics to agree to indicators of success ahead of time for your experiments, pilots, and proofs of concept. Also agree up front to failure criteria to make others comfortable with giving you a chance to try. Whenever possible, transparently show everyone how you are performing against those metrics.

8. **Sweat the Small Stuff.** Detractors will get you in the details. Get as much feedback as you can, as early as you can, about what specifics you need to consider. Even seemingly insignificant things, like having the corporate legal notice in a page footer of a website or white paper, can help stakeholders feel seen and heard, and therefore more willing to show their support.

9. **Make the Bureaucracy Work for You.** Most organizations have more existing resources and flexibility than you might think—learn how to take advantage of them.

10. **Strangle the Mainframe.** Attack an overwhelmingly large problem with smaller wins that let you tackle it in bite-sized, manageable pieces—often without the bureaucracy even realizing it should mount a defense.

Build Your Team

1. **Cultivate the Karass.** You can't go it alone. Find and grow your karass—your informal group of people who want to get stuff done together. Armed with an understanding of which "guild" you belong to, build bridges with those who share your vision—especially those who have attempted your idea before and failed.

2. **Give Credit Liberally.** Give credit to others—authentically, generously, and publicly. You'll generate goodwill and trust by recognizing their contributions. Welcome when others take credit for your initiative, because it means you'll have more champions and allies in the long term.

3. **Find the Doers.** Find the people who can actually do the work, and pair up with them.

4. **Make It Easy for the Other Person.** Help other people help you by making it as easy as possible for them to do what you need.

5. **Don't be a Tourist.** Find a way to help or get out of the way.

6. **Make Your Job.** Bureaucracies are mostly filled with people hired to satisfy a specific, and sometimes outdated, job description. With some creativity and entrepreneurial spirit, you can create a new role that better leverages your specific skills and passions.

7. **Create People Flow.** Add people to your project through fellowships, internships, in-residence programs, and other temporary, nontraditional, and part-time mechanisms. New talent, paired with experienced teams and mentors, can create breakthrough momentum for your project—and just might make an even larger impact over time.

8. **Give People a Choice, and a Chance.** You won't win everyone over to your way of thinking, but you may win over some by giving them an honest chance to join you. For example, if you are trying to convert to a new technology system, the current team needs a genuine opportunity to learn the new application and be part of the roll-out.

9. **Stab People in the Chest.** Be open and honest with your detractors about where and how you disagree. This builds a unique sort of trust, where, despite your difference of opinion, your colleagues will gain confidence that you won't blindside them down the line.

Make It Stick

1. **Use the Bureaucracy Against Itself.** Use the routine practices of your organization—like committees, approvals, and reviews—to formalize your changes within the bureaucracy's current ways of doing business.

2. **Pick Up the Pen.** Large organizations depend on written rules, processes, and plans. Find opportunities to help those who are writing down the rules. Where possible, volunteer to write the rules yourself for long-term influence.

3. **Use Leadership Changes to Your Advantage.** Changes in leadership bring new opportunities to gain a champion. Shape an incoming leader's agenda by talking with them directly and influencing what they learn early in their tenure. Even if they have a long history with your organization, once in a new role, a leader is less likely to see constraints as truly fixed and more likely to be open to bold ideas.

4. **Always Be Ready for Five Minutes with the Head Honcho.** You never know when you are going to run into your big boss or another important stakeholder outside your chain of command. Having a few talking points prepared will serve you well in a chance encounter.

5. **Don't Waste a Crisis.** Bureaucracies are more receptive to change during times of crisis, especially if your idea is related to fixing or recovering from the problem at hand. Being prepared with a one-pager—or even a full plan that's ready to go—will best position you to take advantage of an unexpected opening.

6. **Leverage the Big Bosses.** Large organizations are hierarchical, with a lot of focus on what the big boss thinks, says, and does. Use this to your advantage and find ways to gain attention and air cover from your higher-ups.

7. **Work from the Outside In.** Leverage external stakeholders who can provide outside support for your initiative, or even own part of the solution.

8. **Get Public Commitments.** Get your organization to publicly commit to specific actions—and find ways to leverage that commitment to generate momentum for your initiative. If your organization also has the power to convene and celebrate other groups, ask others to make public commitments on shared goals that you can unveil and collaborate on together.

9. **Pay the Box Guy.** Honor the promises you make to people— or they may be the one to take your entire project down.

10. **Pick Your Battles.** You need a clear understanding of what you can compromise on, and what you can't, to achieve your objectives. Consider the extent of the disagreement and the players involved to help figure out whether you should give in or fight back over a particular detail.

11. **Don't Try to Make the Bureaucracy Care.** Bureaucracies, unlike the people that inhabit them, don't have feelings. You cannot persuade your bureaucracy to change through emotional arguments. Instead, understand exactly the criteria that are going to be used to make a decision—and meet them.

12. **Play the Long Game.** Your bureaucracy isn't going anywhere, and no change is going to happen overnight. Expecting that your entire project or initiative will be adopted quickly and at scale is unrealistic. If you have your endgame in mind, you can make strategic chess moves that get you closer and closer to that goal, one bureaucracy hack at a time.

13. **Create a New Org.** Consider whether your idea might flourish faster somewhere beyond your home bureaucracy.

14. **Stay Calm and Carry On.** It's not a matter of if something is going to go sideways, it's a matter of when. If you can stay calm when you hear unpleasant news, or when a crisis comes out of nowhere, you'll build credibility and trust among your colleagues. Bureaucracy hacking requires grit and patience.

15. **Leave Your Bureaucracy Better Off.** Consider how your changes will persevere after you leave the organization, and what you can put in place now to make lasting change after you're gone.

SOURCES

The firsthand stories in this book, with Marina and Nick as protagonists, are to their best recollections, validated by friends and colleagues who were present. The other stories in the book are from either public sources or from friends and colleagues who provided quotes and reviewed the chapter or section. While we are careful to not disclose any confidential information, many of the stories came from places we work, advise, or consult.

Introduction

Davis, Lynda, Laura Prietula, and Charles Worthington. *Veterans Experience with VA.gov FY 2020, Q4 Update*. US Department of Veterans Affairs. Accessed January 30, 2022. https://trumpadministration.archives.perfor mance.gov/veterans_affairs/FY2021_january_Veteran%E2%80%99s _Experience_with_VA_dot_gov.pdf.

Merriam-Webster Dictionary. S.v. "hack." Accessed December 11, 2021. https:// www.merriam-webster.com/dictionary/hack.

Office of Strategic Services. *Simple Sabotage Field Manual*. No. 3. Washington, DC: Office of Strategic Services, 1944. https://www.hsdl.org /?abstract&did=750070.

A Bureaucratic Note

Downs, Anthony. *Inside Bureaucracy: A Rand Corporation Research Study*. Boston: Little, Brown, and Company, 1967.

Edmondson, Amy C., and Ranjay Gulati. "Agility Hacks." *Harvard Business Review*, November–December 2021. https://hbr.org/2021/11/agility-hacks.

Rockman, Bert. *Britannica*. S.v. "bureaucracy." Last modified July 4, 2021. https://www.britannica.com/topic/bureaucracy.

Talk to Real People

Pérez-Peña, Richard. "Scorecard for Colleges Needs Work, Experts Say." *New York Times*, February 13, 2013. https://www.nytimes.com/2013/02/14/education/obamas-college-scorecard-needs-works-experts-say.html.

Stewart, James B. "How Much Graduates Earn Drives More College Rankings." *New York Times*, October 20, 2016. https://www.nytimes.com/2016/10/21/business/how-much-graduates-earn-drives-more-college-rankings.html.

Be Your Own Customer

Meyer, Harris. "Collaborative Efforts Can Save Money and Improve Care." *KHN*. Kaiser Family Foundation. January 5, 2012. https://khn.org/news/collaborative-efforts-can-save-money-and-improve-care/.

"Test with the minister." In "Digital Service Standard (pre-July 2019)." *GOV. UK Service Manual*. June 30, 2019. https://www.gov.uk/service-manual/service-assessments/pre-july-2019-digital-service-standard#test-with-the-minister-1.

Remember Employee Needs

Hudson, Sara, and Hana Schank. *The Government Fix: How to Innovate in Government*. Self-published, 2019.

Lopez, Steve. "A Veteran of Fighting Bureaucracy Tries to Tame L.A.'s Red Tape." *Los Angeles Times*, August 23, 2014. https://www.latimes.com/local/la-me-0824-lopez-stone-20140824-column.html.

Beware of Red Teams and Problem Lists

Ibsen, Henrik. *An Enemy of the People*. New York: Charles Scribner's Sons, 1915.

Understand Incentives and Risks

"#127 The Crime Machine, Part I." Produced by Gimlet. *Reply All*. October 12, 2018. Podcast, MP3 audio. https://gimletmedia.com/shows/reply-all/o2hx34.

"#128 The Crime Machine, Part II." Produced by Gimlet. *Reply All*. October 12, 2018. Podcast, MP3 audio. https://gimletmedia.com/shows/reply-all/n8hwl7.

Committee on Education and Labor US House of Representatives. *Hidden Tragedy: Underreporting of Workplace Injuries and Illnesses*. Washington, DC: US House of Representatives, 2008. https://www.bls.gov/iif/laborcomm report061908.pdf.

Hartley, Dale. "The Cobra Effect: No Loophole Goes Unexploited." *Psychology Today* (blog), October 14, 2020. https://www.psychologytoday.com /us/blog/machiavellians-gulling-the-rubes/202010/the-cobra-effect-no -loophole-goes-unexploited.

Know the Consequences

"5 CFR § 1320.3: Definitions." *Code of Federal Regulations*, title 5 (2013), https://www.law.cornell.edu/cfr/text/5/1320.3.

"Understand what people need." In "Digital Services Playbook." *U.S. Digital Service*. https://playbook.cio.gov/#play1.

Understand Why

"Life's Like That." *Reader's Digest Canada*, February 2001: 192.

Prasad, Vinayak K. *Malignant: How Bad Policy and Bad Evidence Harm People with Cancer*. Baltimore: Johns Hopkins University Press, 2020.

Roberts, Russ, and Vinay Prasad. "Vinay Prasad on Cancer Drugs, Medical Ethics, and Malignant." Produced by EconLib. *EconTalk*. February 6, 2020. Podcast, MP3 audio. https://www.econtalk.org/vinay-prasad -on-cancer-drugs-medical-ethics-and-malignant/.

Try the Normal Way First

Amann, Denise. "An Introduction to Mobile Slaughter Units." *U.S. Department of Agriculture* (blog), February 21, 2017. https://www.usda.gov/media /blog/2010/08/30/introduction-mobile-slaughter-units.

Relax Fixed Constraints

Cowen, Tyler. "The High-Return Activity of Raising Others' Aspirations." https://marginalrevolution.com/marginalrevolution/2018/10/high-return -activity-raising-others-aspirations.html.

Heil, Emily. "Furloughed White House Staffer Turns Bartender" *Washington Post*, October 3, 2013. https://www.washingtonpost.com/blogs/in-the-loop /wp/2013/10/03/furloughed-white-house-staffer-turns-bartender/.

Kalil, Tom. https://www.youtube.com/watch?v=MJkhH83Bw4A (emphasis ours).

Universal Service Administrative Company (USAC) Open Data, FCC Form 471 Application Data from the FCC's Schools and Libraries Program ("E-rate"), Funding Year 2020.

Beware the Obvious Answer

Explain xkcd. S.v. "1831: Here to Help." Last edited December 11, 2021. https://www.explainxkcd.com/wiki/index.php/1831:_Here_to_Help.

Richardson, Yolanda, and Jennifer Pahlka. *Employment Development Department Strike Team Detailed Assessment and Recommendations*. September 16, 2020. https://www.govops.ca.gov/wp-content/uploads/sites/11/2020/09/Assessment.pdf.

Write a One-Pager

Homans, John. "Reading Roone's." *New York*. Vox Media. April 30, 2003. https://nymag.com/nymetro/arts/books/reviews/n_8682/.

Think of the End at the Beginning

Bryar, Colin, and Bill Carr. *Working Backwards: Insights, Stories, and Secrets from Inside Amazon*. New York: St. Martin's Press, 2021.

Use the Power of Visual Design

Bargas-Avila, Javier. "Users Love Simple and Familiar Designs—Why Websites Need to Make a Great First Impression." *Google AI Blog* (blog), August 29, 2012. https://ai.googleblog.com/2012/08/users-love-simple-and-familiar-designs.html.

Kahneman, Daniel. *Thinking, Fast and Slow*. New York: Farrar, Straus and Giroux, 2011.

Consult a Thesaurus

Dekker, Sidney. *The Field Guide to Understanding 'Human Error.'* Boca Raton: CRC Press, 2014.

Heath, Chip, and Dan Heath. *Made to Stick: Why Some Ideas Survive and Others Die*. New York: Random House, 2007.

Ries, Eric. *The Startup Way: How Modern Companies Use Entrepreneurial Management to Transform Culture and Drive Long-Term Growth*. New York: Currency, 2017.

Show the Hard Numbers

Haden, Jeff. "How Does a Company Worth Over $1 Trillion Teach Its Employees to Communicate? 5 Ways to Write Like Amazon" *Inc.*, April 14, 2021. https://www.inc.com/jeff-haden/how-does-a-company-worth-over-1 -trillion-teach-its-employees-to-communicate-5-ways-to-write-like-amazon .html.

Do the Work Outside the Meeting

McCoy, Kevin. "'Condo Wars': Surfside Association Fighting in Florida Was Extreme, But It's a Familiar Battle for HOAs." *USA Today*, July 11, 2021. https://www.usatoday.com/story/news/2021/07/10/surfside-condo -building-collapse-associations-fights-plans/7840468002/.

Sell, Baby, Sell

Pink, Daniel. *To Sell Is Human: The Surprising Truth About Moving Others.* New York: Riverhead Books, 2012.

Act "As If"

Docket No. DE 19-197: Development of a Statewide, Multi-use Online Energy Data Platform, Before the New Hampshire Public Utilities Commission. 116th Cong. 2d (2020). Statement of Michael Murray, President of Mission:data Coalition.
Wikipedia. S.v. "Stone Soup." Last edited December 12, 2021. https://en.wiki pedia.org/wiki/Stone_Soup.

Delivery Is the Strategy

Behavioural Insights Team. *Annual Report 2017–18.* London: Behavioural Insights Team, 2018. https://www.bi.team/wp-content/uploads/2019/01 /Annual-update-report-BIT-2017-2018.pdf.
Hargreaves, Steve. "One Sentence Can Make You Pay All Your Taxes." *CNN Business*, May 29, 2015. https://money.cnn.com/2015/05/29/news /economy/bloomberg-taxes.
Hudson, Sara, and Hana Schank. *The Government Fix: How to Innovate in Government.* Self-published, 2019.

Pilot Is the Password

Thomke, Stefan H. *Experimentation Works: The Surprising Power of Business Experiments*. Boston: Harvard Business Review Press, 2020.
Wallace, Mark, "The U.S. Air Force Learned to Code—and Saved the Pentagon Millions." *Fast Company*, July 5, 2018. https://www.fastcompany .com/40588729/the-air-force-learned-to-code-and-saved-the-pentagon -millions.

Sweat the Small Stuff

Gawande, Atul. "The Checklist." *New Yorker*, December 10, 2007. https://www .newyorker.com/magazine/2007/12/10/the-checklist.
Horton, Alex. "A Court Official Failed to Click a Box—and a Witness Paid with His Life." *The Washington Post*, February 22, 2019. https://www .washingtonpost.com/nation/2019/02/22/court-official-failed-click-box -witness-paid-with-his-life.

Make the Bureaucracy Work for You

Pavuluri, Rohan. "An App That Empowers People to Solve Their Legal Problems." TED video, May 2021. https://www.ted.com/talks/rohan_pavuluri_an_app _that_empowers_people_to_solve_their_legal_problems?language=en.

Strangle the Mainframe

Richardson, Yolanda, and Jennifer Pahlka. *Employment Development Department Strike Team Detailed Assessment and Recommendations*. September 16, 2020. https://www.govops.ca.gov/wp-content/uploads/sites/11/2020/09/Assess ment.pdf.
Rowling, J. K. *Harry Potter and the Deathly Hallows*. New York: Arthur A. Levine Books, 2007.
Virgil. *Aeneid*. Oxford: Clarendon, 1918.

Find the Doers

Kalil, Thomas. "Policy Entrepreneurship at the White House: Getting Things Done in Large Organizations." *Innovations: Technology, Governance, Globalization* 11, no. 3–4 (2017): 4–21. https://doi.org/10.1162/inov_a_00253.

Make It Easy for the Other Person

Clear, James. *Atomic Habits: An Easy & Proven Way to Build Good Habits & Break Bad Ones*. New York: Avery, 2018.

Create People Flow

"Meet the Presidential Innovation Fellows." The Obama White House. *Medium*, August 17, 2015. https://medium.com/@ObamaWhiteHouse/meet -the-presidential-innovation-fellows-194dec20442b.

Weiss, Mitchell B., Nick Sinai, and Michael Norris. *U.S. Digital Service*. Boston: Harvard Business School, 2016.

Use Leadership Changes to Your Advantage

Downs, Anthony. *Inside Bureaucracy: A Rand Corporation Research Study*. Boston: Little, Brown, and Company, 1967.

Don't Waste a Crisis

Miller, Ron. "How AWS Came to Be." *TechCrunch*, July 2, 2016. https://tech crunch.com/2016/07/02/andy-jassys-brief-history-of-the-genesis-of-aws/.

Tepperman, Jonathan. *The Fix: How Countries Use Crises to Solve the World's Worst Problems*. New York: Tim Duggan Books, 2016.

Work from the Outside In

Electric Consumer Right to Know Act. H.R.4860. 111th Congress (2009–2010).

Get Public Commitments

Kalil, Thomas. "Policy Entrepreneurship at the White House: Getting Things Done in Large Organizations." *Innovations: Technology, Governance, Globalization* 11, no. 3–4 (2017): 4–21. https://doi.org/10.1162/inov_a_00253.

Play the Long Game

Gonnerman, Jennifer. "Larry Krasner's Campaign to End Mass Incarceration." *New Yorker*, October 22, 2018. https://www.newyorker.com/magazine /2018/10/29/larry-krasners-campaign-to-end-mass-incarceration.

Hurdle, Jon, and Jonah E. Bromwich. "Victory in Philadelphia Buoys Supporters of Progressive District Attorney." *New York Times*, May 20, 2021. https://www.nytimes.com/2021/05/19/us/krasner-vega-philadelphia.html.

Smith, Jamil. "'Progressive Prosecutors' Are Working Within the System to Change It. How Is That Going?" *Vox*, July 30, 2021. https://www.vox.com/2021/7/30/22600669/larry-krasner-philadelphia-reform-prosecutors-crime.

Create a New Org

Mehta, Neel. "Introducing the Civic Digital Fellowship." *Coding It Forward* (blog), April 3, 2017. https://blog.codingitforward.com/the-first-tech-internship-program-in-a-federal-agency-13bfacff3f5c.

Leave Your Bureaucracy Better Off

Niccol, Brian. "The CEO of Chipotle on Charting a Culinary and Digital Turnaround." *Harvard Business Review*, November–December 2021. https://hbr.org/2021/11/the-ceo-of-chipotle-on-charting-a-culinary-and-digital-turnaround.

ACKNOWLEDGMENTS

Writing a book is hard! We were motivated to write about many of our friends and colleagues who we admire. There are hundreds more people and stories we would have liked to profile, but the challenge of any book is keeping it focused and readable. We take solace in the idea that this book can be a "living document"—a starting point for others to tell their stories. We've also created a website (HackYourBureaucracy.com) where we can blog about other bureaucracy-hacking stories that didn't make the final version (e.g., Biden's promised pool party), and feature ones from new and old friends. We hope you refine and amend the tactics in this book—and share stories of your own.

We can't thank enough our friends, family, mentors, colleagues, and fellow bureaucracy hackers who took the time to review stories, chapters, or even review the full manuscript. Your comments and astute observations made this book much better, and you caught so many mistakes. Thank you—in alphabetical order: Becca A., Katrina Abhold, Mike Andrews, Shawn Arnwine, Brian Basloe, Lee Becker, Bill Bender, Rohan Bhobe, Mary Bissell, Jonathan Black, Scott Blackburn, Mary Ann Brody, Berkeley Brown, Afua Bruce, Sixto Cancel, Aneesh Chopra, Chris Cleary, Rosye Cloud, Ben Collins, Dan Correa, Lucia Coulter, Curt Coy, Richard Culatta, Matt Cutts, Kara DeFrias, Mikey Dickerson, Rachel Dodell, Evan Doomes, Deesha Dyer, Courtney Eimermann-Wallace, Jennifer Erickson, John Paul Farmer, Anjali Fernandez, Katie Fogg, Brian Forde, Jim Fruchterman, Caitlin Gandhi, Kumar Garg, Alex Gaynor, Carla Geisser, Lisa Gelobter, David Gergen, Greg Gershman, Sloan Gibson, Robert Gordon, Vivian Graubard, Sam Gray, Dave Guarino, Ilan Gur, Blake Hall, Cyd Harrell, Dan Hon, Mina Hsiang, Josh Jacobs, Clementine Jacoby, Tom Kalil, Ian Kalin, Michael Kannan, Eliza Kelly, Kelsey Kennedy, Lauren Knausenberger,

Eric Koester, David Koh, Chris Kuang, Mary Lazzeri, Steve Levitt, Jonathan Lipman, David Litt, Lauren Lockwood, Alex Loehr, Howard Look, Jeff Maher, Carl Malamud, Josh Marcuse, Evan Marwell, AJ McCray, Bob McDonald, Tara McGuinness, Bethany McKenzie, Jeff Meisel, Erie Meyer, David Miller, Bret Mogilefsky, Natalie Moore, Adam Moorman, Giuseppe Morgana, Marshall Moriarty, Nina Moriarty, Barbara Morton, Jonathan Mostowski, Cecilia Munoz, Stephanie Nguyen, Charles Nitze, Janie Nitze, Paul Nitze, Beth Noveck, Kelly O'Connor, Liz Odar, Enrique Oti, Lynn Overmann, Jen Pahlka, Ryan Panchadsaram, Todd Park, Kevin Parker, Rohan Pavuluri, Tom Power, Angel Quicksey, Kathy Rice, Melanie Rice, Alec Ross, Mike Saintcross, David Saunders, Heidi Thompson Saunders, Hana Schank, Shannon Scott, Alla Seiffert, Raj Shah, Jack Shanahan, Amir Shevat, Jim Sinai, Michael Sinai, Vanessa Sinai, Jess Skylar, Mike Slagh, Anne-Marie Slaughter, Paul Smith, Robert Sosinski, Ariana Soto, Tommy Sowers, Michael Steffen, Amos Stoltzfus, Sarah Sullivan, Dana Suskind, Emily Tavoulareas, Nicholas Thompson, Phyllis Thompson, Steve VanRoekel, Abi Vladeck, Traci Walker, David Waltman, Matthew Weaver, Mitch Weiss, Albert Wong, Rob Wood, Charles Worthington, Emily Wright-Moore, Marie Zemler Wu, Cori Zarek, and Jen Zug. Apologies to whomever we left out, as this book was truly a collaborative effort.

Thank you to our fearless agent, Bridget Wagner Matzie, at Aevitas Creative Management, who helped us craft a book out of a series of stories and sayings, pushing us to rewrite the proposal many times, each time for the better, and who saw this idea as much more than a government book. If you are lucky enough to get Bridget on your team, don't hesitate!

We very much appreciate our ever-thoughtful editors, Dan Ambrosio and Alison Dalafave, our publisher, Mary Ann Naples, and the entire Hachette Go team. You saw the potential in our proposal and encouraged us to make it widely accessible across business, government, academia, and more; and you patiently endured our endless questions about the process. We hope that you can use some of the tactics in the book to change the publishing industry for the better!

A bittersweet note: we've lost, too soon, two amazing bureaucracy hackers that were so clearly going to change the world: Jake Brewer and Erica Pincus. They both worked in the Obama White House at various points after us. Jake was a young father who was killed in a bike accident during a charity race for cancer. President Obama called him "one of the best," and aptly described him as having a brilliant mind, a big heart, and an insatiable desire to give back. Jake hadn't worked long in the White House, but it was already clear to everyone that he understood instinctively how to use the platform of the presidency to empower people; as one small example, he had just led an event in the Bronx to help underprivileged young people learn to code. Erica Pincus served in the Domestic Policy Council toward the end of the Obama administration and later became one of Nick's star students at Harvard Kennedy School. Her kindness, brightness, and humanity were immediately apparent—as was her passion for using technology to improve the public good. Both Jake and Erica had an incredible joy for life and an authentic idealism that was magnetic. They inspire us to see the best in people, dream big, and be kind.

For me (Marina), any of my bureaucracy-hacking successes are all a direct credit to my amazing colleagues and mentors, starting with my fellow fry sauce aficionado, Richard Culatta, who took a big chance picking me as his first Presidential Innovation Fellow and who has been beyond generous with his wisdom, time, and network with me over the years. At the White House, I had the great fortune to learn not only from Nick, but also from my "work husband" Ryan Panchadsaram, and from Todd Park's bottomless enthusiasm and belief in a better world (and in me). And not a day goes by when I don't benefit from the calm and stoic leadership of Secretary Shinseki, Secretary Bob, Sloan Gibson, Bob Snyder, Scott Blackburn, John Spinelli, and Josh Jacobs, and from my predecessor, Peter Levin, for opening such an amazing door.

I am eternally grateful to my Digital Service team at the VA, a group of the most talented and dedicated people I've ever met, all of whom took a crazy chance to come try to hack the VA bureaucracy with me. Not only am I grateful for their sacrifices and hard work, but also for all the times they gently shared constructive criticism and feedback to help make me a better leader, person, and bureaucracy hacker. I would also like to acknowledge my Layer Aleph partners, Weaver, Mikey, and Carla; you are the three best possible colleagues and friends.

I would especially like to thank my husband, Charles, for patiently putting up with my working on this book over vacations and holidays, well after I promised to cut back on work. I'm also grateful to Melanie for reading random excerpts of the book over many months; to my cousins Heidi, Nick, Dave, and Phyllis for their thoughtful feedback; and to Aunt Nina and Uncle Marshall for sacrificing an oak tree in order to print out an early draft.

Finally, I'd like to recognize my late father-in-law, Bill, for his endless faith and support in my bureaucracy hacking over the years. It still doesn't quite feel real that you never got to read this.

I (Nick) know that this book would not be possible if not for the generosity of Insight Partners and the Harvard Kennedy School. Individuals from each—including Deven Parekh, Hilary Gosher, Richard Wells, Jeff Horing, and many more at Insight, and David Ellwood, Archon Fung, Suzanne Cooper, Alex Jones, Nicco Mele, Ash Carter, Eric Rosenbach, Laura Manley, and many more at HKS—have made a place for me, supported me, and given me the opportunity to learn, teach, write, and much more. It is truly a privilege to work with such talented people at two unique organizations. I'm similarly indebted to the entrepreneurs that I have the privilege of working with; especially those who include me on their boards (a special thanks to Hisham Anwar, Chris Lynch, John Serafini, Dan Ceperley, and Josh Lospinoso). The students at Harvard—those I've have the chance to teach, mentor, or simply meet—have been an inspiration, and I've gotten far more from them than they could hope to learn from me. I couldn't help but write about a few in this book and could fill an entire book with their stories.

I'm also especially grateful for my bosses and mentors in federal government who believed in me and showed me how to bureaucracy hack with the best of them: Blair Levin, Kristen Kane, Aneesh Chopra, Phil Weiser, Todd Park, Megan Smith, Tom Kalil, and John Holdren.

My twin daughters, Ellis and Georgia, were mostly accepting of my book writing, but insisted that I credit Wallace and Goose, our loyal canine companions, past and current, in the Sinai household. I hope that you one day read and use this book, or better yet, write your own! And of course, a special thank you to my loving family in Berkeley, California. Mom, your love of politics and current events inspires me, still. Dad, your devotion and kindness are a role model for me as a father. Jim, thank you for enduring me as a big brother, and I couldn't resist telling one of your stories in this book, even if you couldn't be bothered to read the entire manuscript. Vanessa, my wise and soulful sister, may you hack bureaucracies with empathy and inclusiveness as you embark on your path to be a leader and change agent in the education system.

Finally, but most importantly, thank you to my loving firecracker of a wife, Christine Clinton—fierce, funny, and fabulous! Your advice on my speeches or writing is always right: stop trying to impress people, explain what you mean, and make it easy for the listener or reader to understand. Thank you for being (mostly) patient and supportive as I devoted nights and weekends to writing this book. I love you, appreciate you, and promise not to write another one for a while!

INDEX

INDEX